# Paul:

## Apostle of Secrets

But now being made free from sin, and become servants to God,
you have your fruit unto holiness, and the end everlasting life.

For we preach not ourselves, but Christ Jesus the Lord; and
ourselves your servants for Jesus' sake. For God, who
commanded the light to shine out of darkness, has
shined in our hearts, to give the light of
the knowledge of the glory of God
in the face of Jesus Christ.

For all who love the LORD Jesus Christ,
desire to understand the Scriptures,
and look for the blessed hope
of His glorious appearing.

Amen.

# Paul:

# Apostle of Secrets

By

Don Samdahl

Thy word is a lamp unto my feet,
and a light unto my path.
Psalm 119.105

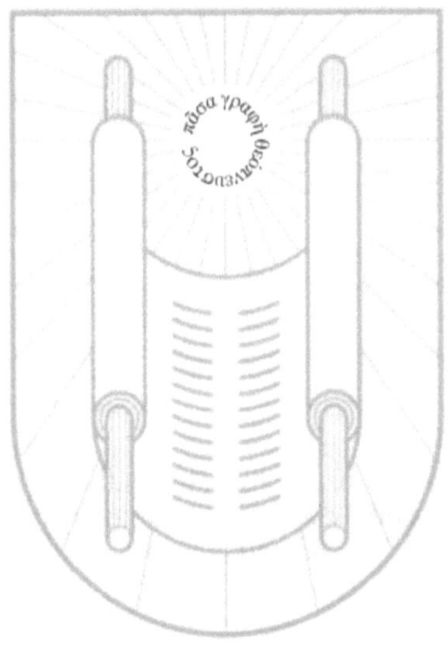


A Doctrine Publication
Doctrine.org

New Testament quotations are from the author's *The New Testament Study Bible (BDV)*. Old Testament quotations are from the KJV with updated language.


First Edition: November 2018
Fifth Printing: Revised and with corrections.
Printed in the United States of America
ISBN: 978-0-9994689-5-1

# Table of Contents

# Preface

Most recognize Paul as "the apostle of grace" (Acts 20.24) and "the apostle of the Gentiles" (Romans 11.13). Both appellations are true. But the *defining* nature of his apostleship is that Paul was the "apostle of secrets." He was God's "secret agent" who founded the Church, the body of Christ, and revealed all its doctrines.

Paul wrote the Corinthians of the "abundance of revelations" he received from the risen Christ. But after nearly two millennia, Christendom remains almost completely ignorant of them. Rarely does one read or hear about the revelations God gave to Paul. This reality may be shown by asking the following questions: How many sermons have you heard on "Paul's secrets?" How many articles or books have you seen on Paul as the founder of the Church and the revelator of all its doctrines? For most, the answer will be: none.

Because Christendom remains ignorant of these truths it has fractured into thousands of church affiliations and denominations. The vast majority of theologians, pastors, and Bible teachers, most with advanced degrees, do not understand *why* God chose Paul when He had twelve chosen, trained apostles. The question, "Why Paul?" is the most critical question in New Testaments studies. Answer it correctly and everything falls into place. Seeming contradictions and confusions vanish. Answer it incorrectly and we have our present state of confusion and division.

Thousands of books and tens of thousands of articles have been written about Paul's life and theology. But almost none of them understand that Paul was the *sole* revelator of the Church and all its doctrines and that Paul is to the Church what Abraham, Moses, and the Prophets were to Israel.

This book comes with a guarantee. Passages that seem perplexing, confusing, and difficult will be revealed. The veil will lift and the reader will see why God chose Paul and what God's saving him meant—the beginning of a new program: The Church, the body of Christ—a secret God had kept hidden for millennia.

**Note:** This printing, in addition to minor corrections and revisions, expands the Conclusion in Chapter 12, Paul and Sign Gifts.

# Prologue

The Bible reveals five great programs: Mankind, Israel, Church, Kingdom, and Eternity. Each program has its own administration and environment. Each constitutes a part of God's plan. Together, they tell the story of how God will accomplish His purposes and reveal His glory. It is a drama like no other, compassing heaven and earth, men and women, spirit beings, and God Himself. And like all dramas, it has crises, misunderstandings, victories, setbacks, reversals of fortune, failures, regrets, good, and evil. It is a love story like no other. God makes the ultimate sacrifice to win mankind. It is also a war story—God has determined enemies. But when God fights, He fights to win. And win He will. Though wounded, He will decisively defeat His adversaries.

The focus of this book is Paul. That is to say, the focus of this book is on God's program known as the Church, the body of Christ. The story of Paul is the story of the Church. The Church is God's creation of grace and no one deserved God's grace less than Saul of Tarsus. He was Jesus of Nazareth's most resolute enemy. But God demonstrated His matchless grace to Gentiles by saving Saul, to become Paul, the apostle of the Gentiles.

Paul was *not* a thirteenth apostle appended to the Twelve. Paul was God's apostle who began a whole new program: the Church, the body of Christ. As the founder of the Church, *all* Church doctrine is found in Paul's letters.

The roots of Christendom's theological perplexities go back over 1,900 years. Shortly before his execution, Paul wrote these sad words to Timothy: "This you know, that all they who are in Asia are turned away from me; of whom are Phygellus and Hermogenes" (2 Timothy 1.15). Paul spent years tirelessly ministering in Asia Minor (Turkey). Despite his labors, the region abandoned his teachings. The great progress he made with the Asian churches—Ephesus, Colossae, Galatia, Iconium, Derbe, Lystra, Antioch Pisidia, and Laodicea—proclaiming Christ's death and resurrection, teaching salvation by faith alone, instructing believers about their relationship to Christ and how to live the Christian life—all these churches abandoned his teachings. How, why, what occurred, and how it affected the Church is examined throughout the book.

## The Framework of Scripture

Theologians recognize God revealed His plan systematically and progressively. The most basic divisions of the Bible are called the Old Testament and the New Testament. This division, however, is an arbitrary construct and provides little help for understanding the Bible. The "Old Testament" is the "Old Covenant," the Mosaic Law, given in Exodus. Technically, the "Old Testament" begins in Exodus 20. The "New Testament" is the "New Covenant," prophesied by Ezekiel and Jeremiah, and inaugurated by Christ at the end of His earthly ministry. But in His earthly ministry, Jesus ministered under the Mosaic Law, the Old Testament. Thus, the Gospels are Old Testament but are called "New Testament."

Augustine stated, "the New Testament is hidden in the Old, the Old Testament is revealed in the New" (*Novum Testamentum in Vetere latet, Vetus Testamentum in Novo patet*). This axiom, known and quoted widely, fails to recognize that the Old Testament gave no hint of the organism known as the Church, the body of Christ. Its creation was unforeseen.

A better approach is required. The Scriptures reveal five distinct periods, administrations, or programs to reveal how God has structured His progressive revelation. Every believer in Christ should understand this layout or framework since it is the foundation for understanding the Scriptures and one's place in them.

To understand the Scriptures, one must recognize this foundational principle: All Scripture is FOR us but not all is TO us. The focus of this book is upon God's program of the Church, the body of Christ. Paul's letters are TO us and everything else is FOR us. Paul expressed this thought, thus:

> For what was written before was written for our instruction, so through the endurance and the encouragement of the Scriptures we might have the hope (Romans 15.4).
>
> Now these things happened to them *for* examples and were written for our instruction, to whom the ends of the ages have arrived (1 Corinthians 10.11).

**Framework of the Divine Programs Through the Ages**

| **Program** | Mankind | Israel | Church | Israel Redux | Kingdom | New Heavens and New Earth |
|---|---|---|---|---|---|---|
| **Key Figure** | Adam | Abraham | Paul | Antichrist | Christ | God the Father |
| **Length** | Adam to Abraham | Abraham to Paul | Paul to Rapture | 7 Years | 1,000 Years | Eternal |
| **Revelation** | Revealed by the Prophets | | Unrevealed by the Prophets | Revealed by the Prophets | | |

See doctrine.org/chart-of-gods-programs/ for a detailed chart.

# Chapter 1
# Paul's Early Life

*Are they Hebrews? I too! Are they Israelites? I too! Are they descendants Abraham? I too (2 Corinthians 11.22)!*

God always has a plan and the implementation of His plan is always on time. God also always chooses the right person at the right time to accomplish His plan. Such was Saul of Tarsus. Our biographical information about Paul comes from Luke's history, Acts, Paul's letters, and from a brief mention by Peter in his second epistle to the Jews. These are our primary sources.

## Paul's Birth

Saul of Tarsus was a Jew's Jew. Born into the tribe of Benjamin, he was likely named after Israel's first king. He was also given a Roman name, Paul, a practice common among Hellenized Jews.[1] Paul's Roman name was particularly appropriate since he was also a Roman citizen. Proud of his Jewish heritage, he often used it to defend his ministry. He wrote:

> [3] For I kept wishing that I myself might be *a* curse, separated from the Christ for my brethren, my kindred according to *the* flesh, [4] who are Israelites, whose *is* the adoption, and the glory, and the covenants, and the law-giving, and the service, and the promises—(Romans 9.3-4).
>
> Are they Hebrews? I too! Are they Israelites? I too! Are they descendants Abraham? I too (2 Corinthians 11.22)!
>
> [5] In circumcision—eighth day! Of *the* race of Israel! Of *the* tribe of Benjamin! Hebrew of Hebrews! Regarding Law—Pharisee! [6] Regarding zeal, I persecuted the congregation! Regarding righteousness which is by Law, I was irreproachable (Philippians 3.5-6)!

## Paul's City

Saul was born in Tarsus, in the Roman province of Cilicia, what is now Turkey. Tarsus was situated inland about 12 miles from the Mediterranean and strategically located between land and sea trade routes. It was a robust commercial center and during the time of Pompey the Great it became the capital of Cilicia (67 B.C.). Mark

---

[1] Jews became Hellenized after Alexander the Great. His conquests made. Greek the universal language and many Jews took Greek and Roman names, e.g., Luke, Mark, Apollos, Steven, etc.

Antony[2] declared it a free city in 42 B.C.[3] and Augustus exempted it from imperial taxation because Athenodorus, his teacher and friend, was a Tarsian.

Tarsus was culturally sophisticated and a renowned intellectual center. Strabo (64 or 63 B.C.—c. A.D. 24), described it in his *Geography*:

> The people at Tarsus have devoted themselves so eagerly, not only to philosophy, but also to the whole round of education in general, that they have surpassed Athens, Alexandria, or any other place that can be named where there have been schools and lectures of philosophers. But it is so different from other cities that there the men who are fond of learning, are all natives, and foreigners are not inclined to sojourn there; neither do these natives stay there, but they complete their education abroad; and when they have completed it they are pleased to live abroad, and but few go back home (*Geography* 14.5.13).

Luke wrote the following concerning Paul's association with Tarsus:

> Then the Lord *said* to him, After you get up, go to the street that is called Straight, and seek in *the* house of Judas, *for one* named Saul of Tarsus. For behold, he is praying (Acts 9.11).

> Then Barnabas went to Tarsus to look for Saul, (Acts 11.25).

> Then Paul said, I am *a* Jew from Tarsus of Cilicia, *a* citizen of *an* important city. Now I implore you, let me speak to the people (Acts 21.39).

> I am *a* Jew, born in Tarsus of Cilicia, who was educated in this city at the feet of Gamaliel, taught according to the strictest manner of the Law of the fathers, and was zealous for the God, even as you all are today, (Acts 22.3).

## Paul's Education

Saul undoubtedly demonstrated academic promise and enthusiasm for Judaism as a young man. As a result, he was sent to Jerusalem to study under the famous rabbi, Gamaliel, grandson of the great Hillel. Under his tutelage, Paul became an expert in Jewish law as taught by the Pharisees. Concerning Gamaliel, Luke wrote:

> But when one of them arose in the Sanhedrin, *a* Pharisee named Gamaliel, *a* teacher of the Law, honored by all the

---

[2] Antony met Cleopatra in Tarsus.

[3] A free city under Rome had the right of self-government during the Hellenistic and Roman Imperial eras. Legal cases between natives were tried under their own laws and several cities could issue civic coinage bearing the name of the city.

> people, he ordered the apostles to be put outside briefly (Acts 5.34).
>
> I am *a* Jew, born in Tarsus of Cilicia, who was educated in this city at the feet of Gamaliel, taught according to the strictest manner of the Law of the fathers,[4] and was zealous for the God,[5] even as you all are today, (Acts 22.3).

## Paul's Trade

In addition to academic pursuits, Jewish boys, including those from prominent families, learned a trade. Paul learned tentmaking and this skill provided him with financial support throughout his ministry, Paul lived a life above board. He worked to provide for his needs throughout his ministry to allay accusations by his enemies that he was a greedy huckster. Paul worked with Aquila and Priscilla, fellow Jews who had fled Rome due to Claudius' decree which expelled Jews from Rome. Together they sewed tents and discussed the Scriptures. Luke recorded:

> And since they were of the same trade, he stayed with them and worked (for they were tentmakers by trade) (Acts 18.3).

## Paul's Roman Citizenship

Paul suffered as few have, but his Roman citizenship spared him some unjust suffering and saved his life. On Paul's second missionary journey with Silas, they were arrested in Philippi when they fell afoul with soothsayers (Acts 16.16-19). These men accused them before the city officials, stirred up a mob, and they were whipped and imprisoned. At midnight, while Paul and Silas prayed and sang hymns, a great earthquake occurred. The disturbance freed them from their bonds along with all the other prisoners. Terrified by what had occurred, the jailer was going to kill himself for he thought his prisoners had fled.[6] Paul stopped him and used the occasion to lead the jailer and his household to Christ (Acts 16.27-34). The next morning, the magistrates, probably thinking Paul and Silas had suffered enough and perhaps also thinking they had been overly hasty to punish them on the soothsayers' word, decided to release them. Luke recorded:

> 36 Then the jailor reported these words to Paul: The magistrates have sent *orders* that you should be released. So now, when you go, depart in peace. 37 But Paul began saying to them, They beat us publicly—unconvicted men! Though Roman citizens, they threw *us* into prison. And now,

---

[4] Luke used ἀκρίβεια to describe "the perfect manner of the law of the fathers." Paul followed the Mosaic Law with exactness.

[5] The word "zeal," ζηλωτής, indicated Paul vigorously contended for the Law and Pharisaic traditions. It consumed his mind, will, and emotions.

[6] Under Roman law, jailers were responsible for their prisoners. If prisoners escaped, a jailer would forfeit his life.

> secretly, they throw us out? No way! No, they must come themselves and escort us out! [38] Then the officers reported these words to the magistrates. Now they became afraid when they heard that they were Roman citizens. [39] So when they came, they apologized to them. And after they escorted them out, they kept asking them to leave the city. [40] Now after they left the prison, they went to Lydia's *house*. And after they saw the brethren, they encouraged them and departed (Acts 16.36-40).

Paul's reaction to the magistrates reveals the nature of his character and personality. The officials wished to release Paul and Silas secretly. Paul would have none of it. The magistrates had acted unjustly, especially since Paul and Silas were Roman citizens.[7] Paul told them they would not skulk out of jail like criminals—the officials had to come and release them. To accuse and imprison a Roman citizen without a trial was a serious offense. But they had also beaten them. Paul now had them at a disadvantage.

Why did Paul and Silas not assert their rights as Romans initially? The most reasonable answer is they wished to set a courageous example for the new Philippian church by enduring suffering and persecution. After Paul did stand up for his rights the officials would remember this. They would be less hasty in accepting accusations against Philippian believers and more cautious in judging without due process.

After Paul determined to go to Jerusalem for Pentecost (Acts 20.16), he gave his testimony to the Jews of how he met the risen Christ on the road to Damascus. The Jews listened until he uttered the words, "Then He said to me, Go! For I will send you far away to *the* Gentiles'" (Acts 22.21). When they heard the word "Gentiles," they exploded (Acts 22.22-23). As a result, the Roman battalion commander (χιλίαρχος),[8] had to intervene to keep Paul from being torn apart. Upset by the riot, [9] the commander was going to have Paul whipped and questioned. Luke recorded the conversation between Paul and the commander:

> [25] But as he stretched him out with the straps, Paul said to the centurion[10] standing by, Is it legal for you to flog, if a man *is* an untried Roman *citizen*? [26] Now when the centurion heard *this*, he went to the commander and reported, saying, Be careful about what you are about to do. For this man is *a* Roman *citizen*. [27] So when the commander approached, he said to him, Tell me, are you *a* Roman *citizen*? And he said,

---

[7] Lex Porcia and Lex Valerian exempted Roman citizens from degrading punishments such as scourging. Verse 37 indicates both Paul and Silas were Roman citizens.

[8] A χιλίαρχος commanded a thousand soldiers, a U.S. heavy battalion.

[9] The primary responsibility of Roman governors of conquered territories was to keep order and collect taxes.

[10] A centurion, ἑκατόνταρχον, commanded one hundred soldiers.

> Yes. [28] Then the commander replied, I purchased this citizenship with *a* large sum *of money*. But Paul said, I was born *so* (Acts 22.25-28).

Roman citizenship conferred important rights. The commander had purchased his citizenship with a lot of money and was impressed that Paul had been born with it.[11]

## Paul the Pharisee

Paul was proud of his Pharisaic Jewish heritage. He wrote:

> [5] In circumcision—eighth day! Of *the* race of Israel! Of *the* tribe of Benjamin! Hebrew of Hebrews! Regarding Law—Pharisee! [6] Regarding zeal, I persecuted the congregation! Regarding righteousness which is by Law, I was irreproachable (Philippians 3.5-6)!

Paul's family was evidently of the Pharisaic tradition and he was sent to study under Gamaliel, the great Pharisee rabbi, to continue in this tradition. Writing the Galatians, Paul revealed his zeal for Judaism:

> [13] For you heard of my former way of life in the Judaism, that beyond measure I used to persecute the congregation of the God, and used to destroy it. [14] And I kept advancing in Judaism above many contemporaries among my race, since I was intensely zealous for the traditions of my fathers (Galatians 1.13-14).

The word "profited," προκόπτω, is an imperfect active indicative and means "increase" or "advance." The imperfect indicates continuing action: "kept advancing." Paul had been recognized as a "rising star" among the Pharisees and this undoubtedly meant promotion and financial reward.

Two major theological parties existed during this period: Sadducees and Pharisees. The Jewish upper-class largely composed the Sadducees. They accepted the five books of Moses while the Pharisees accepted all of the Old Testament: the five books of Moses, the Prophets, and the Writings. The Sadducees favored Hellenization and incorporation of Greek philosophy in their interpretations. The Pharisees rejected this. The Sadducees rejected the supernatural and the resurrection but the Pharisees accepted these. Generally, the Pharisees were the religious conservatives, the Sadducees, the liberals.

On one occasion, after being arrested in Jerusalem, Paul used the theological antagonism between the Sadducees and Pharisees to his advantage. Luke recorded:

---

[11] Paul inherited Roman citizenship but specifics are unknown. Normally, citizenship was granted for making a significant contribution to Rome or purchased.

> 6 Then Paul, because he knew that one part was of Sadducees and the other Pharisees, began shouting in the Council, Men, brethren, I am *a* Pharisee, son of *a* Pharisee. I am being tried for *the* hope and resurrection of *the* dead! 7 Now after he said this, *an* argument arose between the Pharisees and Sadducees and the crowd was divided. 8 (For Sadducees say there is no resurrection, or angel, or spirit. But Pharisees recognize them all). 9 Then great clamor arose and some of the scribes of the Pharisees' party got up and began protesting, saying, We find nothing wrong with this man! What if *a* spirit or angel spoke to him? Let us not fight against God (Acts 23.6-9)!

## Introduction of Paul

Luke introduced Paul in Acts 7, at the stoning of Stephen by the Sanhedrin. Stephen, one of the original seven deacons chosen by the Jerusalem assembly to assist the Twelve, is described as a man "full of faith and the Holy Spirit" (Acts 6.5) and "full of faith and power, [who] did great wonders and miracles among the people" (Acts 6.8). In addition to working miracles, Stephen knew the Scriptures and was a powerful orator. Luke wrote:

> 9 However, some of those from what was called the Synagogue of the Libertines, and Cyrenians, and Alexandrians, and of those from Cilicia,[12] and Asia, argued with Stephen. 10 And they kept not being able to withstand the wisdom and the Spirit by whom he kept speaking (Acts 6.9-10).

Stephen was an annoying embarrassment to the scholars of the synagogue of the Libertines, Cyrenians, Alexandrians, and of those of Cilicia and Asia. Despite their learning, they could not refute his knowledge and understanding of the Scriptures. So, they attacked him personally. Luke recorded:

> 11 Then they conspired with men who said, We have heard him saying blasphemous words against Moses and the God. 12 They also incited the people, and the elders, and the scribes, so when they came against *him*, they seized him and brought *him* to the Sanhedrim. 13 They also put up false witnesses who said, This man does not stop saying blasphemous words against this holy place and the Law. 14 For we have heard him saying, This Jesus of Nazareth will destroy this place and will change the customs that Moses gave us. 15 And while everyone who sat on the Council stared at him, they saw his face as *the* face of *an* angel (Acts 6.11-15).

---

[12] Could Paul have been one of the Cilicians who argued against Stephen?

As is often the case, when men cannot answer arguments, they attack the messenger by maligning his character and twisting his words. What must these men have thought as Stephen began his defense with his face shining like that of an angel?

Stephen gave a brilliant review of Israel's history to the Council. He did not try and defend himself. Instead, he accused them of unbelief. He told them they were no different from their ancestors who had killed the prophets (Acts 7.51-53). Stung and enraged by his accusation, the Council members turned on him like feral beasts and dragged him from the city. Laying their robes at a young man's feet—Saul—they stoned him to death (Acts 7.58).[13]

## Paul's Response to Stephen's Stoning

Saul applauded Stephen's stoning.[14] Because of his zeal for Judaism's traditions, he assumed the lead in identifying and imprisoning Jews who had believed Jesus of Nazareth was the Messiah. His assault was so fierce that all the believers in Jerusalem fled—except the Twelve (Acts 8.1).[15] They steadfastly remained in Jerusalem to continue to witness to the Jews that Jesus was the Messiah and await His return (Acts 1.8).

Not content to limit his activities to Jerusalem and Judea, Saul obtained legal authority from the high priest to pursue followers of "the way"[16] to foreign cities. Paul began at Damascus, probably because he had intelligence reports that many believers had fled there. Luke described Paul's purpose:

> [1] Now Saul, who was still breathing out threats and murder towards the Lord's disciples, went to the high priest [2] and asked him *for* letters to Damascus, to the synagogues, so if he should find anyone who was of the Way, both men and women, he might bring them bound to Jerusalem (Acts 9.1-2).

## Paul: Jew and Gentile

As will become clear, God used Paul in a tremendous way for both Jews and Gentiles. His Jewishness qualified him to be proxy Israel, "a

---

[13] Saul was a young member of the Sanhedrin, probably advanced to this position by Gamaliel. In Acts 26.10, Paul wrote he voted (ψῆφος, a pebble) for the death penalty against those who believed Jesus was the Messiah.

[14] Paul fully agreed (συνευδοκῶν) with Stephens' stoning (Acts 8.1, 22.20).

[15] Luke wrote that Paul "made havoc" (ἐλυμαίνετο, imperfect middle indicative) with these believers. Paul was relentless (Acts 8.3).

[16] Believers in the Messiah at this time were not called Christians but followers of "the way" (Acts 9.2, 19.9, 23, 22.4, 24.14, 22). This appellation probably came from Jesus' statement that He was "the Way" (John 14.6) and because John had preached, "Prepare the way of the Lord" (Matthew 3.3; Mark 1.3). The term "Christian" was first used in Antioch, Syria, outside the borders of Israel, with a primarily Gentile congregation (Acts 11.26).

light to the Gentiles" in agreement with the Abrahamic Covenant. As one with Roman citizenship, he could identify with Gentiles as "the apostle of the Gentiles (Romans 11.13).

Saul of Tarsus epitomized unbelief and Jewish national rejection of Jesus of Nazareth. Paul the Apostle epitomized believing Israel and portrayed the nation's role and destiny in blessing Gentiles.

# Chapter 2

# Luke's Record: Acts

*[28] Therefore, know this: This salvation of the God is sent to the Gentiles. And they will listen! [29] And after he said these things, the Jews went away and had a great argument among themselves. (Acts 28.28-29).*

## The Purpose of the Book of Acts

Acts is volume two of Luke's[1] historical record which continues his Gospel account of Jesus' earthly ministry to Israel. Acts is a bridge between the Gospels and Paul's letters.[2] Luke's primary purpose in writing Acts was to explain to Jews why the kingdom of God promised by the prophets and proclaimed by John the Baptist, Jesus, and the Twelve did not come upon the earth.

To understand this purpose, one must understand Jewish hope. Two great themes comprised their theology. They were the wrath of God, described by the prophets as the Day of the Lord,[3] and the kingdom of God.[4] One can hardly read a page of the prophets without encountering these two themes. Throughout the prophetic writings, these themes were intertwined with warnings of impending judgment.[5] The Messiah was the key player in these two great themes. He is the one who will

---

[1] Luke was a Jewish physician and companion of Paul. Some maintain Luke was a Gentile but little support exists for this claim. One argument is his name: Luke. But Jews frequently had Graeco-Roman names, e.g., Paul, Apollos, Stephen, since the region was Hellenized after Alexander the Great. Another argument is Luke gave Hebrew words their Greek equivalents, e.g., Kranion for Golgotha, Master for Rabbi, etc. But Luke was far too familiar with Jewish law, tradition, Scriptures, and employed too many Semitisms to be a Gentile. See H.F.D. Sparks, "The Semitisms of St. Luke's Gospel," *The Journal of Theological Studies*, Vol. XLIV n175-176 (1943): 129-138. The only substantive argument is that Paul's phrase "of the circumcision" (Colossians 4.10-11) referred to Jews and since Luke was not included, he was not a Jew. But Paul was not identifying Jews *per se*, but Jews of the "party of the circumcision," τοὺς ἐκ περιτομῆς (Galatians 2.12-13) who joined his ministry from the Jerusalem assembly (Acts 15.1-5). If Luke was a Gentile, he would be the only non-Jew to write Scripture and contradict Romans 3.1-2.

[2] Acts is a transitional and historical book, not a doctrinal book. Luke's purpose in writing Acts was to show Jews why the kingdom of God did not come. All Church *doctrine* comes from Paul's letters, not from Acts.

[3] The Day of the Lord is God's great judgment upon Israel and the nations before Christ returns to establish the kingdom of God on earth. Jesus called this period the Tribulation and it is the subject of the book of Revelation.

[4] This was the earthly kingdom God promised Israel (Matthew 6.10).

[5] The primary challenge in interpreting the prophets is to determine what the prophet is talking about among three subjects: 1) impending judgment, 2) future judgment, i.e., the Day of the Lord, and 3) the earthly kingdom.

exercise wrath upon humanity (Psalm 2.4-5, 9-12; Isaiah 63.1-6; Revelation 19.11-16), destroy His enemies, and then set up His earthly kingdom (Psalm 2.6-8, 110.1; Daniel 7.13-14; Zechariah 14.9, 16).

The Gospels begin with God's commission of John the Baptist to proclaim a message of repentance to Israel and announce that the kingdom of God was near (Matthew 3.2). This message was known as the "gospel of the kingdom." Inwardly, it required repentance and belief that Jesus was the Christ, the Son of God (John 1.47-49, 11.23-27; Matthew 16.15-16). The outward expression of this faith was water baptism. As priests washed to prepare for their daily service in the Temple, John's baptism was to prepare the entire nation to serve as a kingdom of priests (Exodus 19.6).

Jesus continued John's message, "Repent: for the kingdom of heaven is at hand" (Matthew 4.17) and instructed the Twelve to do the same (Matthew 10.7). Few passages have been more abused than Luke 17.20-21. The KJV renders these verses thus:

> [20] And when he was demanded of the Pharisees, when the kingdom of God should come, he answered them and said, The kingdom of God comes not with observation: [21] Neither shall they say, Lo here! or, lo there! for, behold, the kingdom of God is within you.

A more accurate translation is the following:

> [20] Now after He was asked by the Pharisees when the kingdom of the God was coming, He answered them and said, The kingdom of the God does not come with close scrutiny. [21] Nor will they say, Behold, here! Or, There! For behold, the kingdom of God is in your midst!

Jesus' words, "The kingdom of God comes not with observation" has led some to think the kingdom of God was an invisible, spiritual kingdom. Jesus' next words, "the kingdom of God is within you" seemed to confirm this. This is to misread and misunderstand the passage. Nothing was more established than a visible kingdom confirmed by signs. The prophets wrote hundreds of verses about an earthly kingdom. The whole point of Jesus' miracles (Luke 7.20-23) was to confirm He was the Messiah, the King, who was ready to establish His kingdom on earth. The words translated "with observation," μετὰ παρατηρήσεως, mean "with close scrutiny," "with careful observation." Jesus was mocking the Pharisees. Despite all their religious training, they could not recognize He was the Messiah. Jesus certainly did not tell these unbelieving Pharisees the kingdom was within *them*. Soon, they would plot His arrest and demand His crucifixion. The words "within you," ἐντὸς ὑμῶν, mean "in your midst." What Jesus was saying to them was, "You don't have to strain your eyes, fellows. The kingdom is standing in your midst in the person of the King." Truly, the kingdom was "at hand."

## Peter at Pentecost

Rather than believe Jesus was the Christ, the Jewish nation conspired with the Romans to have Him executed. But amazingly, He had risen from the dead. Thus, on Pentecost, Peter continued to proclaim repentance and the gospel of the kingdom. Jesus had risen from the dead and the Holy Spirit had come in anticipation of fulfilling the New Covenant (Ezekiel 11.16-20, 36.24-28; Jeremiah 31.31-34).

As a result, Israel had another opportunity to have its Messiah and kingdom. Peter quoted Joel 2.38-32, not only because it foretold the coming of the Holy Spirit, but because it prophesied the Day of the Lord. Peter expected the attendant signs of the sun being darkened and the moon turning to blood to come soon. After this, Jesus would return to establish His kingdom. Peter declared:

> 16 But this is what has been spoken through the prophet Joel:
> 17 And it will be in the last days, says the God, I will pour
> out of My Spirit on all flesh. And your sons and your
> daughters will prophesy. And your young men will see
> visions. And your old men will dream dreams. 18 And on My
> men servants and My women servants in those days, I will
> pour out of My Spirit, and they will prophesy. 19 And I will
> give wonders in the heaven above and signs on the earth
> below—blood and fire and billows of smoke. 20 The sun will
> be turned into darkness and the moon into blood before the
> great and glorious Day of *the* Lord comes. 21 And it will be,
> everyone who should call on the name of *the* Lord will be
> saved (Acts 2.16-21).

Peter concluded his address to the nation with the words, "Assuredly, therefore, let all *the* house of Israel know: The God made Him both Lord and Christ—this Jesus whom you crucified" (Acts 2.36). Convicted of their sin, they asked, "What shall we do?" Peter responded:

> 38 Then Peter said to them, Repent and be baptized, every
> one of you, in the name of Jesus Christ, for forgiveness of
> your sins and you will receive the gift of the Holy Spirit.
> 39 For to you is the promise, and to your children, and to all
> those far away, as many as the Lord our God will call (Acts
> 2.38-39).[6]

Peter addressed *Jews* at Pentecost. He did *not* speak to Gentiles. He told Jews if they wanted the King and the kingdom, they must repent and believe Jesus was the Christ. Those "far away" were Jews in dispersion.

---

[6] Peter addressed *all* Israel and told the nation that *every* Jew must repent (Acts 2.36, 38).

## Peter at the Temple

After healing the lame man at the Temple (Acts 3.1-11), Peter again confronted the Jewish people with the crime of murdering their Messiah (Acts 3.13-15). He told them:

> [19] Therefore, repent and return so your sins might be wiped out, [20] so that the season of refreshment might come from the presence of the Lord and He might send the One chosen for you, Christ Jesus, [21] whom heaven must receive until *the* times of restoration of all things, of which the God spoke through the mouth of all His holy prophets, from long ago (Acts 3.19-21).

Peter told the Jews that if they repented, God would send Jesus to establish Israel's kingdom. Shortly before His crucifixion, Jesus addressed the nation and said:

> [37] Jerusalem, Jerusalem, the one who kills the prophets and stones the ones who have been sent to her! How often I wished to gather your children, as *a* hen gathers her chicks under her wings, and you would not! [38] Behold, your house is left to you desolate! [39] For I tell you, you should never see Me from now until you should say, Blessed *is* the One who comes in *the* name of *the* Lord (Matthew 23.37-39).

The phrase, "Blessed is the One who comes in the name of the Lord" is a statement of repentance and faith that Jesus of Nazareth is the Messiah. Until the entire Jewish nation, every Jew does this, Christ will not, indeed, cannot return and establish His earthly kingdom.

Acts explains why God could not establish His earthly kingdom: the nation refused to repent, even after Jesus had risen from the dead. For the past 2,000 years, national Israel has been blinded spiritually to this great truth (Romans 11.25). This condition is *temporary*. The nation, every Jew, *will* repent for Paul declared "all Israel will be saved" (Romans 11.25). In the final hours of the Tribulation, every Jew on earth will repent and believe Jesus is the Messiah. When they do, the Lord will keep His promise and return (Mathew 23.37-39). The Lord's instruction to His disciples when they asked how to pray: "Your kingdom come, Your will be done on earth as it is in heaven" (Matthew 6.10) will be fulfilled.

## Prophecy Concerning Gentile Blessings

All of this was Jewish. The reader may wonder what God's plan was for Gentiles. Were Gentiles excluded from God's blessings?

God dealt with the entire human race for the first 2,000-3500 years of human history.[7] Those years ended in disaster. Due to mankind's

---

[7] The Masoretic Text (MT) and the Septuagint (LXX), the Greek translation of the Hebrew text, disagree regarding the genealogies of Genesis 5 and 11. If

inordinate wickedness, God destroyed the human race with the Flood except for eight people (Genesis 6.17-18). After this, mankind continued its disobedience and rebellion in building the Tower of Babel (Genesis 11.1-9).

Because of this global rebellion, God called Abram from Ur of the Chaldees and made a covenant with him. This covenant, the Abrahamic Covenant, established a new divine program (Genesis 12.1; Acts 7.2-3). The importance of this covenant cannot be overstated. The Abrahamic Covenant is the foundation for all God's covenants with Israel and the basis for how He would bless all mankind. The covenant reads:

> 1 Now the Lord had said to Abram: Get out of your country, from your family and from your father's house, to a land that I will show you. 2 I will make you a great nation; I will bless you and make your name great; and you will be a blessing.
> 3 I will bless those who bless you, and I will curse him who curses you; and in you all the families of the earth shall be blessed (Genesis 12.1-3).

God told Abraham ten things: 1) leave your country, 2) leave your relatives, 3) go to a land God would show him, 4) God would make Abram a great nation (people), 5) God would bless him, 6) God would make his name great, 7) Abram would be a blessing to others, 8) God would bless those who blessed Abram, 9) God would curse the one who cursed Abram, 10) Through Abram, all peoples would be blessed.

The provision that concerns Gentiles is the last statement, "in you all the families of the earth shall be blessed." The Abrahamic Covenant revealed that from this point forward, ALL divine blessing to mankind *would be mediated through a covenant people*—the Jews.

The Abrahamic Covenant and the succeeding covenants God gave Israel—Land, Mosaic, Sabbatic, Davidic, and New—assumed Israel would accept their Messiah. Once they accepted Him, they would fulfill their destiny and become a holy nation and a kingdom of priests (Exodus 19.4-6; Isaiah 61.6; 1 Peter 2.9). In this role, they would go to the nations and proclaim the Messiah (Isaiah 42.6, 60.3; Matthew 28.18-20; Acts 1.8). That was what the "great commission" was all about.

Peter and the Twelve did not foresee a lengthy rejection of the Messiah. How could God bless Israel apart from the Messiah? How could the kingdom come without its King? How could Gentiles be

---

one accepts the MT, the date of Adam's creation was about 4000 B.C. If one accepts the LXX, God created Adam about 5500 B.C. The Dead Sea Scrolls (DSS) mostly agree with the LXX. The MT is dated between around the 10th and 11th centuries A.D. and the LXX was translated between 300 and 200 B.C. The DSS provide Hebrew texts 1,000 years older than the MT. The agreement of the LXX with the DSS indicates translators of the LXX copied from an earlier Hebrew text than the MT.

blessed if Israel rejected their Messiah? The *prophetic answer* to these questions was God could *not* bless Gentiles apart from Israel. God had no *revealed plan* to bless Gentiles apart from the Messiah and Israel.

Acts explains why the kingdom of God did not come on earth. Luke structured his argument through several threefold repetitions. The chart shows how the Jews rejected the Messiah three times under the ministry of the Twelve and how they rejected Christ three times under Paul's ministry. Paul's salvation and defense before Gentile rulers were also recounted three times.

| Repetition of Threes | Passage | Result |
|---|---|---|
| Three Rejections of the King by the Jews Under the Twelve's Ministry | Acts 4.5-31 | Threat |
| | Acts 5.12-42 | Imprisonment |
| | Acts 7.1-60 | Execution |
| Three Rejections of the King by the Jews Under Paul's Ministry | Acts 13.44-52 | Turns to Gentiles |
| | Acts 18.1-7 | Turns to Gentiles |
| | Acts 28.17-29 | Turns to Gentiles |
| Three Accounts of Paul's Salvation | Acts 9.1-16 | Initial account |
| | Acts 22.1-21 | To Jews (Jerusalem) |
| | Acts 26.1-32 | To Agrippa (Caesarea) |
| Three Accounts of Paul's Defense Before Gentile Rulers | Acts 24.10-27 | To Felix (Caesarea) |
| | Acts 25.1-12 | To Festus (Caesarea) |
| | Acts 25.13-32 | To Agrippa (Caesarea) |

## Paul's Conversion

When God repeats, we should pay special attention. Luke repeated Paul's conversion three times in Acts. The first account reads:

> 3 Now while he traveled, it happened as he neared
> Damascus, suddenly, light from the heaven enveloped him.
> 4 And after he fell on the ground, he heard *a* voice say to
> him, Saul, Saul, why do you persecute Me? 5 Then he said,
> Who are you, Lord? Then the Lord said, I am Jesus whom
> you are persecuting. *It is* hard for you to kick against the
> goads. 6 And while he trembled and was astonished, he said,
> Lord, what do you want me to do? And the Lord said to him,
> Get up and go into the city. And it will be told to you what
> you must do. 7 (Now the men who traveled with him stood
> speechless, for they heard the voice, but saw no one). 8 Then
> Saul got up from the ground. But when he opened his eyes,

> he could see nothing. So, leading him by the hand, they brought *him* to Damascus. 9 And for three days he could not see. And he did not eat or drink.
>
> 10 Now *a* certain disciple named Ananias was in Damascus. And the Lord said to him in *a* vision, Ananias. And he said, I am here, Lord. 11 Then the Lord *said* to him, After you get up, go to the street that is called Straight, and seek in *the* house of Judas, *for one* named Saul of Tarsus. For behold, he is praying 12 and he saw *a* man in *a* vision named Ananias, who came and put his hands on him so he might see again. 13 But Ananias replied, Lord, I heard from many about this man, how many evil *things* he did to your saints in Jerusalem. 14 And here, he has authority from the chief priests, to bind all those who call on your name. 15 But the Lord said to him, Go. For this man is *a* chosen vessel to Me, to carry My name before the Gentiles, and kings, and the sons of Israel. 16 For I will show him how many things he must suffer for My name. 17 So Ananias left and entered the house. And when he put his hands on him, he said, Brother Saul, the Lord has sent me—Jesus, the one who appeared to you on the road on which you were coming— so you might see again and be filled with *the* Holy Spirit. 19 And after he received food, he became strengthened. Now Saul was with the disciples for some days in Damascus (Acts 9.3-19).

Paul gave the second account of his conversion to the Jews after his arrest in Jerusalem:

> 1 Men, brethren, and fathers, listen to my defense to you now. 2 Then, when they heard that he began addressing them in the Hebrew dialect, they became even quieter. And he said, 3 I am *a* Jew, born in Tarsus of Cilicia, who was educated in this city at the feet of Gamaliel, taught according to the strictest manner of the Law of the fathers, and was zealous for the God, even as you all are today, 4 who persecuted this Way unto death, by binding and delivering both men and women to prisons, 5 as also the high priest and the whole council of elders can testify of me, from whom I also received letters to the brethren in Damascus. I was on my way to also bring those who had been bound to Jerusalem so they might be punished.
>
> 6 Now it happened as I was traveling and approaching Damascus, about noon, powerful light suddenly surrounded me from the heaven. 7 I fell to the ground and heard *a* voice saying to me, Saul, Saul, why do you persecute Me? 8 Then I replied, Who are you, Lord? He said to me, I am Jesus of Nazareth whom you are persecuting. 9 Now those who were with me saw the light but did not understand the voice of the One who spoke to me. 10 Then I said, What should I do, Lord? And the Lord said to me, After you get up, go to

> Damascus. And there it will be told about everything that
> has been appointed for you to do. 11 Now since I could not
> see due to the intensity of that light, as I was led by the hand
> by those who were with me, I came to Damascus.
>
> 12 Then Ananias, *a* devout man according to the Law, who
> was attested to by all the Jews who lived *there*, 13 when he
> came and stood by me, he said to me, Brother Saul, receive
> you sight. And at that moment I saw him. 14 Then he said,
> The God of our fathers previously handpicked you to know
> His will and to see the Righteous One and to hear *the* voice
> from His mouth. 15 For you will be His witness to all men of
> what you have seen and heard. 16 So why delay? When you
> get up, be baptized and wash away your sins after you call
> on the name of the Lord.
>
> 17 Now it happened after I returned to Jerusalem and while I
> was praying in the Temple, I fell into *a* trance. 18 And I saw
> Him saying to me, Hurry and quickly leave Jerusalem. For
> they will not accept your testimony about Me. 19 And I said,
> Lord, they themselves know that I kept imprisoning and
> beating in every synagogue those who believed on you.
> 20 And when the blood of your witness Stephen was shed, I
> myself stood by and agreed to his death, and kept the clothes
> of those who killed him. 21 Then He said to me, Go! For I
> will send you far away to *the* Gentiles. 22 Now they kept
> listening to him until this word. Then they raised their voice,
> saying, Away from the earth with such! He is not fit to live
> (Acts 22.1-21)!

The third account of Paul's conversion was Paul's testimony before King Agrippa.[8] For two years Paul had been imprisoned at Caesarea[9] under the rule of Felix[10] and then Festus.[11] Festus wanted to send Paul

---

8 Agrippa was the eighth and last client ruler of Rome from the Herodian dynasty, the fifth (after Herod the Great, Agrippa I, Herod of Chalcis and Aristobulus of Chalcis) who bore the title of King. He was the son of the first and better-known Herod Agrippa, the brother of Berenice, Mariamne, and Drusilla, second wife of the Roman procurator Antonius Felix.

9 The Roman battalion commander moved Paul from Jerusalem to Caesarea when he learned of a Jewish plot to kill him (Acts 23.12-22). Since Paul was a citizen of Rome, the commander was especially concerned for his safety and assembled a large protective force to escort him to Caesarea. They left at the third hour of the night (9 p.m.) on horseback (Acts 23.23-24) and carried a letter to Felix, which Luke recorded (Acts 23.26-35).

10 Felix was appointed Roman procurator of Judea in A.D. 53 by the emperor Claudius. He ruled the province in a cruel, profligate manner marked by trouble and sedition. He kept Paul imprisoned at Caesarea with the hope of extorting money from him (Acts 24.26-27).

11 Porcius Festus was appointed to supersede Felix, who, on his return to Rome, was accused by the Jews in Caesarea. His brother, Pallas prevailed with Emperor Nero to spare him. Felix's third wife was Drusilla, daughter of Herod Agrippa I. He persuaded her to leave her husband and marry him.

back to Jerusalem to be judged. Paul knew if this occurred the Jews would kill him. Because of this, he appealed his case to Caesar, his right as a Roman citizen (Acts 25.9-12). During the last days of Paul's imprisonment, Agrippa and Bernice[12] visited Festus and heard his case. Luke recorded their conversation:

> 1 Then Agrippa said to Paul, It is permitted for you to speak for yourself. Then Paul extended his hand and began his defense. 2 About everything of which I am accused by *the* Jews, King Agrippa, I consider myself fortunate that I am about to defend myself before you today, 3 especially since you are knowledgeable about all the customs and disputes of Jews. Therefore, I implore you to listen to me patiently. 4 Now all the Jews indeed know my manner of life from adolescence, from its beginning among my nation, and in Jerusalem. 5 They know about me from the first, (if they would be willing to testify) that I lived *as a* Pharisee according to the strictest party of our religion. 6 And now, for the hope of the promise God made to the fathers, I stand trial, 7 for which, our twelve tribes, who serve earnestly, night and day, hope to attain. It is about this hope I am accused by *the* Jews, O king. 8 Why is it considered incredible by you, if the God raises *the* dead? 9 Indeed, I myself thought I must do many things against the name of Jesus of Nazareth, 10 which I did in Jerusalem. And I locked up many of the saints in prisons after I received the authority from the chief priests and cast *a* vote against *them* when they were sentenced to death. 11 And in all the synagogues, often punishing them, I kept forcing them to blaspheme. And because I was exceedingly furious with them, I kept persecuting *them*, even to foreign cities.
>
> 12 In all this, while I traveled to Damascus, with authority and full power of the chief priests, 13 at midday on the road, O king, I saw light from heaven above, brighter than the sun, surrounding me and those traveling with me. 14 And after all of us fell to the ground, I heard *a* voice saying to me in the Hebrew dialect, Saul, Saul, why do you persecute Me? *It is* hard for you to kick against goads. 15 Then I said, Who are you, Lord? And He said, I am Jesus whom you persecute. 16 But get up and stand on your feet. I appeared to you for this purpose: To handpick you *a* servant and *a* witness both of the things you saw from Me and of the things I will show to you, 17 by rescuing you from the people and from the Gentiles, to whom I send you, 18 to open their eyes, so they

---

[12] Bernice or Berenice, was daughter of Herod Agrippa the elder. Her first marriage was to her uncle Herod, king of Chalcis. After he died, she married Polemon, king of Cilicia. Deserting him soon afterward, she returned to her brother Agrippa, with whom she was said to have lived incestuously. Later, she became mistress of the emperor Titus.

> might turn from darkness to light, and from the power of Satan to the God, that they might receive forgiveness of sins and inheritance among those who have been sanctified by faith that is in Me.
>
> [19] So then, King Agrippa, I was not disobedient to the heavenly vision, [20] but began telling those in Damascus first, and those in Jerusalem, and all the region of Judea, and the Gentiles, to repent and to turn to the God and do works worthy of repentance. [21] Because of these things, the Jews seized me when I was in the Temple and began trying to kill *me*. [22] Therefore, since I obtained help from the God until this day, I have stood witnessing to small and to great, saying nothing except what the prophets and Moses said about what was to happen: [23] that the Christ would suffer and be *the* first to rise from the dead and to proclaim light to the people and to the Gentiles (Acts 26.1-23).

The detailed accounts of Paul's conversion are repeated three times—6% of the content of Acts. Why did Luke devote so much attention to this event?

## Paul: The Apostle of the Gentiles

Saul of Tarsus was on the "fast-track" of Pharisaic Judaism. A "rising star" to succeed his teacher Gamaliel, he would probably have been one of the great rabbis of Israel. He had the intelligence and the zeal for the position. But God had something much greater in mind for him.

Saul's conversion was the most important and dramatic event in his life. Far more important was how God would use him. Paul became the founder of a new, previously unrevealed theological program: the Church, the body of Christ.

The last time God had created a new theological program had been 2,000 years before when He called Abraham. God chose Abraham and made a covenant with him and revealed how He would bless Gentiles. By refusing to respond to the gospel of the kingdom, Israel rebuffed their position in the Abrahamic Covenant as God's channel to bless Gentiles. But though they failed, God determined He would bless Gentiles through an *unrevealed* plan. This plan began with the salvation of Saul of Tarsus. Paul, as "the apostle of the Gentiles" (Romans 11.13), became proxy Israel. He represented true Israel, believing Israel. Through him, God would bless Gentiles.

| Paul's Commission as the Apostle of the Gentiles | |
|---|---|
| But the Lord said to him, Go. For this man is *a* chosen vessel to Me, to carry My name before the Gentiles, and kings, and the sons of Israel. | Acts 9.15 |
| Then He said to me, Go! For I will send you far away to *the* Gentiles. | Acts 22.21 |

| | |
|---|---|
| [16] But get up and stand on your feet. I appeared to you for this purpose: To handpick you a servant and a witness both of the things you saw from Me and of the things I will show to you, [17] by rescuing you from the people and from the Gentiles, to whom I send you, [18] to open their eyes, so they might turn from darkness to light, and from the power of Satan to the God, that they might receive forgiveness of sins and inheritance among those who have been sanctified by faith that is in Me. | Acts 26.16-18 |

Why did God not use the Twelve as apostles to Gentiles? Had he not told them to go to Gentiles with the words, commonly known as the "Great Commission?" Matthew wrote:

> [18] Now when Jesus approached, He spoke to them, saying, All authority is given to Me in heaven and on the earth. [19] Therefore, as you go, teach all the nations, baptizing them in the name of the Father, and of the Son, and of the Holy Spirit, [20] as you instruct them to observe all things, whatever I commanded you. And behold, I am with you all the days, until the completion of the age (Matthew 28.18-20).

Jesus commissioned the Twelve as *apostles of Israel*. This is clear from the Lord's answer to Peter, who asked Him after His conversation with a rich, young Jew, "Behold, we have forsaken all, and followed you; what shall we have therefore" (Matthew 19.27)? Jesus answered:

> [28] And Jesus said to them, Truly I tell you, You who followed Me, in the regeneration, when the Son of the Man should sit on *the* throne of His glory, you too will sit on twelve thrones, ruling the twelve tribes of Israel (Matthew 19.28).

Jesus chose the Twelve as representatives of God's prophetic program based upon the Abrahamic, Land, Mosaic, Sabbatic, Davidic, and New Covenants. The prophetic program assumed Israel would accept their Messiah. The nation would then inherit the blessings of the kingdom and become a channel of blessings to Gentiles (Micah 4.1-2; Zechariah 8.21-23).

The Lord gave specific instruction to the Twelve for the their ministry:

> But you will receive power when the Holy Spirit comes on you. And you will be My witnesses in Jerusalem, and in all Judea, and Samaria, and to the ends the earth (Acts 1.8).

The Lord's marching orders to the Twelve was that they were to start at Jerusalem, then go to Judea (the south), then go to Samaria (the north), and lastly, go to the nations (Gentiles).

Acts 1.8 explains Acts 8.1:

> Now Saul agreed with killing him. Then, on that day, *a* great persecution rose against the congregation in Jerusalem. So all were scattered throughout the regions of Judea and Samaria—except the apostles (Acts 8.1).

Acts 8.1 is at least five years after Pentecost. Where are the Twelve? They are in Jerusalem. They remained in Jerusalem, even under tremendous threat and danger from Saul's persecution. They refused to leave Jerusalem because it had not yet responded to the gospel of the kingdom. They would not go to Judea or Samaria, much less to foreign counties and Gentiles, until Jerusalem responded. Because Israel would not repent, *they could not fulfill* the "Great Commission." God had to make another way to bless Gentiles apart from the Twelve.

The idea the Twelve went to evangelize Gentiles after Pentecost is a myth which has become tradition. It never happened. This is clear from Luke's account of Peter's vision in Acts 10. Peter argued with the Lord about going to the house of the Gentile Cornelius. Why would he argue if he and the Twelve had been ministering to Gentiles? Why, after he returned to Jerusalem, would the leaders there upbraid him for going to the house of a Gentile (Acts 11.1-3)? Why would the Lord *need* to give him a vision if he was already evangelizing Gentiles? Lastly, Luke plainly stated no Gentile evangelism had occurred. The text reads:

> Therefore, those who were scattered by the persecution which occurred over Stephen, traveled as far as to Phoenicia, and Cyprus, and Antioch, speaking the word to no one except Jews only (Acts 11.19).

The key thing to understand is that *no* Gentile ministry occurred until *after* Paul's salvation. *After* Paul's salvation, Peter received his vision to go to the house of Cornelius. *After* Paul's salvation is the following account:

> [20] But some of them, men of Cyprus and Cyrene, who came
> to Antioch, began speaking also to the Greeks,[13] proclaiming
> the gospel—the Lord Jesus. [21] And *the* hand of *the* Lord was
> with them. *A* great number believed and turned to the Lord.
> [22] Now the news about them was heard in the ears of the
> congregation that was in Jerusalem. So they sent Barnabas
> to go to Antioch, [23] who, after he came and saw the grace of
> the God, rejoiced, and began encouraging everyone to
> remain true to the Lord, with devoted hearts. [24] For he was *a*
> good man and full of *the* Holy Spirit and faith. And *a* large

---

[13] Some manuscripts have "Hellenists" or "Grecians" (Ἑλληνιστής), Greek-speaking Jews. Better textual evidence exists for "Greeks" (Ἕλλην), i.e., Gentiles. Greek-speaking Jews had been saved from the beginning. Gentiles were being evangelized.

> group was added to the Lord. [25] Then Barnabas went to Tarsus to look for Saul (Acts 11.20-25).

The Jewish believers from Cyprus and Cyrene went to Antioch and began witnessing to Gentiles. We do not know the circumstances that prompted this but the Lord blessed their efforts and "*A* great number believed and turned to the Lord" (Acts 11.21). When the leaders in Jerusalem (the Twelve) heard this, they were shaken. What did this mean? How were Gentiles coming to know the Lord apart from Israel's repentance? To learn what was happening, they sent Barnabas to Antioch to investigate.

Barnabas discovered these Gentiles were believers. How much he understood about what had happened and why is unknown. What he did understand, however, was that he had to find Paul for he knew God had commissioned Paul to minister to Gentiles. Thus, he set out for Tarsus to find Paul.

After his salvation on the road to Damascus, Paul spent three years in Arabia and Damascus. He then wished to go to Jerusalem to meet with the believers there. Everyone was terrified of him (Galatians 1.18-19) but Barnabas bravely took Paul to see them. Luke recorded:

> [26] Now when Saul came to Jerusalem, he kept trying to join the disciples. But everyone was afraid of him because they did not believe that he was *a* disciple. [27] But Barnabas received him and brought *him* to the apostles and described to them how he saw the Lord on the road and that He spoke to him, and how he had spoken boldly in Jesus' name in Damascus (Acts 9.26-27).

Paul was God's man to minister to Gentiles. Barnabas found him and Luke wrote:

> And when he found *him*, he brought *him* to Antioch. So it happened that they met with the congregation for a whole year and taught a large group. Now in Antioch, the disciples were first called Christians (Acts 11.26).

Antioch was the place where believers first became known as Christians. The name, "Christian," originated outside Israel, in Gentile territory, in what became a mostly Gentile congregation.

The further one goes into Acts, the more Peter and the Twelve fade away. Acts has 28 chapters. Acts 15 is the last time Peter is mentioned. Why? Peter and the Twelve's disappearance shows how the prophetic, kingdom program was passing away. It was being supplanted by Paul's gospel and God's program of the Church, the body of Christ. Peter's visit to Cornelius' house is the *only* Biblical record of any of the Twelve going to Gentiles. Despite tradition, the record is clear: Peter and the Twelve *never had a ministry to Gentiles*.

In Acts 21, we read the following concerning Paul's visit to Jerusalem for Pentecost:

> [17] Now when we arrived in Jerusalem, the brethren warmly welcomed us. [18] And the next day Paul went with us to James and all the elders arrived. [19] And after he greeted them, he began describing in detail the things the God had done among the Gentiles through his ministry (Acts 21-17-19).

When Paul met James[14] in Jerusalem, he told James and his followers how God had saved Gentiles by his ministry. James and the elders rejoiced, but their response showed they had far greater enthusiasm for Jewish salvation and zeal for the Mosaic Law. Luke wrote:

> And when they heard, they began praising the Lord. Then they said to him, You see, brother, how many myriads of those who have believed are among the Jews. And they are all zealous for the Law (Acts 21.20).

This passage shows that while James and company rejoiced Gentiles had been saved, they had little interest in Gentile evangelism. The agreement forged at the Jerusalem Council had formalized what was already a reality: Peter and the Twelve would minister to the Jews and Paul would go to Gentiles. Recounting this event, Paul wrote the Galatians:

> [7] But, on the contrary, when they saw that I had been entrusted with the gospel of the uncircumcision, even as Peter with that of the circumcision, [8] for the One who worked with Peter for *the* apostleship of the circumcision, also worked in me for the Gentiles. [9] And after they understood the grace that was given to me, James, and Cephas, and John, those who were recognized to be pillars, gave me and Barnabas *the* right hands of fellowship, so we *might go* to the Gentiles, but they, to the circumcision (Galatians 2.7-9).

## The Sign of Elymas

Luke recorded Paul's first missionary journey (circa A.D. 45) in Acts 13. Accompanying Paul were Barnabas and John Mark.[15] Barnabas and Saul left Antioch and went southwest to Selucia, then to the island of Cyprus. While at Salamis[16] they preached in the synagogues to the Jews (Acts 13.5). They then traveled to the other side of the island, to

---

[14] This was James the half-brother of Jesus, known as James the Just. The apostle James of Peter, James, and John had been executed in 44 A.D. by Herod Agrippa I (Acts 12.1-2). By the time of the Jerusalem Council, 51 A.D., this James had supplanted Peter as the head of the Jerusalem assembly.

[15] John Mark had the Jewish name "John" and the Roman name "Mark" as his surname (Acts 12.12, 25, 15.37). His mother was Mary, the Mary in whose house the disciples prayed when Peter was imprisoned by Herod Antipas I. Mark was Barnabas' nephew (Colossians 4.10).

[16] Salamis was an important port and commercial center with a large Jewish community.

Paphos,[17] and encountered a Jewish false prophet named Bar-Jesus,[18] also known as Elymas.[19] This "magi" (μάγος) of the gods was an advisor to Sergius Paulus, Proconsul of Cyprus,[20] who had learned of Barnabas and Saul's presence and wished to hear them (Acts 13.7).

Elymas tried to prevent the proconsul from hearing Paul. In response, Paul, full of the Holy Spirit, fixed his eyes upon him,

> 10 said, O full of every deceit and all cunning, son of *the*
> Devil, enemy of all righteousness, will you not stop
> perverting the right ways of the Lord? 11 So now behold, *the*
> hand of *the* Lord *is* on you and you will be blind, not able to see the sun for *a* season. Then, immediately, dimness and darkness descended on him. And he went seeking someone to lead him by the hand (Acts 13.10-11).

The result was that Sergius Paulus, "astonished at the doctrine of the Lord" (Acts 13.12), became a believer. He recognized Paul's teaching and power were greater than Elymas'.

Luke's larger point in is that Elymas represented unbelieving Israel. Because of his unbelief and opposition to Jesus and the gospel, Paul declared he would be blind for "a season." Elymas is a "type" of "blind Israel." Paul wrote in Romans 11:

> 7 What therefore? What Israel seeks, this it did not obtain.
> But the chosen obtained *it*. And the rest became hardened.
> 8 As has been written: The God gave them *a* spirit of stupor,
> eyes which cannot see and ears which cannot hear, to this
> very day. 9 And David says: Let their table become for *a*
> snare, and for *a* trap, and. for *a* stumbling block, and for *a*
> retribution to them. 10 Let their eyes become darkened, not
> to see, and let their back become continually bent over. (Romans 11.7-10).

Israel's national blindness is temporary and partial (Romans 11.25). It was also a secret. God had not revealed it through His prophets.

## Acts: The Fall of Israel

Most believe Luke wrote Acts to tell the story of the birth of the Church and its growth. But Luke's primary message was to show the fall of Israel so Jews would understand why God could not establish His kingdom on earth. Luke wrote in early Acts of the three rejections by the Jews of Peter's ministry (Acts 4.5-31, 5.12-42, 7.1-60).

Paul's ministry also had three Jewish rejections. He first went to the Jews and when they refused his words he would turn to the Gentiles.

---

[17] Paphos was the Roman capital of Cyprus and important port.
[18] "Bar," בַּר, is Aramaic for "son" and corresponds to the Hebrew, "ben," בֵּן.
[19] "Elymas" most likely derives from the Aramaic, אֶלִימָא, "powerful."
[20] Sergius Paulus was Rome's ranking officer on the island.

These testimonies fulfilled the Law's requirement to the Jews of establishing a matter by two or three witnesses (Deuteronomy 17.6, 19.15; Matthew 18.16; 2 Corinthians 13.1).

## Acts 13

Leaving Paphos, Paul and Barnabas sailed to Perga and traveled to Antioch Pisidia where they taught in the synagogue.[21] Acts 13 ends with the following statement:

> 45 But when the Jews saw the crowds, they were filled with envy and began opposing the things spoken by Paul, contradicting and reviling. 46 And after they spoke boldly, Paul and Barnabas said, It was necessary for the word of the God to be spoken to you first. But since you push it away and do not consider yourselves worthy of the eternal life, behold, we turn to the Gentiles. 47 For so the Lord has commanded us: I have set you for *a* light of the Gentiles—for you to be for salvation to the ends of the earth. 48 Now when the Gentiles heard this, they began rejoicing and praising the word of the Lord, and believed, as many as were appointed to eternal life. 49 Then the word of the Lord was spread through the whole region (Acts 13.45-48).

Paul told the Jews that he and Barnabas were required to give the word of God to them first. Since they would not receive their message, they turned to the Gentiles.

## Acts 18

On his second missionary journey, after Paul visited Athens and spoke to the philosophers on Mars Hill (Acts 17), he traveled to Corinth where he met Aquila and Priscilla. While in Corinth, Paul went to the synagogue and taught. Luke wrote:

> 4 Now on every Sabbath he kept lecturing in the synagogue and kept persuading both Jews and Greeks. 5 And after Silas and Timothy came down from Macedonia, Paul was burdened in the spirit, and testified to the Jews *that* Jesus was the Christ. 6 But when they kept opposing and reviling *him*, he shook his clothes *and* said to them, Your blood *be* on your head. I am clean. From now on, I will go to the Gentiles (Acts 18.4-6).

This was Paul's second great declaration to the Jews. They again rejected the Messiah and he declared he would go to the Gentiles.

---

[21] In Perga, John Mark left them. His departure led to a sharp quarrel between Paul and Barnabas. Barnabas went with Paul to the Council of Jerusalem in 51 A.D., but no longer accompanied him in missionary trips (Acts 15.36-39).

## Acts 28

Acts began with great promise. The Jews had murdered their Messiah but He had risen from the dead. The Holy Spirit had come at Pentecost as God's enabler of the New Covenant so Israel could be a kingdom of priests. Peter told the nation to repent. If they would, God would send the Messiah to establish the kingdom of God on earth (Acts 3.12-21). But it was not to be. The nation would not listen. It continued to reject the Messiah. As a result, Acts ends in tragedy for national Israel.

Having narrowly escaped being murdered by the Jews, Paul spent two years in prison in Caesarea and finally reached Rome, surviving a harrowing sea voyage. Under house arrest, he invited the chief Jews along with others to hear him. Luke wrote:

> 23 So, when they scheduled *a* day for him, many more came
> to his lodging, to whom he kept expounding and testifying
> about the kingdom of the God, persuading them about Jesus,
> from both the Law of Moses and the prophets, from morning
> until evening. 24 And some became convinced about the
> things he spoke. But some refused to believe. 25 And when
> there was discord with one another, they began leaving after
> Paul spoke one word: The Holy Spirit correctly spoke
> through Isaiah the prophet to our fathers, 26 saying, Go to this
> people and say, Hearing you will hear so you might never
> understand. And seeing you will see so you might never
> perceive. 27 For the heart of this people is thick and they
> barely hear with their ears, and they closed their eyes, lest
> they should see with their eyes and hear with their ears, and
> perceive with their heart, and turn so I will heal them.
> 28 Therefore, know this: This salvation of the God is sent to
> the Gentiles. And they will listen! 29 And after he said these
> things, the Jews went away and had *a* great argument among
> themselves (Acts 28.23-29).

This ended Paul's dealings with the Jews. Heartbroken because of their unbelief, he recognized God had judicially blinded the nation. This was a bitter lesson but the Lord had told him early in his ministry, "Hurry and quickly leave Jerusalem. For they will not accept your testimony about Me" (Acts 22.18). Paul thought that of all people, they would listen to him (Acts 22.19-20). The Lord knew otherwise. He told Paul, "Go! For I will send you far away to *the* Gentiles" (Acts 22.21).

Paul finally recognized this reality. During his two years of house arrest in Rome, he wrote Ephesians, Colossians, Philippians, and Philemon. Recognizing his Gentile ministry, he wrote:

> For this reason, I Paul, the prisoner of Christ Jesus for you Gentiles (Ephesians 3.1).

> Therefore, I, the prisoner in *the* Lord, urge you to walk worthily of the calling to which you were called, (Ephesians 4.1).

Who imprisoned Paul? Paul was certainly a prisoner of Rome. But he wrote he was the prisoner of Jesus Christ. For what purpose? For Gentiles. The Lord had been patient with Paul in his ministering to Jews. But the time had come for him to focus on his primary commission: the apostle of the Gentiles.

# Chapter 3
# Paul: Proxy Israel

*[16] But get up and stand on your feet. I appeared to you for this purpose: To handpick you a servant and a witness both of the things you saw from Me and of the things I will show to you, [17] by rescuing you from the people and from the Gentiles, to whom I send you, [18] to open their eyes, so they might turn from darkness to light, and from the power of Satan to the God, that they might receive forgiveness of sins and inheritance among those who have been sanctified by faith that is in Me (Acts 26.16-18).*

## Paul's Role

The above verses declare the Lord told Paul that He had saved him to be a minister and witness of the things he had seen and also of things He would later disclose to him. In verse 16 above, the word translated "handpick," προχειρίζω, literally means choose before with the hand. It is used only twice, both times of Paul (cf. Acts 22.14). Also, both times it is in the middle voice, thus, "handpick you Myself beforehand." God told Paul He would deliver him from both Jews and Gentiles and that He was sending him specifically to the Gentiles that they might receive the forgiveness of sins and be heirs with those who had believed in Him.

Paul's salvation and commission qualified him to assume the role repentant, believing Israel was supposed to have played. Over 700 years earlier, God had revealed this role to Isaiah. He wrote:

> [6] I the Lord have called you in righteousness, and will hold your hand, and will keep you, and give you for a covenant of the people, for a light of the Gentiles; [7] To open the blind eyes, to bring out the prisoners from the prison, and them that sit in darkness out of the prison house (Isaiah 42.6-7).
>
> And he said, It is a light thing that you should be my servant to raise up the tribes of Jacob, and to restore the preserved of Israel: I will also give you for a light to the Gentiles, that you may be my salvation to the end of the earth (Isaiah 49.6).

Zechariah also described this ministry:

> [20] Thus says the Lord of hosts; It will yet come to pass, that there will come people, and the inhabitants of many cities: [21] And the inhabitants of one city will go to another, saying, Let us go speedily to pray before the Lord, and to seek the Lord of hosts: I will go also. [22] Yea, many people and strong

> nations will come to seek the Lord of hosts in Jerusalem, and to pray before the Lord. [23] Thus says the Lord of hosts; In those days it will come to pass, that ten men will take hold out of all languages of the nations, even will take hold of the skirt of him that is a Jew, saying, We will go with you: for we have heard that God is with you (Zechariah 8.20-23).

The prophet Micah depicted the same:

> [1] But in the last days it will come to pass, that the mountain of the house of the Lord will be established in the top of the mountains, and it will be exalted above the hills; and people will flow to it. [2] And many nations will come, and say, Come, and let us go up to the mountain of the Lord, and to the house of the God of Jacob; and he will teach us of his ways, and we will walk in his paths: for the law will go forth of Zion, and the word of the Lord from Jerusalem (Micah 4.1-2).

National Israel, guided by the Light of the World, the Messiah, was to be the light to the nations, the Gentiles. This was the message of the Lord's "Great Commission" to the Twelve. Because the nation refused to accept Jesus as the Messiah, Israel lost this opportunity at that time.

## Paul and the Abrahamic Covenant

The Abrahamic Covenant stated God would bless Gentiles through Israel, God's covenant people. God had *not* revealed what would happen with Gentiles if Israel rejected its Messiah other than that the Day of the Lord, God's wrath would occur. God had revealed nothing about creating a new entity, the Church, the body of Christ, in which Jew and Gentile would be equal. Had Israel accepted the Messiah, the Church would not have come into existence. There would have been no need.

Because national Israel refused its commission articulated in the "Great Commission" during the time of the apostles, Paul became proxy Israel and served in that capacity in three important roles: 1) as a light to the Gentiles, 2) as a priest, and 3) as the minister of the New Covenant. He wrote the Corinthians:

> [3] For I delivered to you first, what I also received: Christ died for our sins, according to the Scriptures, [4] and that He was buried, and that He has been raised on the third day, according to the Scriptures, [5] and that he appeared to Cephas, then to the Twelve. [6] Afterwards he was seen by more than five hundred brethren at once, of whom the majority remain until now. Some, however, fell asleep. [7] Then He appeared to James, then to all the apostles. [8] And last of all, as by the untimely birth, he appeared also to me (1 Corinthians 15.3-8).

Paul was the last to see the resurrected Christ and described his coming to Christ as an "untimely birth."[1] Paul's "birth" was untimely in that it preceded the birth of the Jewish nation. His "birth" anticipated Israel's spiritual birth when it recognizes Jesus as the Messiah. Isaiah wrote:

> Who has ever heard of such things? Who has ever seen things like this? Can a country be born in a day or a nation be brought forth in a moment? Yet no sooner is Zion in labor than she gives birth to her children (Isaiah 66.8).

At the Lord's return, the al Israel will repent and be "born in a day."

| Paul's Roles as Proxy Israel | |
|---|---|
| Light of the Gentiles | Acts 13.46-47 |
| Priest of the Gentiles | Romans 15.15-16 |
| Minister of the New Covenant | 2 Corinthians 3.4-6 |

## Paul: Light of the Gentiles

During Paul's first missionary journey, he and Barnabas traveled to Antioch Pisidia and went to the synagogue on the Sabbath. After the Scripture reading, the rulers asked if anyone would like to say a word of encouragement. Paul stood and addressed the people. They were blessed by his words and wished to hear him the following Sabbath. Luke recorded what transpired:

> 43 So when the synagogue dismissed, many of the Jews and the devout proselytes followed Paul and Barnabas, who, as they spoke to them, kept persuading them to continue in the grace of the God. 44 So on the next Sabbath, almost the whole city gathered to hear the word of the God. 45 But when the Jews saw the crowds, they were filled with envy and began opposing the things spoken by Paul, contradicting and reviling. 46 And after they spoke boldly, Paul and Barnabas said, It was necessary for the word of the God to be spoken to you first. But since you push it away and do not consider yourselves worthy of the eternal life, behold, we turn to the Gentiles. 47 For so the Lord has commanded us: I have set you [σε] for *a* light of the Gentiles—for you [σε] to be for salvation to the ends of the earth. 48 Now when the Gentiles heard this, they began rejoicing and praising the word of the Lord, and believed, as many as were appointed to eternal life (Acts 13.43-48).

Paul's words, "I have set you to for *a* light of the Gentiles, that you should be for salvation to the ends of the earth" (τέθεικά **σε** εἰς φῶς

---

[1] The word translated "untimely birth" is ἔκτρωμα, a premature birth.

ἐθνῶν τοῦ εἶναί **σε** εἰς σωτηρίαν ἕως ἐσχάτου τῆς γῆς) is a quote from Isaiah 42.6 and 49.6.[2] Who is "you" in verse 47? Isaiah revealed "the light to the Gentiles" was Israel. But because the Jews continued to reject their Messiah, Paul declared *he* was that light. Did Paul not mean both Barnabas and himself? No. Paul meant *himself.* Paul used σέ, the *singular* second person accusative pronoun of "you" twice in the passage. Had Barnabas been included, he would have used ὑμᾶς, the *plural* pronoun. Jesus chose *Paul* as the apostle of the Gentiles. [3]

## Paul: Priest of the Gentiles

Paul wrote about Church offices, gifts, and ministries. He noted apostles, prophets, bishops/elders, deacons, pastors, teachers, evangelists, and mentioned numerous gifts—administration, mercy, teaching, giving, faith, healing, tongues, etc. The one office, so prominent to Israel, unmentioned in the Church, is "priest."[4] Except once. Paul wrote *he* served as a priest. Romans 15.15-16 reads:

> 15 Now I wrote to you more freely brothers on some matters, so as to remind you, because of the grace given to me by the God: 16 that I might be the minister [λειτουργὸν] of Jesus Christ for the Gentiles, serving as a priest [ἱερουργοῦντα] the gospel of the God, so the offering of the Gentiles might become acceptable, since it has been sanctified by *the* Holy Spirit (Romans 15.15-16).

Paul used the noun λειτουργός in verse 16, "minister of Jesus Christ to the Gentiles." This word was used for public servants (Romans 13.6), persons who rendered general service (Philippians 2.25), angelic service (Hebrews 1.7), and Christ as High Priest (Hebrews 8.2). Paul included the definite article, τὸ λειτουργὸν "the minister" to emphasize *he* was the minister to the Gentiles. The second part of the verse reveals specifically how Paul served. Paul used the present active participle ἱερουργοῦντα of the verb ἱερουργέω (cf. כָּהַן), "ministering the gospel of God." This verb means to minister as a priest.

---

[2] Jesus' statement to the Jews, "You are the light of the world" (Matthew 5.14) and "Let your light so shine before men" (Matthew 5.16) anticipated Israel's role as God's channel of blessing to Gentiles.

[3] One may argue Luke rendered Paul's quote with the singular σέ because that was the reading of the LXX. But Paul sometimes changed a reading to make an application. As an apostle and writer of Scripture he had that authority.

[4] The Church has *no* priests. Some have taught that every believer is a priest, an idea from 1 Peter 2.9. But Peter wrote to *Jews* (1 Peter 1.1) who believed the gospel of the kingdom in fulfillment of Exodus 19.6 and Isaiah 61.6, *not* members of the Church, the body of Christ. Members of the Church are saints (Romans 1.7) and ambassadors (2 Corinthians 5.20), but *not* priests.

Paul was of the tribe of Benjamin, not Levi, not a descendant of Aaron and could not serve as a priest under the Mosaic Law (Exodus 28.1; Numbers 3.10; Hebrews 5.1-4). What did he mean by his statement?

God's destiny for Israel was to be a holy nation, a kingdom of priests (Exodus 19.6; Isaiah 61.6). That destiny went beyond the service of the Levitical priesthood. The main role of a priest is a go-between, a representative. One day, every Jew will serve in this role. Zechariah wrote:

> 22 Many people and strong nations will come to seek the Lord of hosts in Jerusalem, and to pray before the Lord. 23 Thus says the Lord of hosts; In those days it shall come to pass, that ten men shall take hold out of all languages of the nations, even shall take hold of the skirt of him that is a Jew, saying, We will go with you: for we have heard that God is with you (Zechariah 8.22-23).

Repentant, believing Israel will fulfill its Exodus 19.6 destiny. Every Jew will be a priest. Until then, Paul serves this role to Gentiles. Paul's commission and office, as proxy Israel, complied with God's promise to bless Gentiles *through Israel* according to the Abrahamic Covenant.

## Paul: Minister of the New Covenant

God promised to establish the New Covenant with Israel.[5] Jeremiah 31, Ezekiel 11, and 36 state this clearly. As "new," it was to replace the "old" covenant, the Mosaic Covenant. Unlike the other covenants God gave Israel, which included the physical blessings of land, kingdom, and preeminence, New Covenant blessings were spiritual.

The New Covenant is mentioned infrequently in the New Testament. Outside of Christ's statement at the Last Supper, "This is My blood of the new covenant, which is poured out for many." (Mark 14.24; cf. Matthew 26.28; Luke 22.20) Paul is the only New Testament writer who mentioned it (1 Corinthians 11.23-36; 2 Corinthians 3.5-6; Hebrews 7.22, 8.6-13, 9.15-20, 10.16, 29, 12.24). Peter, James, John, and Jude never discuss it. Why? Paul was proxy Israel. He wrote the Corinthians:

---

[5] The New Covenant has been a difficult subject for those who believe God established His covenants with Israel alone and that He will literally fulfill these promises to national Israel despite their unbelief in rejecting the Messiah. Those who hold this view are known as Dispensationalists. Others, who hold to Reformed or Covenant theology, teach the Church has assumed God's promises to Israel. For the Church to fulfill the New Covenant is no problem to them since they teach Israel's covenants are fulfilled *figuratively* by the Church. This handy solution comes at an exorbitant price: abandoning a hermeneutic with rigor and loss of God's integrity. If God will not literally fulfill His promises to Israel, why should the Church think He will literally fulfill His promises to it?

> [23] For I received from the Lord what I also delivered to you: the Lord Jesus, in the night in which he was betrayed, took bread, [24] and when He gave thanks, He broke *it* and said, Take eat, this is My body, broken for you. Do this in the remembrance of Me. [25] Likewise also the cup. After dining, He said, This cup is the new covenant in My blood. Do this as often as you should drink *it* for My remembrance. [26] For as often as you should eat this bread and should drink this cup, you proclaim the Lord's death until He should come (1 Corinthians 11.23-26).

The Lord communicated directly with Paul and validated the Lord's Supper for the Church. Additionally, He revealed to Paul that it was a memorial: "you proclaim the Lord's death until He should come."

The other passage Paul wrote concerning the New Covenant was in his second letter to the Corinthians:

> [4] Now we have this confidence through the Christ to the God—[5] not that we are sufficient from ourselves to consider anything as from ourselves—rather our sufficiency *is* from the God, [6] who also qualified us *as* ministers of *a* new covenant, not of *the* letter, but of *the* Spirit. For the letter kills, but the Spirit gives life (2 Corinthians 3.4-6).

Paul identified himself[6] as a minister[7] of a new covenant and noted its spiritual nature. The "blood of the New Covenant" (Matthew 26.28) was shed not only to redeem Israel but to replace the Mosaic Law with a "better covenant" (Hebrews 8.6). Paul wrote Christ's death (His shed blood) blotted out and removed the ordinances (Mosaic Law) against us, nailing them to His cross (Colossians 2.14).

| New Covenant—Established by the Blood of Christ<br>Matthew 26.28; 1 Corinthians 11.25; Ephesians 2.13 | |
|---|---|
| Provisions | Application to the Church |
| Forgiveness of sins (Jeremiah 31.34; Ezekiel 36.25, 29) | Ephesians 1.7, 4.33; Colossians 1.14, 2.13 |
| God's people (Jeremiah 31.33) | Titus 2.14 |
| Indwelling Holy Spirit (Ezekiel 36.26-27) | 1 Corinthians 2.12, 6.19; 2 Corinthians 1.22, 5.5; Ephesians 1.14 |

God promised these blessings to *Israel.* Gentiles were not included. Gentiles were *separated* from Israel's covenants (Ephesians 2.11-12).

---

[6] The context of the passage indicates Paul was using "we" as a nosism and meant "himself."

[7] The word here for "minister" is the general word διάκονος.

But members of the Church, the body of Christ, have received the spiritual blessing of the New Covenant—the indwelling Holy Spirit and the forgiveness of sins *by grace*. Christ's death and resurrection reconciled the world (2 Corinthians 5.18-19) to God. Both Jews and Gentiles who believe Paul's gospel receive these blessings. Paul wrote:

> For they were happy and they are their debtors. For if the Gentiles shared in their spiritual things, they ought to minister to them in the material things (Romans 15.27).

Gentiles share in Israel's *spiritual* blessings, the forgiveness of sins, the indwelling Holy Spirit, by grace, as "the seed of Abraham" through Paul's gospel and ministry.

## Paul's Apostleship

Paul highlighted and defended his apostleship throughout his letters. Nine of his epistles begin with his apostolic identification. He declared his apostleship was through Jesus Christ, according to the will of God, not from man. The following verses note Paul's apostolic greeting:

| Paul's Apostleship |
|---|
| Paul, servant of Jesus Christ, **called apostle**, who has been set apart for *the* gospel of God (Romans 1.1). |
| Paul, **called apostle of Jesus Christ** through *the* will of God, and Sosthenes our brother (1 Corinthians 1.1). |
| Paul, **apostle of Jesus Christ through *the* will of God**, and Timothy, our brother, to the church of the God which is in Corinth, with all the saints who are in all Achaia (2 Corinthians 1.1) |
| Paul, **apostle, not from men, or through man, but through Jesus Christ**, and God *the* Father, who raised Him from the dead (Galatians 1.1). |
| Paul, **apostle of Jesus Christ through *the* will of God**, to the saints which are in Ephesus, and to *the* faithful in Christ Jesus (Ephesians 1.1). |
| Paul, **apostle of Jesus Christ through *the* will of God**, and Timothy our brother (Colossians 1.1). |
| Paul, **apostle of Jesus Christ, according to the command of God our Savior, even of Lord Jesus Christ**, our hope (1 Timothy 1.1). |
| Paul, **apostle of Jesus Christ, through *the* will of God**, according to the promise of life that *is* in Christ Jesus (2 Timothy 1.1). |
| Paul, servant of God, **apostle of Jesus Christ**, according to the faith of the elect of God, and full knowledge of *the* truth which *is* according to godliness (Titus 1.1). |

Paul omitted an apostolic declaration in 1 and 2 Thessalonians, Philippians, Philemon, and Hebrews. Why did he not cite his apostleship in *all* his letters? The Thessalonians and Philippians regarded Paul dearly and Paul had no need to assert his apostleship to them. Paul omitted it from Philemon because it was a personal letter. Hebrews did not include his apostolic designation because Paul did not wish to broadcast his authorship of the letter.

We have examined how the risen, glorified Christ commissioned Paul to reveal His grace to Gentiles and serve as proxy Israel. The next chapter will examine the things God revealed to Paul alone—His secrets.

# Chapter 4
# Paul the Revelator

*So, let a man reckon us as officers of Christ, and stewards of the secrets of God (1 Corinthians 4.1).*

## Paul: "To Me"

Paul used the phrase "to me" to emphasize the exclusive nature of the revelations he received from the risen Lord. Even as God made the Abrahamic Covenant exclusively with Abraham and gave the Mosaic Law exclusively through Moses, God revealed His secrets concerning the Church, the body of Christ, exclusively to Paul (Galatians 1.11-12; 1 Thessalonians 4.2).

| "To Me" |
|---|
| For **I** say, through the grace given **to me**, to everyone who is among you, do not think more highly of yourself than you should think, but think so you might be sound-minded, as the God allotted to each *a* measure of faith (Romans 12.30 |
| 15 Now **I** wrote to you more freely brothers on some matters, so as to remind you, because of the grace given **to me** by the God: 16 that **I** might be the minister of Jesus Christ for the Gentiles, serving as a priest the gospel of the God, so the offering of the Gentiles might become acceptable, since it has been sanctified by *the* Holy Spirit (Romans 15.15-16) |
| According to the grace of the God given **to me**, as *a* wise master-builder, **I** laid *the* foundation, and another builds on *it*. But let each one who builds take heed how he builds (1 Corinthians 3.10) |
| 16 For if **I** should proclaim the gospel, no boasting is for **me**. For necessity is laid **on me**. Woe is me if **I** should not proclaim the gospel! 17 For if **I** do this willingly, **I** have *a* reward. But if unwillingly, **I** have been entrusted with *a* stewardship! (1 Corinthians 9.16-17) |
| 7 But, on the contrary, when they saw that **I** had been entrusted with the gospel of the uncircumcision, even as Peter with that of the circumcision, 9 And after they understood the grace that was given **to me**, James, and Cephas, and John, those who were recognized to be pillars, gave me and Barnabas *the* right hands of fellowship, so we *might go* to the Gentiles, but they, to the circumcision (Galatians 2.7, 9). |

| [1] For this reason, *I* Paul, the prisoner of Christ Jesus for you Gentiles, [2] seeing that you heard of the dispensation of the grace of the God, which was given **to me** for you, [3] that by revelation He made known **to me** the secret, as **I** briefly wrote before, [4] by which, you can by reading understand **my insight** in the secret of the Christ, [7] of which **I** became servant, according to the gift of the grace of God, which was given **to me**, according to the working of His power. [8] **To me**, to the least of all saints, was this grace given: to preach to the Gentiles the incomprehensible riches of the Christ, [9] and to enlighten everyone about the dispensation of the secret, which has been hidden from the ages in the God, the One who created all things through Jesus Christ, (Ephesians 3.1-3, 7-9) |
|---|
| of which **I** became *a* servant according to the dispensation of the God, which was given **to me** for you, to complete the Word of the God, (Colossians 1.25) |
| but in His own season revealed His word by proclamation with which **I** was entrusted according to *the* command of God our Savior, (Titus 1.3) |
| And consider the patience of our Lord *is* salvation, even as also our beloved brother Paul, according to the wisdom given **to him** wrote to you (2 Peter 3.15). |

Peter wrote the last verse in the table. He recognized God had revealed things exclusively to Paul that He had not shown the Twelve and told the Jews who had believed the gospel of the kingdom to listen to Paul.

## By Commandment

Believers should recognize everything Paul wrote in his letters he received by direct command from the risen Lord, *except when he expressly declared this was not the case*. Paul wrote the Thessalonians and the Corinthians:

> For you know what commands we gave you by the Lord Jesus (1 Thessalonians 4.2).
>
> If anyone thinks he is *a* prophet, or spiritual, he must recognize the things that I write to you are the commands of the Lord (1 Corinthians 14.37).

On occasion, Paul wrote he had not received a direct command from the Lord about a particular matter (1 Corinthians 7.6, 25; 2 Corinthians 8.8). This does not mean Paul's words are not God-breathed or not authoritative for He wrote under the direction of the Holy Spirit. It simply means the risen Lord Himself did not directly address the matter to Paul by revelation. Paul also wrote that his apostleship was by the command of Christ (Romans 16.25-26; 1 Timothy 1.1; Titus 1.3). The letters of Paul are the words of Christ even as the words of the prophets are the words of Christ.

## Why Paul?

The question, "Why Paul?" is the *most critical question* in New Testament studies. Why did God save Paul? This question is not about Paul's salvation—God wishes all to be saved (1 Timothy 2.4)—but a question of ministry. God had twelve apostles to proclaim the gospel. Why did He need a thirteenth? The Lord taught and trained the Twelve for three years to proclaim the gospel of the kingdom. He promised they would rule the twelve tribes of Israel (Matthew 19.28). And, He had empowered them with the Holy Spirit. They were adequate to the task. They did not need Paul to help them.

What God did need, however, because Israel continued to reject its Messiah, was an apostle of an entirely different sort. He needed someone to begin a *new program* to bless Gentiles in light of Israel's disobedience. Instead of initiating the Day of the Lord, the Tribulation, God suspended His judgment and dealt with the world in mercy and grace. He determined to save Gentiles in spite of Israel's failure. That was the significance of Paul's salvation. Paul wrote God had appointed him from his mother's womb for this task (Galatians 1.15-16).

God has revealed five great programs in the Bible. In Program One, Mankind, Adam was the key figure. He represented all mankind and during this program, God dealt with the entire human race.

In Program Two, Israel, Abraham was the key figure. Through Abraham, God created a new, covenant people to bless all mankind.

In Program Three, the Church, God saved Paul to become the key figure and revelator of and to the Church, the body of Christ.

In Program Four, Jesus the Messiah is the key figure. He will reign from Zion as King (Zechariah 14.9; Matthew 6.10), fulfill Israel's covenant promises, and bless the nations.

In the final program, Program Five, God the Father will become the key figure. Christ will hand over all rule to Him in an eternal New Heavens and New Earth.[1]

| Key Figures | God's Programs |
|---|---|
| Adam | Mankind |
| Abraham | Israel |
| Paul | Church |
| Jesus the Messiah | Kingdom |
| God the Father | Eternity |

[1] These programs are covered in detail in the author's book: *God's Programs: An Introduction to Understanding the Bible*.

## Paul's Secrets: Key to His Theology

WITHOUT UNDERSTANDING PAUL'S SECRETS, ONE CANNOT UNDERSTAND CHURCH THEOLOGY

This statement should be fixed firmly in every believer's mind. Paul's "secrets" (μυστήριον) *are* Church theology. Paul's secrets are the vehicles God used to reveal his new program of the Church, even as God's covenants were the vehicles through which He revealed His program to Israel.

| Paul's Secrets |
|---|
| For I do not wish you to be ignorant brethren of this secret [μυστήριον]—so you may not be wise in yourselves—partial hardening has happened to Israel, until the completion of the Gentiles might enter in (Romans 11.25). |
| Now to Him who can establish you according to my gospel, even the preaching of Jesus Christ according to secret [μυστήριον] revelation, which has been kept silent in *the* times in the ages (Romans 16.25). |
| Rather, we speak *the* wisdom of God by *a* secret, [μυστήριον] what has been hidden, which the God predetermined before the ages for our glory (1 Corinthians 2.7). |
| So, let *a* man reckon us as officers of Christ and stewards of the secrets [μυστήριον] of God (1 Corinthians 4.1). |
| And if I should have prophecy, and know all the secrets, [μυστήριον] and all the knowledge, and if I should have all the faith, so as to remove mountains, but should not have love, I am nothing (1 Corinthians 13.2). |
| Behold! I tell you *a* secret: [μυστήριον] we will not all sleep but we will all be changed (1 Corinthians 15.51). |
| by making known to us the secret [μυστήριον] of His will, according to His pleasure, that He set forth in Him (Ephesians 1.9). |
| [3] that by revelation He made known to me the secret, [μυστήριον] as I briefly wrote before, [4] by which, you can by reading understand my insight in the secret [μυστήριον] of the Christ (Ephesians 3.3-4). |
| and to enlighten everyone about the dispensation of the secret, [μυστήριον] which has been hidden from the ages in the God, the One who created all things through Jesus Christ (Ephesians 3.9). |
| This secret [μυστήριον]: is great, but I speak as to Christ and as to the Church (Ephesians 5.32). |
| and for me, so I might be given *a* message with boldness in opening my mouth, to make known the secret [μυστήριον] of the gospel (Ephesians 6.19). |

| |
|---|
| the secret [μυστήριον] which has been hidden from the ages and from the generations, but now was manifested to His saints, [27] to whom the God wished to make known, what *is* the glorious riches of this secret [μυστήριον] among the Gentiles, which is Christ in you, the hope of the glory (Colossians 1.26-27). |
| so their hearts might be encouraged, since they have been united in love, and for all *the* riches of the full assurance of the understanding, for *the* full knowledge of the secret [μυστήριον] of the God, Christ (Colossians 2.2). |
| praying at the same time also for us, that the God might open *a* door to us for the word, to speak the secret [μυστήριον] of the Christ, for which I have also been bound (Colossians 4.3). |
| For the secret [μυστήριον] of the lawlessness is already at work, only the One who now restrains *him* will continue until it should be removed out of *the* way (2 Thessalonians 2.7). |
| who hold the secret [μυστήριον] of the faith with *a* pure conscience (1 Timothy 3.9). |
| And, admittedly, great is the secret [μυστήριον] of the godliness: God was revealed in *the* flesh, declared righteous by *the* Spirit, seen by angels, preached among Gentiles, believed on in *the* world, taken up in glory (1 Timothy 3.16)! |

| Paul's Secrets | Scripture |
|---|---|
| The Body of Secrets | 1 Corinthians 2.7, 4.1, 13.2; Colossians 4.3;1 Timothy 3.9 |
| The Church, the Body of Christ | Ephesians 3.3, 4, 9, 5.32; Colossians 1.26 |
| The Gospel of the Grace of God | Romans 16.25; Ephesians 6.19 |
| The Blinding of Israel | Romans 11.25 |
| The Rapture of the Church | 1 Corinthians 15.51 |
| Gathering All Things in Christ | Ephesians 1.9-10; Colossians 2.2 |
| The Secret of Godliness | 1 Timothy 3.16 |
| The Secret of Iniquity | 2 Thessalonians 2.7 |

The word rendered "mystery" (μυστήριον) in almost all translations is a *transliteration*, not a *translation*. The word μυστήριον *does not mean* "mystery."[2] It means a "secret," what was previously hidden and unknown. To translate it as "mystery" creates confusion because "mystery" connotes something entirely different than "secret." Paul wrote the Corinthians:

> So let a man reckon us as officers of Christ and stewards [οἰκονόμος][3] of the secrets [μυστήριον] of God (1 Corinthians 4.1).

Paul was God's officer and steward, His "secret agent" to disclose the *new revelations* he had received directly from the risen Lord. These revelations were *new theology.*[4] *All* of Paul's theology was a new revelation whether he specifically identified it with the word μυστήριον or not. Paul was *not* an addition to or extension of the Twelve. Rather, he was God's unique apostle who began an entirely new program: the Church, the body of Christ. Apart from this recognition, it is *impossible* to understand Church theology.

## The Revelation of Paul's Secrets

Paul wrote about the *body of secrets* the risen Lord gave him in several passages. They include the following:

> So let a man reckon us as officers of Christ and stewards of the secrets [μυστήριον] of God (1 Corinthians 4.1).

> And if I should have prophecy, and know all the secrets, [μυστήριον] and all the knowledge, and if I should have all the faith, so as to remove mountains, but should not have love, I am nothing (1 Corinthians 13.2).

> praying at the same time also for us, that the God might open *a* door to us for the word, to speak the secret [μυστήριον] of the Christ, for which I have also been bound (Colossians 4.3).

> who hold the secret [μυστήριον] of the faith with *a* pure conscience (1 Timothy 3.9).

---

[2] Most Bibles translate μυστήριον incorrectly because the translators do not understand Paul's secrets. Prior to Paul, the word μυστήριον was used in only three passages (Matthew 13.11; Mark 4.11; Luke 8.10) and concerned Israel's earthly kingdom. The other occurrences are in Revelation (Revelation 1.20, 10.7, 17.5, 7) and concern God's program for Israel and the nations, not the Church.

[3] An οἰκονόμος was a manager or a superintendent in charge of running the affairs of an estate.

[4] Christendom's greatest error is its failure to recognize that what Paul taught was unknown before him and that the ascended Christ revealed all Church doctrine exclusively to Paul.

Paul also used the word "revelation" (ἀποκάλυψις) to describe the secrets he received from the risen Lord (Romans 16.25; 2 Corinthians 12.1, 7; Galatians 1.12, 2.2; Ephesians 3.3 cf. Acts 22.16).

> Now to Him who can establish you according to my gospel, even the preaching of Jesus Christ according to secret revelation [ἀποκάλυψιν μυστηρίου],[5] which has been kept silent in *the* times in the ages (Romans 16.25).

> I must boast. Though it is not appropriate I will go on to visions and revelations [ἀποκάλυψις] from *the* Lord (2 Corinthians 12.1).

> And so I might not become arrogant because of the superiority [ὑπερβολή] of the revelations, [ἀποκάλυψις] *a* thorn in my flesh, *an* angel of Satan, was given to me so he might torment me, so I might not become arrogant (2 Corinthians 12.7)

> [11] Now I want you to know to you, brethren, the gospel I proclaimed, it is not according to man. [12] For I neither received nor was taught from man but through revelation [ἀποκάλυψις] of Jesus Christ (Galatians 1.11-12).

> [1] Then, after fourteen years, I went up again to Jerusalem with Barnabas and also took Titus. [2] Now I went up by revelation, [ἀποκάλυψις] and explained to them the gospel that I proclaim among the Gentiles, but privately to those who were recognized, so I should not run or did run in vain (Galatians 2.1-2).

## Paul Secrets Remain Secret

Sadly, like Poe's letter,[6] Paul's secrets reside in plain sight unperceived by most of Christendom. The ignorance of understanding Paul by the vast majority can be discovered by asking how many sermons, articles, or books has one heard or read concerning his secrets. Most would say they had *never* heard a sermon or read a book about them. Paul's secrets are universally ignored by most of Christendom. If asked, most pastors and church-goers can tell you nothing about Paul's secrets. One will most likely be met with a puzzled expression and the reply, "What are you talking about?" Paul's secrets are the *key* to understanding Christianity. Thus, anyone who writes about the Church in which Paul's secrets are not the centerpiece *does not understand Church theology*. The reader may think I am overstating the case. I am not.

---

[5] The genitival phrase, ἀποκάλυψιν μυστηρίου, has been translated as an attributive genitive, adjectivally.

[6] Poe, Edgar A., "The Purloined Letter" 1844.

Paul's revelations, his secrets, were new divine vehicles through which God revealed the Church, the body of Christ, salvation by faith alone, the believer's identification with Christ, how believers are to live the Christian life, and Israel's future in light of the nation's rejection of their Messiah.

Theological controversies about Israel and the Church, the Rapture, prophecy, and God's program with Israel result from theologians not knowing and understanding Paul's secrets. This problem began in Paul's lifetime and has continued for over 1,900 years. Paul wrote Timothy shortly before his execution:

> You know this: everyone in Asia deserted me—among whom are Phygellus and Hermogenes (2 Timothy 1.15).

Paul declared that *all* the churches of Asia Minor—Ephesus, Colossae, Galatia, Iconium, Derbe, Lystra, Antioch Pisidia, Laodicea, etc. abandoned his teachings.

The writings of the early Church fathers provide a rich history of this desertion and its consequences. Perhaps no better example exists than the *Didache*.[7] Its first line reads, "The teaching of the Lord to the Gentiles (or Nations) by the twelve apostles." This statement is stunning. Anyone who has read the New Testament knows the Twelve *had no ministry to Gentiles*. None. Not one word of Scripture supports the idea the Twelve had a ministry to Gentiles—ever. But here we read a text, written about 100 A.D., with this glaring falsehood.

The *Didache* does not mention Christ's death on the cross for our sins, His resurrection, or salvation by faith alone. It has nothing of Paul's teachings about the Church, the body of Christ, the truths Paul taught about the believer's identification with Christ in His death and resurrection. It contains no mention of Paul's watchwords—faith, hope, and love. It says nothing about the Holy Spirit. It contains none of Paul's "secrets." In short, the *Didache* contains *nothing* of Paul, as if he never existed. Its focus is wholly on Christ's earthly ministry to Israel under the Mosaic Law and the teaching of the Twelve to Jewish believers.

The *Didache* reveals those whom Paul described as "fallen away from the grace" (Galatians 5.4). It is the earliest extra-Biblical example of documented Church heresy and vividly exposes how the apostasy that began in Paul's lifetime continued through the early Church fathers and through Church history. This apostasy has continued for over 1900 years and dominates Christendom.

---

[7] The *Didache,* "Teaching" was one of the earliest writings (c. 100 A.D.) of the Apostolic Fathers.

# Paul's Secrets:

## 1. The Church, the Body of Christ

Most have been taught the Church began with Jesus' declaration to Peter, "You are Peter and on this rock will I build my church" (Matthew 16.18) or on the Day of Pentecost in Acts 2. Both views are wrong. The reason it is wrong is because the Scriptures explicitly state when the Church began—and it was not with Peter or Pentecost.

The Church is the body of Christ (Ephesians 1.22-23; 1 Corinthians 12.12-13; Romans 12.3-5; Colossians 1.24). We learn this *only* from Paul. Paul wrote that one becomes a member of the Church, the body of Christ by: 1) Believing Paul's gospel (1 Corinthians 15.1-4) and by 2) the Baptism of the Holy Spirit (1 Corinthians 12.13; Galatians 3.27).[8] Jews and Gentiles who believe Paul's gospel are equal in Christ (Romans 10.12; Galatians 3.28), members of the Church, the body of Christ. This is a Pauline truth.

Paul wrote the Ephesians:

> 1 For this reason, **I** Paul, the prisoner of Christ Jesus for you Gentiles, 2 seeing that you heard of the dispensation of the grace of the God, which was given **to me** for you, 3 that by revelation [ἀποκάλυψις] He made known **to me** the secret, [μυστήριον] as **I** briefly wrote before, 4 by which, you can by reading understand **my** insight in the secret [μυστήριον] of the Christ, 5 which, in other generations, was not made known to the sons of men, as now was revealed to His holy apostles and prophets by *the* Spirit: 6 that the Gentiles should be joint heirs, and of the same body, and joint partakers of the promise in the Christ, through the gospel, 7 of which **I** became servant, according to the gift of the grace of God, which was given **to me**, according to the working of His power. 8 **To me**, to the least of all saints, was this grace given: to preach to the Gentiles the incomprehensible riches of the Christ, 9 and to enlighten everyone about the dispensation of the secret, [μυστήριον] which has been hidden from the ages in the God, the One who created all things through Jesus Christ (Ephesians 3.1-9)

The most striking feature of this passage is how often Paul referred to *himself*. The reader is encouraged to focus on this fact in reading the passage. Observe how often Paul used personal and possessive pronouns, "I," "me," and "my" noted in **bold**. Note what Paul wrote concerning the Church from the above passage:

---

[8] Man's part is to believe Paul's gospel. God's part is to baptize the believer with the Holy Spirit. This baptism is a real experience but not attended with signs or feelings. It is a work of God to be believe because God has said it.

1. Paul (not Peter or the Twelve) was a prisoner of Christ for Gentiles (v. 1).
2. God gave the dispensation of God's grace to Paul (not to Peter or the Twelve) (v. 2).
3. God gave Paul (not to Peter or the Twelve) the secret [μυστήριον] (v. 3).
4. Paul (not Peter or the Twelve) had insight into the secret [μυστήριον] of Christ (v. 4-6)
5. Paul (not Peter or the Twelve) was made a minister of this secret by the gift of God's grace (v. 7).
6. Paul (not Peter or the Twelve), the least of saints, was given God's grace to preach to Gentiles (v. 8).
7. Paul (not Peter or the Twelve) was given the mission to reveal the secret [μυστήριον] of the Church which God hid from previous ages (v. 9).

Could words be clearer? The Church was *unknown* before Paul. Some have argued Paul's words, "now been revealed to His holy apostles and prophets in the Spirit" (Ephesians 3.5) refer to the Twelve and therefore the Church, the body of Christ, was not a secret revealed to Paul alone. What of this?

Something cannot be known and unknown at the same time. Paul would not have written that the Church, the body of Christ, was a secret if it had been known. Who were the apostles to whom Paul referred? Most likely Paul meant apostles associated with his ministry: Barnabas (Acts 14.4, 14), Apollos (1 Corinthians 4.6, 9), Timothy and Silvanus (1 Thessalonians 1.1, 2.6), Epaphroditus (Philippians 2.25), Andronicus and Junia (Romans 16.7), and Titus (2 Corinthians 8.23).

The revelation of Jew and Gentile equal in Christ and indwelt by the Holy Spirit was alien to the Twelve. Whatever they learned about the Church, the body of Christ, was *from Paul*. Peter, James, John, and Jude *never* mention the Church, the body of Christ, in their letters. Peter, at the end of his ministry, shortly before his death, wrote that Paul's doctrines were hard to understand (2 Peter 3.15-16). Why did he write this? They were hard to understand because they were *new*. They concerned a new divine program unknown to Israel's prophets.

Paul wrote similar words to the Colossians:

> [24] Now **I** rejoice in my sufferings for you and am filling up the things lacking of the afflictions of the Christ in my flesh for His body, which is the Church, [25] of which *I* became *a* servant according to the dispensation of the God, which was given **to me** for you, to complete the Word of the God, [26] the secret [μυστήριον] which has been hidden from the ages and from the generations, but now was manifested to His saints, [27] to whom the God wished to make known, what *is* the glorious riches of this secret [μυστήριον] among the Gentiles, which is Christ in you, the hope of the glory,

> [28] whom **we** proclaim, warning every man, and teaching every man, in all wisdom, so **we** might present every man complete in Christ Jesus, [29] for which **I** also labor, striving in accord with His energy that works **in me** in power (Colossians 1.24-29).

Paul wrote Gentile believers in Ephesus to remind them that prior to God's revelation of the secret of the Church, they were *excluded* from Israel's covenants and were *without hope*:

> [11] Therefore, remember, that formerly, you, the Gentiles in *the* flesh, the ones called Uncircumcision by those called Circumcision in the flesh made by hands, [12] that you were at that time separated from Christ, having been alienated from the commonwealth of Israel, and strangers to the covenants of the promise, having no hope, and without God, in the world (Ephesians 2.11-12).

God set Gentiles aside with His establishment of the Abrahamic Covenant as far as dealing directly with all humanity. Instead, He would address mankind through a covenant people, Israel. But Paul revealed God had established a new relationship with both Jews and Gentiles based on faith alone in the work of Christ's death and resurrection. He expressed this new reality with "but now," (νυνὶ δὲ), his favorite expression of contrast.[9]

> [13] But now, [νυνὶ δὲ] in Christ Jesus, you, the ones who were once far off, became near by the blood of the Christ. [14] For He is our peace, the One who made both one and broke down the middle wall of the barrier, [15] the hostility, by His flesh, He nullified the Law of the commands in ordinances so He might create the two in Himself into one new man, thus making peace, [16] and might reconcile both in one body to the God through the cross, since He killed the hostility by it. [17] And when He came, He proclaimed good news: peace to you, those far away, and to those near. [18] Because through Him we both have the access by one Spirit to the Father. [19] So then, you are no longer foreigners and aliens, but fellow citizens of the saints and the household of the God, [20] which was built on the foundation of the apostles and prophets, Jesus Christ Himself being *the* cornerstone, [21] in whom *the* whole building, since it is joined together, is increasing into *a* holy temple in *the* Lord, [22] in whom you also are being

---

[9] Paul used the expression νῦν δὲ or νυνὶ δὲ in Romans 3.21, 6.22, 7.6, 11.30, 16.25-26; 1 Corinthians 7.14, 12.18, 20, 13.13, 15.20; Galatians 4.9; Ephesians 2.13, 5.8; Colossians 1.22, 26, 3.8; 2 Timothy 1.10 to reveal the "secrets" of a believer's new relationship to God as "Church." He also used this expression to denote contrast concerning God's relationship with Israel: Hebrews 2.8, 8.6, 9.26, 11.6, 12.26.

> built together for *a* dwelling of the God by *the* Spirit (Ephesians 2.13-22).

Members of the Church, the body of Christ, by virtue of Paul's gospel, become fellow citizens with Jewish believers who are part of God's prophetic program. God's two programs, Israel and Church, are separate, distinct entities, but both compose a building, a "holy temple in the Lord." Each program has its own blessings and glory but both are part of a structure in which Christ is the cornerstone.

Paul described this new creation of the Church as a body—an *organism*—not an organization—the body of Christ. One becomes a member of His body by believing the gospel (1 Corinthians 15.1-4) and through the baptism of the Holy Spirit. Paul wrote the Corinthians:

> [12] For as the body is one and has many members, and all the members of the one body, being many, are one body, so too *is* the Christ. [13] For by one Spirit we were all baptized into one body, whether Jews or Greeks, whether servants or freemen, and all were made to drink one Spirit (1 Corinthians 12.12-13).

Each member of the Body of Christ is vital to its function, even as every part of the human body is needed to function properly. Paul explained:

> [14] For the body is not one member, but many. [15] If the foot should say, Because I am not *a* hand, I am not of the body, it does not mean it is not of the body. [16] And if the ear should say, Because I am not *an* eye, I am not of the body, it does not mean it is not of the body. [17] If the whole body *were an* eye, where *would be* the hearing? If *the* whole *were* hearing, where *would be* the smelling? [18] But the God arranged the members in the body, each one of them, as He wished (1 Corinthians 12.14-18).

Paul revealed several points about the Church in his discussion of marriage in Ephesians 5.22-33:

> [22] Wives! Submit to your own husbands, as to the Lord. [23] For *the* husband is head of the wife, even as the Christ *is* Head of the Church and He Himself *is the* Savior of the body. [24] But as the Church is subject to the Christ, so also the wives to their own husbands in everything. [25] Husbands! Love your wives, even as the Christ also loved the Church and gave Himself for her, [26] so He might sanctify her, for He cleansed *her* by the washing of the water by *the* word, [27] so He might present the Church to Himself in glory, not having spot or wrinkle, or any such things, but that it may be holy and unblemished. [28] So, husbands ought to love their wives as their own bodies: the one who loves his wife, loves himself. [29] For no one ever hated his own flesh, but nourishes

> and cherishes it, even as also the Christ *does* the Church.
> 30 For we are members of His body, from His flesh and from
> His bones. 31 Because of this, *a* man will leave his father and
> mother and will be joined to his wife. And the two will be
> one flesh. 32 This secret is great, but I speak as to Christ and
> as to the Church. 33 So then, you too, each one must love his
> wife as himself so the wife might respect her husband.

Thus:

1. Christ is Head of the Church (v. 23).
2. Christ loved the Church and gave Himself for it (v. 25).
3. Christ's goal is to sanctify the Church by the Word of God (v. 26-27).
4. Members of the Church are members of Christ's body, His flesh and bones (v. 30).
5. The relationship between Christ and the Church was a secret [μυστήριον] (v. 32).[10]

The Church is the body of Christ and Christ is its Head. He did *not* teach the Church is the bride of Christ (Ephesians 1.22; 4.15; 5.23; Colossians 1.18; 2.19). For the Church, the proper titles of Christ are "Lord" and "Head," not "King." Members of the Church are heirs of God and joint-heirs with Christ (Romans 8.17). Joint-heirs share what belongs to the heir. Paul also wrote members of the Church will govern angels (1 Corinthians 6.3). The promises of joint-heirship and ruling angels were never given to Israel. They are exclusive to members of the Church. This is grace!

## What Does the Word "Church" Mean?

The word translated "church" is ἐκκλησία.[11] The simplest definition of ἐκκλησία is a group. Specific meanings depend on context. In Acts 19, the word occurs three times (verses 32, 39, and 41) and provides an example of how context determines meaning. Paul aroused the anger of the silversmiths and other tradesmen who manufactured and sold idols in Ephesus. Demetrius, the silversmith stirred up a riot against Paul because he was hurting business—the people believed in Christ and abandoned their idols. The chart shows the meaning of ἐκκλησία is determined by context:

---

[10] This passage is often used to support the idea the Church is the "bride of Christ" but this is not stated. The phrase "bride of Christ" does not occur in the Scriptures. Paul explicitly stated the Church is the body of Christ, not the bride of Christ. God's bride/wife relationship is with Israel, not the Church.

[11] The Septuagint (LXX), the Greek translation of the Old Testament, used ἐκκλησία most often for קָהָל, (e.g., Deuteronomy 4.10, 9.10, 23.1) and usually rendered it "assembly" or "congregation."

| Ἐκκλησία in Acts 19 | |
|---|---|
| Passage | Meaning |
| Then, some kept shouting one thing and some another, for the mob [ἐκκλησία] was in chaos and the majority did not understand why they had gathered (v. 32). | Mob |
| So if you demand anything more, it will be settled in the legal court [ἐκκλησία] (v. 39). | Court |
| And after he said these things, he dismissed the crowd [ἐκκλησία] (v. 41). | Crowd |

Paul used ἐκκλησία for the Church, the body of Christ. When the term is found in the Gospels or letters of James and John it means a congregation or assembly of Jewish believers.

| Ἐκκλησία in the New Testament | |
|---|---|
| Gospels | Matthew 16.18, 18.17 |
| Acts | Acts 2.47, 5.11, 7.38, 8.1, 3, 11.22, 26, 12.1, 5, 13.1, 14.23, 27, 15.3-4, 22, 18.22, 20.17, 28 |
| Paul | Romans 16.1, 5, 23<br>1 Corinthians 1.2, 4.17, 6.4, 10.32, 11.18, 22, 12.28, 14.4-5, 12, 19, 23, 28, 35, 15.9, 16.19<br>2 Corinthians 1.1<br>Galatians 1.13<br>Ephesians 1.22, 3.10, 21, 5.23-25, 27, 29, 32<br>Philippians 3.6, 4.15<br>Colossians 1.18, 24, 4.15-16<br>1 Thessalonians 1.1<br>2 Thessalonians 1.1<br>1 Timothy 3.5, 15, 5.16<br>Philemon 1.2 |
| Hebrews | Hebrews 2.12, 12.23 |
| James | James 5.14 |
| Peter | 1 Peter 5.13 |
| John | 3 Jo 1.6, 9-10 |
| Revelation | Revelation 2.1, 8, 12, 18, 3.1, 7, 14 |

The noun ἐκκλησία occurs only *twice* in the Gospels. The first is the Lord's well-known statement to Peter, "on this Rock will I build My church" (Matthew 16.18). The second is Jesus' instruction in dealing with a sinning Jewish brother. He said if the brother refused reproof, the "church" was to treat him as a Gentile and a tax collector (Matthew

18.15-17). Such language could not possibly refer to the Church, the body of Christ, in which Jew and Gentile are equal.[12]

## When Did the Church Begin?

Much of Christendom teaches the Church, the body of Christ, began at Pentecost. The logic for this tradition is the following: 1) The Church is the body of Christ; 2) Membership into the body of Christ is through the baptism of the Holy Spirit; 3) The baptism of the Holy Spirit occurred at Pentecost; 4) Therefore, the Church began at Pentecost. This logic *appears* strong but collapses when examined.

Three major problems exist for this view. The first is Paul stated the Church, the body of Christ, was a "secret" [μυστήριον]. If the Church began at Pentecost, Paul was wrong. What occurred at Pentecost, the coming of the Holy Spirit was *not* a secret. Jesus told the Twelve the Holy Spirit would come (John 7.39, 14.16-17, 26; Acts 1.4-5). Jeremiah, Ezekiel, and Joel wrote hundreds of years before of the coming of the indwelling Holy Spirit. Peter stated Pentecost was the "last days" (Acts 2.17) of God's prophetic program, *not* the "first days" of the Church.

The second problem is that Peter addressed Jews, not Jews and Gentiles, at Pentecost. Notice the language in Luke's detailed record:

1. Now **devout Jews from every nation** under the heaven were residing in Jerusalem (Acts 2.5).
2. But Peter, after he stood up with the Eleven, raised his voice and spoke to them, **Men of Judea, and all those residing in Jerusalem**, understand this and pay attention to my words (Acts 2.14)!
3. **Men! Israelites!** Hear these words: Jesus of Nazareth, a man who has been shown by the God to you by miracles, and wonders, and signs, which God did through Him among you, as you yourselves know (Acts 2.22).
4. **Men! Brethren!** It is right to speak to you with freedom about the patriarch David, for he died and was buried, and his tomb is among us to this day (Acts 2.29).
5. Assuredly, therefore, let **all *the* house of Israel** know: The God made Him both Lord and Christ—this Jesus whom you crucified (Acts 2.36).
6. Now when they heard, they were pierced to the heart. Then they said to Peter and the other apostles, What should we do, **men, brethren** (Acts 2.37)?

---

[12] Writing Jews (James 1.1), James used συναγωγή, "synagogue" (James 2.2) and ἐκκλησία (James 5.14) as synonyms for the congregation of believing Jews. John used the word ἐκκλησια in Revelation 2-3 in the same sense. Those "churches" were Jewish congregations or synagogues.

7. For **to you** is the promise, and **to your children**, and **to all those far away**, as many as the Lord our God will call (Acts 2.39).

All these verses concern Jews. Peter only addressed Jews for he had no idea of Jews and Gentiles being equal in Christ, indwelt by the Spirit, the definition of the Church. Peter's focus was the same as it had been the past three years: Israel needed to repent and believe Jesus was the Messiah. This was what was required for Him to return and establish His kingdom (Matthew 23.37-39, Israel's great prophetic hope in which the nation would be supreme among the nations and the Twelve would rule the twelve tribes of Israel (Matthew 19.28; Acts 1.6). The idea of Jew and Gentile being *equal* in Christ was completely alien to Peter and the Twelve.

The last point which proves the Church did not begin at Pentecost is that Peter mentioned nothing in his message at Pentecost or at the Temple about Christ having died for the sins of the world. Peter's message to the Jews was that Jesus' crucifixion was a crime for which they had to repent. He declared:

> Assuredly, therefore, let all *the* house of Israel know: The God made Him both Lord and Christ—this Jesus whom you crucified (Acts 2.36).

How did the Jews respond?

> Now when they heard, they were pierced to the heart. Then they said to Peter and the other apostles, What should we do, men, brethren (Acts 2.37)?

Did Peter tell them to believe Christ died for their sins and rose from the dead for salvation? Not at all. Luke wrote:

> Then Peter said to them, Repent and be baptized, every one of you, in the name of Jesus Christ, for forgiveness of your sins and you will receive the gift of the Holy Spirit (Acts 2.38).

Peter told the nation that *every one* of them must repent and be baptized in the name of Jesus Christ for the forgiveness of sins. When that happened, they would receive the gift of the Holy Spirit.[13] This was the gospel of the kingdom which required national repentance (Matthew 3.2, 4.17).

Is this Church language? Is this the gospel proclaimed by the Church? Is it through repentance from killing the Messiah and water baptism

---

[13] Peter's point in proclaiming Christ's resurrection was that He was alive and could return to establish His earthly kingdom. He knew nothing of the significance of Christ's death and resurrection with regard to solving the problem of sin. That truth was revealed much later by Paul.

that one becomes a Christian? Is it through repentance and water baptism that members of the Church, the body of Christ, receive the Holy Spirit? The idea the Church begin at Pentecost is *tradition*. It is Scripturally *impossible* for the Church to have begun at Pentecost.

## Paul: Founder of the Church

If the Church did not begin at Pentecost, when did it begin? The Scriptures provide a clear answer—so clear it is amazing that hardly anyone teaches it. Paul wrote that the Church, the body of Christ, began with him. Addressing the problem of divisions within the Corinthian church, Paul wrote:

> [10] According to the grace of the God given to me, as *a* wise master-builder, I laid *the* foundation, and another builds on *it*. But let each one who builds take heed how he builds. [11] For no one can lay another foundation besides the one which is laid, who is Jesus the Christ (1 Corinthians 3.10-11).

In verses 1-9, Paul addressed the problem of divisions in the Corinthian church, particularly as it related to Apollos and himself. In verse 10, Paul moved beyond the local church to the Church, the body of Christ. Notice Paul's "to me" declaration. He declared he was a σοφὸς ἀρχιτέκτων, a "wise master builder" or "wise architect." An architect *begins* a building project. He does not come on the scene *after* construction has begun. Paul wrote *he* laid the foundation of the Church and this foundation was Christ.[14] If Paul *laid the foundation*, the Church could not have begun at Pentecost. It began with Paul.

A second passage provides more evidence of this fact. Paul wrote Timothy:

> [15] The saying is trustworthy and worthy of all acceptance: Christ Jesus came into the world to save sinners: of whom I am first [πρῶτος]. [16] But because of this I was shown mercy, that in me first, [πρῶτος] Jesus Christ might demonstrate the full patience as *a* pattern [ὑποτύπωσις] for those about to believe on Him for eternal life (1 Timothy 1.15-16).

Most translations read "of whom I am chief" (KJV) or "foremost" (NASB) or "worst" (NIV, NET) instead of "first." These renderings are *interpretations*, not translations. They *interpret* the verse to mean Paul thought he was the chief or greatest sinner. But the word rendered "chief," "foremost," "worst" is πρῶτος, which Paul always used in its primary sense of "first in a line of succession."

Why have translators interpreted πρῶτος as "chief," "foremost," or "worst" when Paul always used the word in its ordinal sense, "first?"

[14] Some argue Paul was only speaking of the Corinthian church. If one follows this logic, it means Christ was the foundation of only the Corinthian church.

They do so for two reasons. One is they extend Paul's statement of verse 13, in which he wrote he was once a blasphemer, etc. into this verse.[15] The second is they have no idea what Paul meant by his words that he was the "first sinner."

Any translation requires some degree of interpretation. But the primary task of translators is to *translate*. Paul used the word πρῶτος twenty-nine times: Romans 1.8, 16, 2.9-10, 3.2, 10.19, 15.24; 1 Corinthians 11.18, 12.28, 14.30, 15.3, 15.45-47; 2 Corinthians 8.5; Ephesians 6.2; Philippians 1.5; 1 Thessalonians 4.16; 2 Thessalonians 2.3; 1 Timothy 1.15-16, 2.1, 2.13, 3.10, 5.4, 5.12; 2 Timothy 1.5, 2.6, 4.16. In each case, he used it in its primary sense, i.e., "first in time, place, etc." Here, translators have abandoned translation to do exegetical work and have failed. A second-year Greek student should not make such a glaring error. The translators are beyond second-year Greek but force a twisted interpretation on the text because they do not understand Paul's secrets. Like Alexander, let us cut the knot.

The next verse removes all doubt about what Paul meant. He wrote he obtained mercy, "that in me first, (πρῶτος) Jesus Christ might demonstrate the full patience as *a* pattern for those about to believe on Him for eternal life." What Paul meant by stating he was the "first sinner" was that he was the pattern of God's grace for those who would be saved *afterward*. The word ὑποτύπωσις means an "example" or "pattern." Expressed another way, Paul was the model or prototype of salvation in God's new program, the Church. Paul expressed this thought to the Galatians:

> [15] But when it pleased the God, who set me apart from my mother's womb and called *me* through His grace [16] to reveal His Son in me so I might proclaim Him among the Gentiles, I immediately consulted not with flesh and blood (Galatians 1.15-16).

God began a new program, an age of grace with Paul. He saved Paul to demonstrate His love for Gentiles. National Israel in refusing to repent was failing to be a light to Gentiles (Isaiah 42.6, 49.6). According to God's prophetic program, Gentiles were to be blessed through Israel's *obedience*. But in wisdom and grace, God created a new way to bless Gentiles through Israel's *disobedience*. Rather than initiate the prophesied Day of the Lord, God interrupted His prophetic program and saved Paul as the "first," to be the "pattern" of His saving grace for a new entity, the Church, the body of Christ.

## The Church: A New Relationship

When God established the Abrahamic Covenant, He began a new program which divided the human race into two peoples: Jews and Gentiles. With Paul's salvation and commission, God created a third

---

[15] Paul was a great sinner. But that is not the point of the passage.

entity: the Church, the body of Christ. Thus, Paul wrote the Corinthians:

> Do not offend Jews, or Greeks, or the Church of the God (1 Corinthians 10.32).

This verse reveals the human race is now composed of three theological races: Jew, Gentile, and Church. When one believes Paul's gospel (1 Corinthians 15.1-4), one is no longer Jew or Gentile. He is "Church"—a member of the body of Christ—a new creation. Paul expressed this truth in his letters to the Corinthians and the Galatians:

> Therefore, if anyone *is* in Christ: *a* new creation. The old things passed away. Behold, new things have come into existence (2 Corinthians 5.17).

> 27 For as many of you as were baptized into Christ were clothed *with* Christ. 28 There is no Jew or Greek, there is no servant or freeman, there is no male and female. For you are all one in Christ Jesus (Galatians 3.27-28).

In the immediately preceding verse noted above to the Corinthians, Paul wrote:

> Therefore, from now on we know no one in human terms. And if we have known Christ as a human, we now know Him no longer (2 Corinthians 5.16).

What did Paul mean by, "from now on we know no one in human terms?" Many have supposed Paul meant believers no longer know one another in a carnal, unspiritual way. That may be true, but that is not what Paul meant. Paul's point was that those who have believed his gospel now know one another as members of the Church, the body of Christ, not as Jew or Gentile. This is a new relationship.

The rest of the verse is more challenging. What are we to make of Paul's statement, "if we have known Christ as a human, we now know Him no longer" (εἰ καὶ ἐγνώκαμεν κατὰ σάρκα Χριστόν, ἀλλὰ νῦν οὐκέτι γινώσκομεν)? The first verb, ἐγνώκαμεν, is a perfect active indicative of γινώσκω, "we have known" and the second, γινώσκομεν, is a present active indicative, "we now know." What did Paul mean by κατὰ σάρκα, translated by the KJV as "after the flesh" and above as "human." The straightforward meaning is that Paul meant Christ's earthly ministry.

In His earthly ministry, Jesus set aside His power and glory (Philippians 2.6-8). He humbled Himself and allowed Himself to be mocked, beaten, and crucified to accomplish His work of salvation. But Christ's resurrection demonstrated His victory over sin and death (Romans 1.4). His humiliation was ended.

Members of the Church only know the resurrected, heavenly Christ, not the earthly Christ. The Church, the body of Christ, has a heavenly destiny (Ephesians 1.2, 22; Philippians 3.20).[16] Paul wrote:

> [19] and what *is* the surpassing greatness of His power for us who believe, according to the working of the strength of His might, [20] which He worked in the Christ when He raised him from *the* dead, and sat *Him* at His right hand in the heavenlies, [21] far above every ruler, and authority, and power, and lordship, and every name which is named, not only in this age, but also in the one to come. [22] And He put all things under His feet and gave Him *to be* Head over all things in the Church, [23] which is His body, the fullness of the One who fills the all in all (Ephesians 1.19-23).

He wrote the Colossians similarly:

> [17] So He is before all things and by him all the things hold together. [18] And He is the Head of the body, of the Church, who is *the* beginning, Firstborn from the dead, so He might be preeminent in all things (Colossians 1.17-18).

Paul received his ministry from the heavenly *resurrected* Christ. As members of the Church, the body of Christ, this is what Paul meant when he wrote the Corinthians, "if we have known Christ as a human, we now know Him no longer." Not to know Christ merely as "human" means that Christ's message to the Church is from the risen, glorified Christ, not from Christ in His earthly ministry. *Our* truths concern *heavenly* promises, not *earthly* promises, given to Israel and Gentiles.[17]

## Identification With Christ

Closely related to the revelation of the Church, the body of Christ, is God's identification of the believer in Christ's death and resurrection. When one believes Paul's gospel (1 Corinthians 15.1-4) he becomes a member of the Church, the body of Christ and God baptizes him into His Body. Paul alone taught this baptism. He wrote the Corinthians:

> [12] For as the body is one and has many members, and all the members of the one body, being many, are one body, so too *is* the Christ. [13] For by one Spirit we were all baptized into one body, whether Jews or Greeks, whether servants or freemen, and all were made to drink one Spirit (1 Corinthians 12.12-13).

---

[16] Israel's destiny is the earthly kingdom of God. The Church's destiny is heavenly.

[17] One of the great tragedies in Christendom is that most churches spend most of the time in the Gospels, i.e., Christ's earthly ministry, focusing upon Christ's earthly ministry rather than His heavenly ministry and Church truths.

Romans 6 is Paul's great passage of how the believer is identified with Christ in His death and resurrection. He wrote:

> [3] Or do you not know that as many as were baptized into Christ Jesus, were baptized into His death? [4] Therefore, we were buried with Him through the baptism into the death, so that just as Christ was raised from *the* dead through the glory of the Father, so we also might walk in newness of life. [5] For if we have become united in the likeness of His death, we will also be *in the likeness* of *His* resurrection. [6] For we know this: our old man was crucified with *Him* so that the body of the sin may be rendered inactive, so that we are no longer enslaved by the sin (Romans 6.3-6).

When one believes Paul's gospel, the Holy Spirit baptizes (identifies) him with Christ in His death and resurrection.[18] The identification in Christ's death means the believer's old nature is crucified with Christ. God views the believer's Adamic nature as *dead*. The believer is also identified in Christ's resurrection. God sees the believer as resurrected in Christ.[19] Paul alone taught this secret.

Paul wrote similarly to the Colossians:

> [11] In whom also you are circumcised with the circumcision made without hands, in putting off the body of the sins of the flesh by the circumcision of Christ: [12] Buried with him in baptism, wherein also you are risen with him through the faith of the operation of God, who has raised him from the dead (Colossians 2.11-12).

The baptism of the Holy Spirit is *dry*. It is the "one baptism" of the Church (Ephesians 4.5). Many arguments have waged over water baptism and divided believers. Paul declared *no* water baptism exists for the Church.[20] How unified believers would be if we only believed Paul!

---

[18] The primary meaning of baptism is *identification*. The baptism of the Holy Spirit is unseen and unfelt. The Scriptures declare it and we accept it by *faith*. Christians live by faith, not sight (2 Corinthians 5.7).

[19] Paul's great dissertation on resurrection is 1 Corinthians 15. It contains more about resurrection than is found in the rest of the Bible. One of the great mysteries is how life comes out of death. Nature reveals a seed must die to live (John 12.24). Supernature reveals life comes out of death but at a higher level. Every human being will experience resurrection: some to eternal life; others to eternal condemnation (John 5.29).

[20] Some have taught Paul's phrase, "buried with Him in baptism" involves water. Paul's words, "buried with Him in baptism" is a *spiritual identification* with Christ, *not* an aquatic experience.

| Identification Truths | Scripture |
|---|---|
| Baptized into Christ's death and resurrection | Romans 6.3-5, 8; 1 Corinthians 12.13; Colossians 2.12; 3.3; Philippians 3.10; Titus 3.5-7 |
| Crucified with Christ | Romans 6.6; Galatians 2.20 |
| No longer a slave to sin | Romans 6.6-7, 18, 22 |
| Possessor of eternal life | Romans 6.22-23 |
| Dead to and released from the Law | Romans 7.4, 6 |
| Under Grace, not Law | Romans 6.14, 7.4, 6; Galatians 5.18 |
| No condemnation or separation from God | Romans 8.1, 37-39 |
| Received Spirit of adoption | Romans 8.15 |
| Complete in Christ | Colossians 2.10 |
| Seated with Christ in heaven | Ephesians 2.6; Philippians 3.20 |
| Sons of God and Joint-Heirs with Christ | Romans 8.17 |

In addition to these identification truths, Paul taught that the believer is justified, reconciled, redeemed, regenerated, and forgiven. God's ongoing work is to conform believers into the image of Christ (Romans 8.28-29; 2 Corinthians 3.18). What a package!

## The Transformation

Paul wrote the Corinthians:

> Now we all, with unveiled face, as we view the glory of the Lord as in *a* mirror, we are transformed [μεταμορφούμεθα] to the same image, from glory to glory, even as from *the* Lord, *the* Spirit (2 Corinthians 3.18).

The Word of God reflects and reveals God's nature and glory. It is God's mirror. Paul used the figure of a mirror to illustrate that by the believer's occupation with the Word and through the work of the Holy Spirit, he is transformed into the image of Christ,[21] from glory to glory.[22] Paul wrote:

> [3] But if our gospel has been hidden, it has been hidden to those who perish, [4] in whom the god of this age blinded the minds of those who do not believe, so the light of the

[21] Christ is the image of God. "Image" is the word εἰκών and means a visible representation. Christ visibly manifests the invisible God (John 1.18, 14.9).
[22] Paul discussed "glory to glory" in 1 Corinthians 15.39-49 anticipating the glory of the believer's resurrection body.

> glorious gospel of the Christ, who is *the* image of the God, might not shine forth (2 Corinthians 4.3-4).

> [14] in whom we have the redemption through His blood, the forgiveness of the sins. [15] Who is *the* image of the invisible God, Firstborn over all creation, [16] because all the things were created by Him—in the heavens and on the earth—the visible and the invisible, whether thrones, or dominions, or rulers or authorities. All the things have been created through Him and for Him. [17] So He is before all things and by him all the things hold together (Colossians 1.14-17).

Once one believes the gospel, God begins His work of sanctification, transforming believers into the likeness of Christ. Paul wrote the Thessalonians, Romans, Philippians, and Colossians about this work:

> And because of this, we also continually thank the God, that when you received *the* word of the God when you heard *it* from us, you accepted it, not *as the* word of men, but as it truly is, *the* word of God, which also works [ἐνεργεῖται] in you who believe (1 Thessalonians 2.13).

> [28] Now we know that for those who love the God, all things work together for good, for those who are called after *His* purpose. [29] Because whom He foreknew, He also predestined *to be* conformed to the image of His Son, so He might be Firstborn among many brethren (Romans 8.28-29).

> since I have been persuaded of this very thing: that the One who began *a* good work in you will accomplish *it* until the day of Jesus Christ (Philippians 1.6).

> [10] and since you put on the new, the one who is being renewed in full knowledge, after *the* image of the One who created him, [11] where there is no Greek and Jew, circumcision and uncircumcision, foreigner, Scythian, servant, freeman. Rather, Christ is everything, and in everything (Colossians 3.10-11).

The Thessalonians received and believed the gospel which began God's transforming work. The word translated "works" is the present middle indicative of ἐνεργέω.[23] This verb denotes effective, operative work. The middle voice indicates the word of God itself works in the believer, transforming him. The believer's role in this process is faith, believing what God has said.

In the 2 Corinthians 3.18 passage, Paul wrote "we are transformed (μεταμορφούμεθα) to the same image, from glory to glory," present passive indicative).[24] The passive voice indicates God is doing the

---

[23] Our word "energy" comes from this word.
[24] Our word "metamorphosis" comes from this word.

work. God's purpose is to transform us into the image of Christ. What a remarkable truth! It is a Pauline revelation.

Paul discussed the different types of "glory" in his first letter to the Corinthians.

> 39 Not all flesh *is* the same flesh. One flesh is of men, and
> another flesh of animals, and another of fish, and another of
> birds. 40 And *there are* heavenly bodies and earthly bodies.
> But one *has* heavenly glory and another, earthly. 41 One
> glory is of *the* sun, and another glory *is* of *the* moon, and
> another glory *is* of *the* stars, for star differs from star in
> glory. 42 So too *is* the resurrection from the dead: it is sown
> in corruption; it is raised in incorruption. 43 It is sown in
> dishonor; it is raised in glory. It is sown in weakness; it is
> raised in power. 44 It is sown *a* natural body; it is raised *a*
> spiritual body. If there is *a* natural body, there is also *a*
> spiritual. 45 So also, it has been written: The first man, Adam,
> became *a* living person; the last Adam *became a* life-giving
> spirit. 46 But the spiritual *was* not first, but the natural, then
> the spiritual. 47 The first man *was* from *the* earth, made of
> dust; the second man is the Lord from heaven. 48 As the one
> of earth, so also *are* the ones of the earth. And as the
> heavenly One, so also *are* the ones of heaven. 49 And as we
> bore the image of the earthly, we will also bear the image of
> the heavenly (1 Corinthians 15.39-49).

Every part of God's creation has a unique glory. Mankind's body has a special glory being made in the image of God (Genesis 1.27). But God is in the process of transforming believers into a far greater glory. This is a cooperative work between the believer and God. As the believer is occupied with God's Word and allows the Holy Spirit to control his life, the Holy Spirit transforms him into the image of Christ. The believer *lives* by faith. For members of the Church, this transformation culminates at the Rapture, the Church's resurrection (1 Corinthians 15.51-54).

## 2. The Gospel of the Grace of God

Immediately after Paul was saved, he proclaimed the gospel of the kingdom, the gospel proclaimed by John the Baptist, Jesus, and the Twelve. Luke wrote in Acts 9.20, "And immediately, he began preaching Jesus in the synagogues—that He is the Son of the God." Paul did not preach Christ's death and resurrection for salvation because he, like the Twelve, did not know this truth. All he knew was that Jesus was the Christ, the faith component of the gospel of the kingdom. Paul believed in the *identity* of Christ.

The gospel Paul later proclaimed, that Christ died for our sins and rose from the dead (1 Corinthians 15.1-4), was a secret. It was the gospel of the grace of God (Acts 20.24), the "glorious gospel" (2 Corinthians 4.4; 1 Timothy 1.11). Paul likely received this gospel during his three years in Arabia and Damascus (Galatians 1.15-18) directly from the risen Lord (Galatians 1.11-12).

In his letter to the Ephesians, Paul asked them to pray for him, that he might proclaim the "secret of the gospel." This passage should settle all doubt that Paul's gospel of grace was different from the gospel of the kingdom proclaimed by the Twelve. The passage reads:

> 18 Through every prayer and request, pray at all times in *the* Spirit, even for this very thing, watching with all perseverance and request for all the saints, 19 and for me, so I might be given *a* message with boldness in opening my mouth, to make known the secret [μυστήριον] of the gospel, 20 for which I am *an* ambassador in *a* chain, so by it I might be bold to speak as I must (Ephesians 6.18-20).

Paul wrote a similar message to the Romans:

> 25 Now to Him who can establish you according to my gospel, even the preaching of Jesus Christ according to secret revelation, [ἀποκάλυψιν μυστηρίου] which has been kept silent in the times in the ages, 26 but now was revealed, and through *the* prophetic Scriptures, according to *the* command of the eternal God for obedience of faith, which was made known to all the Gentiles (Romans 16.25-26).

The expression "secret revelation" is an attributive genitive, translated adjectivally. This "secret revelation" was Paul's gospel. In other passages, Paul used the phrase "my gospel" to show his gospel was *different from and not known* by those who were before him (Romans 2.16; 2 Timothy 2.8; 1 Corinthians 15.1; Galatians 1.1, 11-12, 2.2).

The word "gospel" (εὐαγγέλιον) means "good news." Believing Paul's gospel is how one is saved from sin and death today. Paul's gospel was the good news that Christ's death and resurrection had solved the problem of sin and death and removed the barrier between God and man. It was the heart of his ministry.

The clearest definition of Paul's gospel is the following:

> 1 Now I declare to you, brethren, the gospel that I proclaimed to you, which you also received, by which also you stand, 2 through which also you are saved, if you possess[25] that message I proclaimed to you, unless you believed in vain. 3 For I delivered to you first, what I also received: Christ died

---

[25] The word κατέχετε has been translated poorly in verse 2. The KJV, "keep is memory," the NIV, NET "hold firmly," the NASB, ESV "hold fast," imply salvation may be lost unless one "hangs on." The best rendering of κατέχετε is "possess" and agrees with the rest of the verse, "unless you believed in vain" (εἰκῆ), or "did not truly believe." One who truly believes Paul's gospel is eternally secure.

> for our sins, according to the Scriptures, [4] and that He was buried, and that He has been raised on the third day, according to the Scriptures (1 Corinthians 15.1-4).

| Paul's Gospel | |
|---|---|
| "My Gospel" | Romans 2.16, 16.25; 2 Timothy 2.8; 1 Corinthians 15.1; Galatians 1.1, 11-12, 2.2; 1 Timothy 1.11 |
| Paul's Gospel: Content and Response | |
| Content | Christ died for our sins and rose from the dead (1 Corinthians 15.3-4). |
| Response | Salvation is by faith *alone*—believing Christ died for one's sins and rose from the dead (1 Corinthians 15.2). |

Placing one's trust in the work of Christ (His death, burial, and resurrection) is how one is saved from sin and death.[26] God gives the one who trusts in Christ's work *eternal life*. What a gift![27]

Paul wrote the Corinthians:

> [17] For Christ did not send me to baptize but to proclaim the gospel—not by wisdom of speech so that the cross of the Christ might not be nullified. [18] For the message of the cross is foolishness to those who perish. But to the ones who are saved, to us, it is *the* power of God (1 Corinthians 1.17-18).

Water baptism was the centerpiece of the gospel of the kingdom. God sent John the Baptist to baptize with water (Matthew 3.1-6; Mark 1.4). Jesus sent the Twelve to baptize with water (Matthew 28.19). But the risen Lord did *not* send Paul to baptize with water (1 Corinthians 1.17). He sent him to proclaim the gospel, the preaching of the cross. This fact shows how different Paul's ministry was from the Twelve (Matthew 28.19; Acts 2.38). Paul declared his gospel was the power of God for salvation to anyone who *believes* (Romans 1.16-17, 3.22, 26, 4.1-5, 5.1).[28] The gospel is the power of Christianity. He wrote:

> [1] And when I came to you, brethren, I did not come not in ostentatious speech or wisdom proclaiming the secret of the God to you. [2] For I decided not to know anything among you

---

[26] Presentations of the gospel often mention Christ's death for our sins without mentioning His resurrection. Christ's resurrection is essential to the salvation message. If Christ did not rise, we are still in our sins and our faith is in vain (1 Corinthians 15.17). One must believe in Christ's resurrection to be saved.

[27] Paul wrote many verses that establishes salvation is by faith alone. A few are the following: Romans 1.16-17, 3.21-22, 26, 28, 30, 4.5, 5.1).

[28] Paul practiced water baptism early in his ministry but likely had ceased by the time he wrote the Corinthians. He wrote the Ephesians (c. 62 A.D.) there was "one baptism" (Ephesians 4.5)—the baptism of the Holy Spirit (1 Corinthians 12.13), the only valid baptism in the Church, the body of Christ.

except Jesus Christ and Him having been crucified (1 Corinthians 2.1-2).

Paul wrote the Romans:

> 16 For I am not ashamed of the gospel of the Christ[29] for it is *the* power of God for salvation to everyone who believes:[30] to Jew first and to Greek. 17 For by it, *the* righteousness of God is revealed from faith to faith: just as it has been written: The righteous will live by faith (Romans 1.16-17).[31]

## The Gospel of Grace: By Faith Alone

The Scriptures reveal faith has *always* been required for salvation (Hebrews 11). They also reveal men and women were *not* saved by faith *alone* before Paul.[32] Salvation by faith *alone* was a Pauline revelation.

From the time of Paul's return from Arabia until the Council of Jerusalem, two gospels were valid salvation messages: the gospel of the kingdom and the gospel of grace. The gospel of the kingdom began with John the Baptist and continued until the Council of Jerusalem. Paul's gospel began after he returned from Arabia and continues until today. The significance of the Jerusalem Council (51 A.D.) was that it formally set aside the gospel of the kingdom and recognized that only Paul's gospel was valid for salvation (Acts 15.11). Paul wrote the Galatians concerning this about 55 A.D.:[33]

> 6 I am amazed that you are so quickly deserting the One who called you in *the* grace of Christ to another gospel, 7 which is not another, except some are troubling you and wanting to pervert the gospel of the Christ. 8 But even if we or *an* angel from heaven should proclaim *a* gospel to you contrary to what we proclaimed to you, Let him be accursed! 9 As we have said before, and now I say again, If anyone proclaims *a* gospel to you contrary to what you received, Let him be accursed (Galatians 1.6-9)!

Paul's warning was extremely strong. He could not have written such strong words until *after* the Council of Jerusalem's decision regarding the gospel. During God's program of the Church, the body of Christ,

---

[29] Some manuscripts do not have "of the Christ," τοῦ Χριστοῦ.

[30] Paul was the first to proclaim salvation by faith alone in the finished work of Christ. He stated this glorious truth many times in Romans.

[31] Too many in Christendom look for signs and experiences. The true power of God is the gospel. This was Paul's focus and should be ours.

[32] One of God's absolutes is the requirement of faith for salvation. Paul wrote the Jews that apart from faith, it was impossible to please God (Hebrews 11.6).

[33] Paul wrote *all* his letters *after* the Council of Jerusalem. His first letter was to the Thessalonians probably in 52 or 53 A.D. God settled the matter of the gospel before Paul began to write doctrine for the Church.

Paul declared anyone—man or angel—who proclaims a gospel different from his: "let him be accursed" (ἀνάθεμα ἔστω).[34] The phrase is a present active imperative. Anyone who teaches one is saved by anything but by believing Christ died for his sins, was buried, and rose from the dead is cursed. This should strike fear into any who add water baptism, taking Communion, tithing, joining a church, being good, etc. to Paul's gospel. To do so places one under God's curse.

## The Assurance of Salvation

God's salvation is a gift—the greatest possible gift. Paul wrote the Ephesians:

> [8] For by the grace you have been saved through the faith and this [τοῦτο] is not from yourselves: *it is* the gift of God, [9] not from works, so no one might boast (Ephesians 2.8-9).

Some have argued "the faith" or "the grace" in this passage is the gift. But since a pronoun normally agrees with its antecedent in gender and number there is a grammatical problem with "the grace" or "the faith" being "the gift."[35] If Paul meant "the grace" or "the faith" as the antecedent, he would have used the feminine form of "this" (αὕτη) rather than the neuter (τοῦτο), since both "grace" and "faith" are feminine nouns. A neuter pronoun can refer to a phrase or summarize a thought and this is just the case here. The thought of the passage is salvation—the entire salvation package of being saved by the grace (of God) through the faith (Paul's gospel) is "the gift of God." Such a reading agrees with Paul's other statements about salvation as God's gift (Romans 5.15-18, 6.23; 2 Corinthians 9.15; Ephesians 3.7, 4.7).

Nowhere is the assurance of salvation more pronounced than in Paul's writings. Time and again he declared salvation is a present possession for one who has believed his gospel (Romans 3.21-28, 4.1-5; Galatians 2.16, 21; 1 Corinthians 15.1-4). Consider the following:

> [8] But the God shows His love to us: that while we were yet sinners, Christ died for us. [9] Much more, therefore, since we were now declared righteous by His blood, we will be saved from the wrath through Him (Romans 5.8-9).[36]

> in whom we have the redemption through his blood, the forgiveness of the sins, according to the riches of His grace (Ephesians 1.7).

---

[34] The adjective "another," in verse 6, is ἕτερος. In verse 7, the adjective "another" is ἄλλος. The adjective ἕτερος means "another of a different kind" while ἄλλος means "another of the same kind." The Galatians were in danger of abandoning Paul's gospel for a different gospel (verse 7).

[35] Further discussion of this passage is in the chapter, Paul on Faith.

[36] Salvation from wrath is the Lord's deliverance of believers from the Tribulation, not hell (1 Thessalonians 1.10, 5.9). This is a Rapture passage.

> [12] thanking the Father, the One who qualified us for the share of the saints' inheritance in the light, [13] who rescued us from the power of the darkness and transferred *us* into the kingdom of His beloved Son, [14] in whom we have the redemption through His blood, the forgiveness of the sins (Colossians 1.12-14).

> [5] He saved us, not from works in righteousness that we did, but according to His mercy, through washing of regeneration and renewing of *the* Holy Spirit, [6] whom He poured on us richly, through Jesus Christ our Savior, [7] so that, since we were declared righteous by His grace, we might become heirs according to *the* hope of eternal life (Titus 3.5-7).

All these passages speak of the believer's salvation in the past tense. Salvation is both a past event *and* a present possession. Eternal life does not begin when a believer dies. It begins *the moment one believes the gospel*. The believer *has* eternal life. Thanks be to God for His indescribable gift (χάρις δὲ τῷ θεῷ ἐπὶ τῇ ἀνεκδιηγήτῳ αὐτοῦ δωρεᾷ, 2 Corinthians 9.15)!

## Only One Gospel?

One of Christendom's greatest errors has been the teaching, "there has always only been one gospel." Such teaching is so egregiously false one wonders if those who proclaim this have ever opened their Bibles! What is Paul's gospel? It is that Christ died for one's sins, was buried, and rose from the dead (1 Corinthians 15.1-4). Did Abraham believe this? Did Moses? Did David? Did the Twelve? Luke wrote:

> [31] Now after He took the Twelve aside, He said to them, Behold, we are going up to Jerusalem and everything that has been written by the prophets about the Son of the Man will be accomplished. [32] For He will be delivered to the Gentiles, and mocked, and insulted, and spit on. [33] And after they whip Him, they will kill Him. And on the third day He will rise again. [34] And they understood none of these things. And this saying was hidden from them and they kept not understanding the things being said (Luke 18.31-34).

Jesus revealed to the Twelve what was going to happen to Him. The text states, "they understood none of these things." If they did not understand the Lord was going to die and rise from the dead how could they be saved by believing this? The answer is obvious. They couldn't. And they weren't. If they knew Jesus was going to rise from the dead, why weren't they at His tomb? John wrote when he and Peter came to His tomb on resurrection morning, "[9] (For they had not yet understood the Scripture that He must rise from *the* dead)" (John 20.9). Could words be clearer?

Men and women are saved by believing what God has *revealed at a particular time*. Abraham was saved by believing what God told him (Genesis 15.1-6; Romans 4.1-3). The Jews were saved by believing and obeying what God had told them—by the Levitical sacrifices and keeping the Mosaic Law. Salvation during Christ's earthly ministry was by believing in the identity of Christ—He was the Messiah, the Son of God, water baptism, keeping the Law, etc. *Today* there is one gospel—Paul's gospel. That became a reality at the Council of Jerusalem. But Paul's gospel was not known until God revealed it to Paul (Galatians 1.11-12). It was a *secret*.

## The Gospel of the Kingdom Redux

Paul's gospel officially replaced the gospel of the kingdom at the Council of Jerusalem (Acts 15.11).[37] But the gospel of the kingdom will have another day after the Church is completed. Jesus declared the gospel of the kingdom will be proclaimed during the Tribulation until His Second Advent:

> And this gospel of the kingdom will be proclaimed in all the earth for *a* testimony to all the nations. And then the end will come (Matthew 24.14).

Once God has completed and removed His Church, men and women will be saved once again by believing the gospel of the kingdom—that Jesus is the Messiah, the Son of God. The reason for this is twofold. The gospel of the kingdom began with John the Baptist's ministry. Had Israel accepted Jesus as the Christ, this gospel would have been the only gospel since the Church would not have come into existence. The Day of the Lord would have ensued and Jesus would have returned and set up His kingdom. Israel would have received its covenant promises and become a kingdom of priests to bless Gentiles (Exodus 19.6; Micah 4.2; Zechariah 8.20-23).

The second reason is that sometime after God has completed and removed His Church, the Antichrist will emerge. During this time, the great temptation will be to believe the Beast is God. Jesus warned of this deceit: "I have come in My Father's name and you do not receive Me. If another should come in his own name—that one you will receive" (John 5.43). Because this will be the chief temptation, salvation will again be based again on believing in the *identity* of Christ, that Jesus is the Christ, rather than the Beast. This explains the Lord's warning, "But the one who endured to *the* end, this one will be saved" (Matthew 24.13) and His warnings in Revelation 2-3 to the seven Jewish congregations. In those addresses the Lord instructed the Jews to overcome (νικάω)—not to worship the Beast or take his mark which ensures eternal condemnation (Revelation 13.8, 15-16, 14.9-11). Those who overcome inherit eternal life.

---

[37] This matter is dealt with in detail in the chapter, Paul on Faith.

## 3. The Blinding of Israel

Paul wrote in Romans 11.25-27:

> 25 For I do not wish you to be ignorant brethren of this secret [μυστήριον]—so you may not be wise in yourselves—partial hardening [πώρωσις] has happened to Israel, until the completion of the Gentiles might enter in. 26 And so, all Israel will be saved. As it has been written: The Rescuer will come from Zion. He will remove ungodliness from Jacob. 27 And this *is* My covenant with them when I should take away their sins (Romans 11.25-27).

God told the Jews that if they obeyed Him, He would bless them and if they disobeyed, He would discipline them (Deuteronomy 28-30). This truth has been confirmed throughout Jewish history. Beginning with the Assyrian invasion (c. 722 B.C.) and then the Babylonian invasions and captivity (c. 606-587 B.C.), Israel became subject to Gentile powers. Though Israel became a sovereign nation once again in 1948, it is still under the dominion of Gentile powers. This was known. But God revealed to Paul something He had kept secret. He revealed a period of partial "blindness" (πώρωσις) for national Israel (Romans 11.25).[38]

Like Elymas' blindness (Acts 13.9-11), Israel's partial hardening is *temporary*. It will last *until* the fullness of the Gentiles (Romans 11.25), the completion of the Church, the body of Christ. When complete, the Lord will return for it (Rapture) and revisit His program with Israel to remove its hardening.

The gospel of the kingdom required the whole nation to repent, which Peter declared at Pentecost (Acts 2.36, 38).[39] Israel's repentance was taught by the prophets (Isaiah 66.7-9, 25.9; Zechariah 12.10, 13.6), proclaimed in the Gospels, and Paul's quote of Isaiah 59.20, "remove ungodliness from Jacob" above. Jesus told the Jews He would return when they repented (Matthew 23.37-39). This repentance will remove Jacob's ungodliness.[40] At the end of the Tribulation, "all Israel" will be saved (Isaiah 66.8; Jeremiah 30.7; Zechariah 12.10, 13.6; Acts 2.36, 38; Romans 11.25-26), the Lord will return (Matthew 23.37-39), and establish His kingdom (Acts 1.6; Romans 11.16, cf. Deuteronomy

---

[38] A πώρωσις was a callus. Figuratively, it means a hardening or dullness of perception, hence, KJV "blindness." The word is found three times in the New Testament (Mark 3.5; Romans 11.25; Ephesians 4.18).

[39] Μετανοήσατε "repent" in Acts 2.38 is an aorist active imperative—a command. It means a change of mind.

[40] Paul used the name "Jacob," not "Israel." Jacob was Isaac's son's name before the Lord named him "Israel" at Peniel (Genesis 32.27-30). Peniel, פְּנוּאֵל, means "face of God" for Jacob saw God face to face and lived. The Jews will live when they see God face to face at His 2nd Coming. Jacob will become Israel.

28.1-14; Matthew 6.10). The "Tribulation generation" are the "other sheep" of whom Jesus spoke in John 10.16: "And I have other sheep that are not of this fold. I must bring those also. And they will hear My voice and there will become one flock *with* one shepherd" (Deuteronomy 30.1-6; Ezekiel 34.12-14, 36.22-28, 37.19-28; Jeremiah 29.14, 30.1-3, 31.7-10).[41]

## 4. The Rapture: Resurrection of the Church

No Christian doctrine is under greater assault at the present time than the Pre-Tribulational Rapture.[42] This increased spiritual opposition indicates the completion of the Church is growing near (Ephesians 6.12). It also reveals the vast ignorance and apostasy of Christendom.

Opponents state the Rapture is not found in the Old Testament, Gospels,[43] letters of James, Peter, John, or Jude. They are *right*. The fact the Rapture is *not* in the Old Testament, Gospels, letters of James, Peter, John, or Jude *proves* its opponents wrong. If the Rapture *was* in those Scriptures, Paul would be wrong and the doctrine of the Pre-Tribulational Rapture would be an error.

Paul wrote the Corinthians that the Rapture was a *secret*. If the Rapture *could* be found in other Scriptures, it would *not* be a secret. The Rapture was a secret the risen Lord revealed only to Paul. His opening words in 1 Corinthians 15.51 were Ἰδού, μυστήριον ὑμῖν λέγω, "Behold! I tell you *a* secret (μυστήριον)." Such words are *so* clear one wonders how *anyone* can misunderstand them. Christ's Second Advent was *not* a secret. The Rapture was. It was a *new revelation given to Paul*. Since it was new, it cannot be found in the Old Testament, Gospels, or letters of James, Peter, John, or Jude.

Paul wrote:

---

[41] The other sheep are not Gentiles or the Church but a future generation of Jews who will believe Jesus is the Messiah. They will "hear My voice" and become "one flock." God unites the nation as promised (Ezekiel 37.19-22).

[42] The word "rapture" is not in our English Bibles. It comes from St. Jerome's (c. 347-420 A.D.) translation of the Greek New Testament into Latin (the Vulgate). He translated ἁρπάζω "seize" or "snatch away" into the Latin "rapiemur" to be "caught up" or "taken away." Our English word, "rapture" is a transliteration of the Latin. Paul used the verb ἁρπάζω once for the Rapture (1 Thessalonians 4.17) but taught it in several places with other vocabulary. The verb ἁρπάζω and is found 13 times: Matthew 11.12, 13.19; John 6.15, 10.12, 28-29; Acts 8.39, 23.10; 2 Corinthians 12.2, 12.4; 1 Thessalonians 4.17; Jude 1.23; Revelation 12.5.

[43] E.g., Matthew 24.40-42, "Then two men will be in the field: one is taken and one is left. Two women will be grinding in the mill: one is taken and one is left. Therefore, watch. For you do not know what day your Lord comes" has been cited as a Rapture passage. This is to misread the passage. It concerns God's prophetic program with Israel and the nations. One "taken" is taken to judgment; one "left" enters the kingdom.

> [51] Behold! I tell you *a* secret: we will not all sleep but we will all be changed— [52] in *an* instant, in *the* blink of *an* eye, at the last trumpet. For *the* trumpet will sound and the dead will be raised incorruptible. Then, we will be changed. [53] For this corruptible *body* must put on incorruption and this mortal must put on immortality.[54] Now when this corruptible should put on incorruption, and this mortal puts on immortality, then will come to pass the word which has been written: The death was swallowed up in victory (1 Corinthians 15.51-54).

The Rapture is the Church's *resurrection.* If there is no Rapture the Church has no resurrection. Resurrection of Jewish believers was taught in the Old Testament (Job 19.26; Daniel 12.13). The Pharisees believed it; the Sadducees did not. Jesus taught it in His ministry (John 5.25-29, 11.23-27). What was *not taught* was the resurrection of members of the Church, the body of Christ. How could resurrection of the Church be taught when the Church *did not exist?*

In the Rapture, Christ will return in the sky and transform the mortal bodies of members of the Church into eternal, resurrection bodies. This will occur "in *an* instant, in *the* blink of *an* eye, [44] at the last trumpet."[45]

Paul detailed the order of the Rapture in his letter to the Thessalonians:

> [13] But we do not want you to be uninformed, brethren, about those who are asleep, so that you will not grieve as do the rest who have no hope. [14] For if we believe that Jesus died and rose again, even so God will bring with Him those who have fallen asleep in Jesus. [15] For this we say to you by the word of the Lord, that we who are alive and remain until the coming of the Lord, will not precede those who have fallen asleep. [16] For the Lord Himself will descend from heaven with a shout, with the voice of the archangel and with the trumpet of God, and the dead in Christ will rise first. [17] Then we who are alive and remain will be caught up [ἁρπάζω] together with them in the clouds to meet the Lord in the air, and so we shall always be

---

[44] The noun ἄτομος "instant" is the word from which we get the word "atom" and meant the smallest indivisible unit. It was created by the α privative (not) and τόμος (what has been cut off). Thus, ἄτομος was that which could not be cut or divided. The word ῥιπή "blink" means a throw, stroke, or beat.

[45] This "last trumpet" ἐσχάτῃ σάλπιγγι and the trumpet in 1 Thessalonians 4.16 are different from the trumpets in Revelation. Those trumpets concern Israel and the nations and announce judgment. The Church, the body of Christ, is rescued from such judgment. The "last trumpet" of 1 Corinthians 15.52 signifies "last" in the sense of completion, completion of the Church, not last as in a series such as the seven trumpets in Revelation. 1 Thessalonians reveals "the trumpet of God" while the trumpets in Revelation are trumpets of angels.

> with the Lord. [18] Therefore comfort one another with these words. (1 Thessalonians 4.13-18).

Paul's grand message was the gospel. He could not stop talking about it. Here we find it in verse 14. The resurrection sequence of the body of Christ is the following: First, believers of Paul's gospel who have died will be raised and transformed. Second, immediately following these believers, God will transform the bodies of believers who are *alive*. This tremendous doctrine reveals one generation of believers will *escape physical death*. Both groups will meet the Lord in the air.

This return of Christ is an entirely different event from His return at the end of the Tribulation. At the Rapture, the Lord returns in *the air*. It is a heavenly return for a heavenly people, the Church (Ephesians 1.3; Philippians 3.20-21). In the Second Advent, the Lord returns *to earth*: an earthly return for an earthly people, Israel (Zechariah 14.4).

| Passages Teaching the Pre-Tribulation Rapture | |
|---|---|
| Romans 5.9-10, 13.11-12 | 2 Thessalonians 2.1-4 |
| 1 Corinthians 1.4-8, 3.13, 5.1-5, 15.50-51 | Philippians 1.3-6, 8-10, 2.14-16, 3.10-11, 20-21 |
| 2 Corinthians 1.12-14 | Titus 2.13 |
| 1 Thessalonians 1.10, 4.13-18, 5.9 | 2 Timothy 1.16-18, 4.6-8 |

The Rapture is the "blessed hope" (Titus 2.13) of believers in the body of Christ. Paul's earliest letter was 1 Thessalonians and he wrote the Thessalonians to remind them what he had taught them: members of the Church will not experience the Tribulation:[46]

> [9] For they themselves report about how you welcomed us and how you turned to the God from the idols to serve *the* living and true God [10] and to wait for His Son from the heavens, whom He raised from the dead, Jesus, the One who rescues [τὸν ῥυόμενον] us from the coming wrath (1 Thessalonians 1.9-10).

This passage explicitly states members of the Church will *not* experience God's wrath, the Tribulation. The word, "delivered" is the present middle participle of ῥύομαι which means to rescue or deliver. The present tense indicates a deliverance contemporary with the wrath to come, the Tribulation. Paul repeated this teaching later in his letter:

> [8] But since we are of *the* day, let us be sober, having put on the breastplate of faith and love, and as a helmet, the hope of salvation. [9] For God has not destined us for wrath, but

---

[46] As soon as the Thessalonians believed Paul's gospel, he taught them the Rapture. This doctrine is of great comfort to new believers for it is our hope of resurrection and assurance of being delivered from the Tribulation.

> for obtaining salvation through our Lord Jesus Christ, [10] who died for us, so that whether we are awake or asleep, we will live together with Him. [11] Therefore comfort one another and build up one another, just as you also are doing (1 Thessalonians 5.8-11).

Paul stated God has not destined the Church for wrath (the Tribulation) but for salvation (the Rapture).[47] Paul again commanded believers to "encourage one another" with the doctrine of the Rapture.[48] Those who fail to teach the Pre-Tribulational Rapture as an encouragement to believers disobey God.

Paul wrote the Romans:

> [9] Much more then, having now been justified by His blood, we shall be saved from the wrath of God through Him. [10] For if while we were enemies we were reconciled to God through the death of His Son, much more, having been reconciled, we shall be saved by His life. [11] And not only this, but we also exult in God through our Lord Jesus Christ, through whom we have now received the reconciliation. (Romans 5.9-11).

It should be noted that whenever Paul wrote of "wrath," ὀργή, with God as the subject, he meant the Tribulation. The verses above are rarely taught as a Rapture passage but they are one of the *great* Rapture passages. Paul began his dissertation with the words, "Therefore having been justified by faith, we have peace with God through our Lord Jesus Christ (Romans 5.1).[49] Throughout the passage, Paul declared a believer's salvation was sure. No threat of separation from God or "loss of salvation" exists for those who have believed Paul's gospel (Romans 8.31-39). In addition to being saved from sin and death, members of the Church, the body of Christ, are assured of deliverance from the Tribulation. Thus, Paul wrote, "we shall be saved from the wrath of God through Him" and "we shall be saved through His life." This is as clear a declaration of the Pre-Tribulational Rapture as can be made.

---

[47] God's "wrath" is not hell but the Tribulation, the Day of the Lord. Hell and the Lake of Fire are not wrath but penal justice. The Lord will return and remove members of the Church before the horrors of the 7-year Tribulation.
[48] Twice Paul commanded believers to "comfort one another" (παρακαλεῖτε ἀλλήλους) with the doctrine of the Rapture (1 Thessalonians 4.18, 5.11). The word "comfort" in its original sense meant "with fortification." The word παρακαλεῖτε means "strengthen" or "encourage."
[49] A variant reading exists: ἔχομεν, "we have" vs. ἔχωμεν "let us have." Strong external witnesses exist for both readings but ἔχομεν is preferred based on internal evidence. It fits Paul's case of the believer's sure salvation.

Denial of the Pre-Tribulational Rapture was one of the earliest heresies in the Church and has continued in Christendom for over 1,900 years.[50] Paul addressed this false teaching in his second letter to the Thessalonians. Someone, posing as Paul, wrote the Thessalonians that the persecution they were experiencing was the Day of the Lord, the Tribulation.[51] Paul addressed this error:

> 1 Now we ask you, brethren, concerning the coming of our
> Lord Jesus Christ and of our gathering to Him, 2 that you
> might not be easily shaken in your mind or be troubled, by
> neither spirit, or by word, or by *a* letter as if through us, that
> the day of the Lord has arrived. 3 Do not let anyone deceive
> you in any way. For the departure [ἀποστασία] must come
> first and then the man of the sin should be revealed, the son
> of the destruction, 4 the one who opposes and exalts himself
> above every named god or object of worship, so that he will
> sit in the Temple of the God and display himself: that he is
> God. 5 Do you not recall, when I was still with you, I kept
> telling you these things (2 Thessalonians 2.1-5)?

Paul had warned the Thessalonians they would experience testing and tribulations (1 Thessalonians 2.14, 3.4) but that this was *not* the Day of the Lord.[52] He made it clear that Jesus would rescue members of the Church from it. Paul's enemies took advantage of the Thessalonians' sufferings to attack Paul's doctrine of the Rapture. Like all false teachers, they wished to gain control over these believers.

## An Examination of Ἀποστασία

The noun ἀποστασία occurs twice in the Scriptures (2 Thessalonians 2.3; Acts 21.21).[53] In Acts, James and company questioned Paul about what they had heard: he was teaching Jews to depart from or forsake Moses. The verb associated with ἀποστασία is ἀφίστημι and occurs fifteen times in the New Testament. Paul used the verb five times if we include Hebrews. Only Paul and Luke used the verb ἀφίστημι and the noun ἀποστασία (Luke 2.37, 4:13, 8.13, 13.27; Acts 5.37-38, 12.10, 15.38, 19.9, 22.29).

---

[50] It was one of the earliest and easiest ways to detect a false teacher.
[51] This was the beginning of the error of Post-Tribulationalism.
[52] The KJV text of 2 Thessalonians 2.2 reads "day of Christ," a reading with weak textual evidence—only the second corrector of D ($D^2$, 9th century). Earlier evidence (manuscripts, versions, fathers) reads "day of the Lord."
[53] It is rendered in various ways in translations: "falling away," "rebellion," "apostasy," etc. but the primary sense of the word is "departure."

| Pauline Passage | | Qualifier |
|---|---|---|
| ἀποστασία | | |
| 2 Thessalonians 2.3 | Do not let anyone deceive you in any way. For the departure [ἀποστασία] must come first and then the man of the sin should be revealed, the son of the destruction | Physical withdrawal (no preposition) |
| Acts 21.21 | Now they are informed about you that you teach all the Jews among the Gentiles to abandon [ἀποστασία] Moses, telling them not to circumcise their children or to walk in its traditions | "depart from Moses," |
| ἀφίστημι | | |
| 2 Corinthians 12.8 | Three times I pleaded with the Lord about this, that it might leave [ἀποστασία] me. | Physical withdrawal, preposition "from me" |
| 1 Timothy 4.1 | Now the Spirit explicitly says that in later times some will depart [ἀποστασία] from the faith, by adhering to deceitful spirits and demonic doctrines | "depart from the faith" |
| 1 Timothy 6.5 | bickerings of men who have corrupted their mind and are destitute of the truth, who think the godliness is *a* means of gain. Withdraw [ἀποστασία] from such.[54] | Physical withdrawal, preposition "from such" |
| 2 Timothy 2.19 | Nevertheless the foundation of God stands sure, having this seal, The Lord knows them that are his. And, Let everyone that names the name of Christ depart [ἀποστασία] from iniquity. | "depart from iniquity" |
| Hebrews 3.12 | Take heed, brethren, lest there be in any of you an evil heart of unbelief, in departing [ἀποστασία] from the living God. | "depart from the living God" |

1. Paul used the noun ἀποστασία and verb ἀφίστημι to define both physical and figurative departure, sometimes with a preposition, e.g., "depart from *x*."
2. Paul taught the Thessalonians about the Rapture, not apostasy—

[54] Some manuscripts to not have the text, ἀφίστασο ἀπὸ τῶν τοιούτων, "depart from such."

God would rescue believers from His wrath, the Tribulation (1 Thessalonians 4.13-18; 1 Thessalonians 1.10; 5.9).

3. Early English Bibles translated ἀποστασία as "departure" or "departing" e.g., Tyndale (1525), Coverdale (1535), Matthew (1537), Great (1539), Geneva (1560). Jerome's Latin Vulgate (circa 400 A.D.) translated ἀποστασία with "discessio," "departure." What these men believed about end times is irrelevant. What *can* be said is that they translated accurately.
4. Paul included the definite article "ἡ" with ἀποστασία—"ἡ ἀποστασία" (2 Thessalonians 2.3) to emphasize the identity of the noun, "*the* departure," a specific event, the ἁρπάζω of 1 Thessalonians 4.17. "Apostasy" is too vague to be a helpful sign. At the end of his life, Paul wrote all Asia had turned against him (2 Timothy 1.15). Was that not apostasy?
5. Paul wrote, "ἡ ἀποστασία" comes and then the man of the lawlessness is revealed, the son of the destruction" (verse 3). The conjunctive "and" (καὶ) is a resultant temporal conjunction with the sense "and then." This sense is supported by verses 7-8.

Verses 3a and 7 and verses 3b and 8 are parallel. After ἡ ἀποστασία, "the departure," the "man of lawlessness is revealed." After "he who now restrains is removed" the "lawless one is revealed."

| Parallelism of the Man of the Sin in 2 Thessalonians 2 | | |
|---|---|---|
| Verse | Part 1 | Part 2 |
| v. 3 | a) Do not let anyone deceive you in any way. For the departure [ἡ ἀποστασία] must [ἐὰν μὴ] come first [πρῶτον], | b) and then [καὶ] the man of the lawlessness should be revealed, the son of the destruction, |
| vv. 7-8 | 7 For the secret [μυστήριον] of the lawlessness is already at work, only the One who now restrains *him* will continue until [ἕως] it should be done out of *the* way. | 8 And then [καὶ τότε] the lawless one will be revealed, whom the Lord[55] will slay[56] by the breath of His mouth and abolish by the appearance of His coming, |

Verse 3 has the temporal indicators, ἐὰν μὴ "unless" and πρῶτον "first" (in order of succession) in addition to καὶ. Verses 7 and 8 have the temporal indicators ἕως "until" and καὶ τότε "and then."

What did Paul mean by "the One who now restrains him?" This refers to the Lord Himself. The Lord restrains the Beast's appearance until He removes the Church. Hopefully, some will soon believe in Christ

---

[55] Some manuscripts have "Jesus," Ἰησοῦς.

[56] Some manuscripts have the verb ἀνελεῖ, "slay" and others ἀναλώσει, "consume."

after the Rapture but even so their number will be tiny. This is why God will need to seal the 144,000 for a witnessing ministry.

Two key points should be made concerning Paul's statement about the advent of the Antichrist. One is that the Lord currently restrains his advent. The other is that God's removal of the Church signals a strategic move in God's plan. God has been building His Church, the body of Christ, for almost 2,000 years. When God removes it, Satan recognizes God has made a major move and will quickly engage a counter move. He will prepare his man to deceive the nations to rule the world. The Scriptures are silent about how soon the Antichrist will emerge after the Rapture. He may appear immediately. Or, it may take years.[57] A delay would provide time for the world to forget the Rapture, time for more Jews to move to Israel, and time for Satan to prepare his man. Satan is the great counterfeiter. Jesus lived thirty years before He began His ministry. Satan could copy this timetable to position his man to become the Beast. One must keep in mind that forty is a number the Scriptures use for a period of testing.

In 2 Thessalonians 2.5, Paul wrote, "Do you not remember that while I was still with you, I was telling you these things?" To what things did Paul refer? Paul wrote:

> 1 Now about the times and the seasons, [brethren, you] have
> no need for me to write [you]. 2 For [you yourselves] fully
> know that *the* day of *the* Lord comes as *a* thief in *the* night.
> 3 For when **they** should say, Peace and security, then, sudden
> destruction comes on **them**, as she who has the labor pain in
> her womb. And **they** will not escape. 4 But [you, brethren],
> are not in darkness, so the day should overtake [you] as *a*
> thief. 5 For [you] all are sons of light and sons of day. [We]
> are not of night or of darkness. 6 So then, [we] should not
> sleep as **the others**, but should stay alert and be sober. 7 For
> **the sleepers** sleep at night. And **the drunkards** get drunk
> at night. 8 But since [we] are of *the* day, [we] should be
> sober, by putting on *the* breastplate of faith and love, and *the*
> helmet—hope of salvation. 9 Because the God did not
> appoint [us] for wrath but for obtaining salvation through
> our Lord Jesus Christ, 10 the One who died for [us], so that
> whether [we] should watch or should sleep [we] should live
> together with Him. 11 Therefore, encourage [one another]
> and edify [one another], even as [you] are also doing (1 Thessalonians 5.1-11).

The third person pronouns, "they," "them" "those," noted in **bold**, refer to unbelievers. In contrast, Paul cited believers with first and second personal pronouns, "you," "we," "us," noted in [brackets].

[57] What Satan knows is not known. Paul provided insight into this matter with his declaration about the "secret of the lawlessness" in 2 Thessalonians 2.7.

These verses also again reveal believers will not experience God's wrath, the Tribulation, and provide the timetable of the Rapture prior to the advent of the Beast and the Tribulation.

Paul's many attestations that the Lord will return to remove members of the Church before the Tribulation (Romans 5.9-10; 1 Thessalonians 1.10, 5.1-11) along with the grammatical and textual evidence of ἡ ἀποστασία, "the departure," is a sure word of the Church's "blessed hope" (Titus 2.13), the Pre-Tribulation Rapture.

## The Man of the Sin and the Son of the Destruction

Paul wrote the Thessalonians:

> 3 Do not let anyone deceive you in any way. For the departure must come first and then the man of the sin should be revealed, the son of the destruction, 4 the one who opposes and exalts himself above every named god or object of worship, so that he will sit in the Temple of the God and display himself: that he is God (2 Thessalonians 2.3-4).

Paul gave two names to this personage who will come after the Rapture: "the man of the sin" (ὁ ἄνθρωπος τῆς ἁμαρτίας) and "the son of the destruction" (ὁ υἱὸς τῆς ἀπωλείας). Both titles include the definite article and identified him as a specific person. Why two titles?

"The man of the sin," and "the son of the destruction" are the same. But at the midpoint of the Tribulation Satan *indwells* the Beast and the Beast becomes super-human. As "the son of the destruction," he will "sit in the Temple of the God and display himself: that he is God."[58]

The Scriptures name two individuals ὁ υἱὸς τῆς ἀπωλείας, "the son of the perdition" or "the son of the destruction": Judas Iscariot (John 17.12) and the Antichrist (2 Thessalonians 2.3). Judas acquired this title when he was indwelt by Satan. The Beast also acquires this title when Satan indwells him for it is a title that denotes Satan's indwelling presence.

Jesus told His disciples, "one of you is *the* Devil," ὑμῶν εἷς διάβολός ἐστιν (John 6.70). The Lord used the word διάβολός (devil) not δαιμόνιον (demon). Most translations read, "one of you is a devil." This is *not* the reading of the text. *One* Devil exists. The anarthrous noun is definite and should be translated: "one of you is *the* Devil." During the first three and a half years of the Tribulation, the Beast is a

---

[58] Satan is vanquished in heaven and thrown to earth at the midpoint of the Tribulation (Revelation 12.9). Revelation 13 and 17 reveal that at this same time the Beast is assassinated and rises from the dead through the power of Satanic possession (Revelation 13.3-4, 14). The meaning of who "was and is not and will come" in Revelation 17.8, 11 is that the Beast is the 7th king but after he rises from the dead through Satan, he becomes the 8th king.

man directed by Satan. In the last three and a half years he is more—a man Satan possesses, the "son of the destruction."

Paul wrote that the son of the destruction "displays himself: that he is God" (ἀποδεικνύντα ἑαυτὸν ὅτι ἔστιν θεός). The word ἀποδεικνύντα is a present active participle, i.e., "keeps showing himself as God." Peter used this word in his address to the Jews on the day of Pentecost to persuade them that Jesus was the Messiah because of His miracles, wonders, and signs (Acts 2.22). The Antichrist will perform miracles and deceive the world (Matthew 24, 4-5, 11, 24).

Jesus revealed the key sign identifying the Antichrist will be the "abomination of desolation" (Matthew 24.15) and commanded the Jews in Judea to flee to the mountains when they saw it. The "abomination of desolation" is the Beast's entering the Holy of Holies and declaring himself to be God (2 Thessalonians 2.4). He will likely place an image of himself on the mercy seat, between the cherubim.[59] The world will worship him and his image (Revelation 13.14-15, 14.9, 11, 15.2, 16.2, 19.20, 20.4; 2 Thessalonians 2.5).

Throughout the Old Testament, the prophets warned of the "Day of the Lord," יוֹם יְהוָה.[60] During this time God will exercise vengeance upon Israel and the nations for their evil which will climax with the worship of the Antichrist. This is the subject of the book of Revelation. Jesus described the horrors of this time:

> [21] For then, there will be great tribulation, such as has not been from *the* beginning of *the* world until now, nor should be. [22] And unless those days were cut short, no flesh would be saved. But because of the chosen, those days will be cut short (Matthew 24.21-22).

The Lord will judge Israel (Jeremiah 30.7) and the nations for unbelief and rejection of Christ (Psalm 2.4-5). The Tribulation will end with His return when He destroys His enemies (Matthew 24.30; Revelation 19.11-19). He will then establish His earthly kingdom and reign on David's throne (Luke 1.32).

---

[59] The mercy seat represents the throne of God. The Beast will assert he is God (Isaiah 14.13-14) and the world will worship him and his image as God (Revelation 13.14-15, 14.9, 11, 15.2, 16.2, 19.20, 20.4).

[60] See Isaiah 2.12-21; 13.9-13; 26.20-21; 34.1-2, 8; Ezekiel 30.1-8; Joel 1.13-16; 2.1-3, 11; 2.23-32; 3.12-18; Amos 5.18-20; Obadiah 1.15-17; Zephaniah 1.7-18; 2.1-3; Zechariah 12.2-10; 14.1-20; Malachi 4.1-3; Matthew 24; Acts 2.20; Romans 2.5; 1 Thessalonians 5.2; 2 Thessalonians 2.2; 2 Peter 3.10.

<table>
<tr><th colspan="5">Advents of the Messiah</th></tr>
<tr><th colspan="2">Revealed by the Prophets</th><th colspan="2">Revealed by Paul</th></tr>
<tr><td>1st</td><td>Suffer and Serve</td><td rowspan="2">R<br>A<br>P<br>T<br>U<br>R<br>E</td><td rowspan="2">The Rapture Was a NEW Revelation, a Secret, in which the Church is Saved from God's Judgment</td></tr>
<tr><td>2nd</td><td>Judge, Establish Kingdom, and Rule</td></tr>
</table>

## The Day of Christ

Paul taught a day unrevealed by the prophets, by Jesus in His earthly ministry, or by the Twelve. He called it the "day of Christ" or the "day of the Lord Jesus" (1 Corinthians 1.8; 5.5; 2 Corinthians 1.14; Philippians 1.6, 10; 2.16). He also called it "that day" in his last letter.[61] This day is unique to Paul and is in stark contrast to the "day of the Lord." The "day of Christ" is the Rapture.

| The Day of Christ |
|---|
| 11 So *do* this, since we know the time, that *it is* already *the* hour for you to wake from sleep. For our salvation *is* now nearer than when we first believed. 12 The night is advanced, **the day has come near**. Therefore, let us put away the works of the darkness. Let us be arrayed with the weapons of the light (Romans 13.11-12). |
| 4 I thank my God always about you for the grace of God that was given to you in Christ Jesus, 5 that in everything you were made rich in Him, in all speech and all knowledge, 6 as the testimony of the Christ was confirmed in you, 7 so you do not lack in any gift, as you impatiently await the revelation of our Lord Jesus Christ, 8 who also will establish you to *the* end: blameless in **the day of our Lord Jesus Christ** (1 Corinthians 1.4-8). |
| the work of each will become manifest, for **the day** will disclose *it*, for it is revealed by fire and fire will test the work of each, what kind it is (1 Corinthians 3.13). |

[61] The phrase "the day of the Lord" as "that day" is clearly different from "that day," the "day of Christ." Context determines the definition. The "day of the Lord" is God's wrath; the "day of Christ" is God's deliverance.

| |
|---|
| [4] When you gather in the name of our Lord Jesus Christ, with me in spirit, with the power of our Lord Jesus Christ, [5] deliver this one to Satan for the destruction of the flesh, so the spirit might be saved in **the day of the Lord Jesus** (1 Corinthians 5.4-5). |
| [13] For we do not write to you anything except what you read and also understand. But I hope that you will understand completely, [14] just as you partly understood us, that we are your boast, just as also you *are* ours in **the day of our Lord Jesus** (2 Corinthians 1.13-14). |
| since I have been persuaded of this very thing: that the One who began *a* good work in you will accomplish *it* until **the day of Jesus Christ** (Philippians 1.6). |
| [9] And this I pray, that your love may abound still more and more in full knowledge and every discernment, [10] for you to test the things that are different,[62] so you may be pure and blameless **for *the* day of Christ** (Philippians 1.9-10). |
| by holding to the word of life, for my boast on **the day of Christ**, that I did not run or toil for nothing (Philippians 2.16). |
| May the Lord give to him to find mercy from *the* Lord on **that day**! For you know very well how much he served in Ephesus (2 Timothy 1.18). |
| [7] I have fought the good fight. I have finished the race. I have kept the faith. [8] From now on, the crown of the righteousness is reserved for me, which the Lord, the Righteous Judge, will award me on **that day**. But not to me only—but also to all who have loved His appearing (2 Timothy 4.7-8). |

## Contrasting the Two Days

The Day of the Lord is a day of dread, a day of judgment, a day of God's vengeance. The Day of Christ is the blessed hope of the Church, the body of Christ (Titus 2.13), the Rapture, the Church's resurrection.

---

[62] Most translations render διαφέροντα, "excellent," "best." But Paul always used the word to denote *difference* (Romans 2.18; 1 Corinthians 15.41; Galatians 2.6, 4.1). He prayed for the Philippians to have full knowledge and discernment to combat the false doctrine of his opponents.

| The Day of Christ | The Day of the Lord |
|---|---|
| For the Church | For Rejectors of Christ |
| Deliverance and Reward | Terror and Judgment |
| A Heavenly Hope | An Earthly Despair |
| Eagerly Anticipated | Feared and Dreaded |
| Occurs in the Air | Occurs on Earth |

## 5. Gathering All Things in Christ

Paul wrote the Ephesians:

> [9] by making known to us the secret [μυστήριον] of His will, according to His pleasure, that He set forth in Him, [10] for *the* dispensation of the fullness of the times, to head up everything in the Christ: the things in the heavens and the things on the earth (Ephesians 1.9-10).

Paul wrote the Galatians, "But when the fullness of the time came, the God sent His Son, born of *a* woman, born under the Law" (Galatians 4.4). The word "fullness" (πλήρωμα) means that which is complete, i.e., Christ's advent occurred at just the right time.

In Ephesians 1.10, Paul wrote, "fullness of *times*" rather than "fullness of *time*." What is the significance between the singular "time" and the plural "times?" The singular "time" referred to God's revealed, prophetic program concerning Israel and the nations. The plural "times" included God's new program, the Church, the body of Christ. Gathering together in one—things in heaven and things on earth—in Christ encompasses both God's heavenly program, the Church (Ephesians 1.3; Philippians 3.10) and God's earthly program, Israel (Matthew 6.10, 19.28). These two programs are the main components of the "kingdom of God." Both will be gathered together in Christ.[63]

Paul elaborated on this in Ephesians 2 and wrote:

> [19] So then, you are no longer foreigners and aliens, but fellow citizens of the saints and the household of the God, [20] which was built on the foundation of the apostles and prophets, Jesus Christ Himself being *the* cornerstone, [21] in whom *the*

[63] The phrases, "kingdom of God" and "kingdom of heaven" of the Gospels, mean the same—God's earthly kingdom promised to Israel. The phrase, "kingdom of heaven" is a genitive of source, not a genitive of location. Its source is heaven and its location is earth (Matthew 6.10). When Paul wrote "kingdom of God," he meant God's overall realm of heaven and earth.

> whole building, since it is joined together, is increasing into *a* holy temple in *the* Lord, [22] in whom you also are being built together for *a* dwelling of the God by *the* Spirit (Ephesians 2.19-22).

Paul used the phrases, "household of the God" and "holy temple in the Lord" to include both of God's programs: Israel and the Church. This truth was unknown before Paul since the Church did not exist. Concerning God's program with Israel and His program with Gentiles, Paul exclaimed:

> [33] O *the* depth of riches, both of wisdom and knowledge of God! How unsearchable *are* His judgments and incomprehensible His ways! [34] For who knew *the* mind of the Lord? Or who became His adviser? [35] Or who first gave to Him so he will be repaid? [36] For from Him, and through Him, and to Him, *are* all the things. To Him *be* the glory forever. Amen (Romans 11.33-36).

Interwoven in this secret to "gather together in one all things in Christ" is the revelation Paul wrote the Colossians:

> [2] so their hearts might be encouraged, since they have been united in love, and for all *the* riches of the full assurance of the understanding, for *the* full knowledge of the secret [μυστήριον] of the God, Christ, [3] in whom are hidden all the treasures of the wisdom and the knowledge (Colossians 2.2-3).

Similarly, Paul wrote the Philippians that Christ will "subject all things to Himself." The word "subject" is the aorist active infinitive of ὑποτάσσω, more literally, "to arrange under."

> [20] For our citizenship is in the heavens from where we also impatiently awaiting *a* Savior—the Lord Jesus Christ— [21] who will transform our body of the humiliation *to be* conformed to the body of His glory, according to the working by which He can subject all things to Himself (Philippians 3.20-21).

## 6. The Secret of the Godliness

Paul wrote Timothy:

> [16] And, admittedly, great is the secret [μυστήριον] of the godliness: God was revealed in *the* flesh, declared righteous by *the* Spirit, seen by angels, preached among Gentiles, believed on in *the* world, taken up in glory (1 Timothy 3.16)!

This verse reads like a creedal statement or hymn. It summarized Christ's earthly ministry and included Paul's commission as the apostle of the Gentiles. The word "godliness" is εὐσέβεια and means, "piety," "reverence," "holiness" and the "secret of the godliness" is in contrast with "the secret of the iniquity" (2 Thessalonians 2.7). What did Paul mean by "the secret of the godliness?"

God had revealed through His prophets that He would establish His kingdom on earth and that Israel would be the preeminent nation among the nations (Deuteronomy 28.1, 13; Isaiah 60). Specifics about the Messiah, however, were sketchy. Peter wrote:

> [10] About this salvation, *the* prophets searched and investigated diligently, because they prophesied about the grace to you, [11] for they inquired into what or what manner of time the Spirit of Christ that was in them was revealing, by previously testifying the sufferings of Christ and the glory after them, [12] to whom it was revealed, that not to them but to us, they served things that were now declared to you through those who proclaimed the gospel to you by *the* Holy Spirit sent from heaven—into which things angels long to look (1 Peter 1.10-12).

Moses told the nation, "The Lord your God will raise up to you a Prophet from the midst of you, of your brethren, like me; to him you will hearken" (Deuteronomy 18.15). David wrote that God would establish His Messiah as King in Jerusalem to rule the nations (Psalm 2.2, 6-8). Jeremiah wrote God would raise a Righteous Branch from the house of David who would reign as King over the earth, execute justice, and be called "The LORD our righteousness" (Jeremiah 23.5-6). Isaiah wrote of a virgin who would have a Son called Immanuel (Isaiah 7.14) and described His rule (Isaiah 9.6-7, 11.1-5). In Isaiah 53, the prophet revealed His sufferings.

How these prophecies would be fulfilled was not known. While the prophecies of the Messiah's rule were straightforward, the prophecies concerning His sufferings were exceedingly cryptic and vague.[64]

The Jews expected a conquering Messiah who would free them from Gentile domination. But Christ's ministry was wholly different. Even John the Baptist, of whom the Lord said there was no greater prophet (Matthew 11.11) was perplexed. He asked Jesus, "Are you the Coming One? Or do we look for another" (Matthew 11.3)? Details of the Messiah's work were veiled in secrecy. Most recondite of all was His work regarding sin. The Twelve did not understand it, even after His resurrection. The significance of Christ's death and resurrection concerning sin did not become known until the risen Lord revealed it to Paul.

---

[64] The best way to discover what godly Jews believed about God's plan and His Messiah is to read the first two chapters of Luke's Gospel.

Paul wrote Christ was "declared righteous by *the* Spirit." Both Jews and Gentiles condemned Him. The Jews demanded Pilate crucify Him and Pilate consented due to political pressure. Christ was certainly *not* justified by men. God declared Him righteous. Paul wrote:

> who was decreed the Son of God by power, according to *the* Holy Spirit, by resurrection from *the* dead: Jesus Christ our Lord (Romans 1.4).

The Holy Spirit justified Christ when He rose from the dead. His resurrection demonstrated God approved His Son's work on the cross.

Paul's statement of "preached among Gentiles" referred to Jesus' limited interaction with Gentiles. This ministry would have expanded had Israel accepted Jesus as the Messiah. Since they wouldn't, the risen Lord commissioned Paul as "the apostle of the Gentiles." Paul wrote earlier in his letter:

> [3] For this *is* right and acceptable before the God, our Savior,
> [4] who wants all men to be saved and come to *the* full knowledge of *the* truth. [5] For *there is* one God and One agent between God and men, *the* man Christ Jesus, [6] the One who gave Himself *a* ransom for all, the witness in their proper times, [7] for which, I was appointed preacher and apostle. I speak truth. I do not lie: teacher of Gentiles by faith and by truth (1 Timothy 2.3-7).

Thus, "the secret of the godliness" was *how* God had fulfilled His plan to Israel and to Gentiles according to God's prophetic program. God had kept the specifics secret of how He would accomplish His prophetic will. Now, through Paul, God was revealing the secret of the Church, that Christ died for the entire human race, and how He was blessing Gentiles despite Israel's disobedience.

## 7. The Secret of the Lawlessness

> [6] And now, you know what restrains *him*, so he might be revealed in his time. [7] For the secret [μυστήριον] of the lawlessness is already at work, only the One who now restrains *him* will continue until it should be removed out of *the* way (2 Thessalonians 2.6-7).

Paul wrote his second letter to the Thessalonians to repair the damage done by false teachers who had upset them by writing that the trials they were experiencing was the Day of the Lord (the Tribulation). Paul reminded them that the Antichrist cannot appear until after the Rapture (2 Thessalonians 2.1-5). Jesus had warned of false Christs (Matthew 24.5, 15, 24-25; John 5.43) and the Antichrist will be the final false

Christ.[65] His appearance was *not* a secret. Paul described this person as ὁ ἄνθρωπος τῆς ἁμαρτίας, ὁ υἱὸς τῆς ἀπωλείας, "the man of the sin, the son of the destruction." What did Paul mean by his expression, τὸ γὰρ μυστήριον ἤδη ἐνεργεῖται (present middle indicative) τῆς ἀνομίας, "for the secret of the lawlessness is already working?"

The "secret of the iniquity," in contrast to the "secret of the godliness" (1 Timothy 3.16), is how Satan is accomplishing his plan. When Paul wrote, "the secret of the iniquity is already at work" he meant Satan's plan regarding the "man of the sin" was in place. His advent into human history was not a secret except *when* he would come (John 5.43). Paul disclosed he cannot appear until *after the Rapture*. Satan does not know when God will complete His Church. But when it is, and Christ removes it, it signals Satan that his man can emerge to deceive the world. Since Satan does not know when the Rapture will occur, it is reasonable that he must continually be preparing for this event. Satan probably grooms men in every generation for this role.

When Paul stated, "the secret of the lawlessness is already at work" he revealed that Satanic deception is present in the Church and that Satan can transform himself into an angel of light (2 Corinthians 11.14). When the Beast emerges, he will display signs and wonders to deceive the world that he is God.

Those who claim to have divine powers such as the gifts of tongues, prophecy, knowledge, and healing are both deceived and deceivers. Some "sign gifts" and "miracles" in the Church come from Satanic power which he uses to deceive. It is a small thing for him to perform miracles to deceive believers and unbelievers. He does anything to remove attention from the gospel, the power of God (Romans 1.16).[66]

## 8. Other Secrets

If one steps back and reflects on Paul's theology, the conclusion is that *all of it was secret*. Paul's theology is not in the prophets, in the Gospels, or in the writings of Peter, James, John, or Jude. In addition to the secrets examined above, Paul revealed other secrets. They do not have the specific word μυστήριον attached to them but were secrets nevertheless. They include the believer's heavenly citizenship, relationship to the Mosaic Law, the grace of God, and the nature of man.

### Heavenly Citizenship

The truth of believers dying and going to heaven was a Pauline revelation. It is not found in the Old Testament. No Jew had a hope of

---

[65] The particle, ἀντί, preceeding ἀντίχριστος, "antichrist," can mean either "against" or "instead of." The Antichrist will be both: against Christ and a pretender Christ.

[66] More will be said about this in the chapter, Paul and Sign Gifts.

going to heaven. According to the Old Testament, the dead went to the grave, the abode of the dead, Sheol, שְׁאוֹל, and the righteous had the hope of resurrection, to live on *earth* (Job 19.26; John 11.23-24).

Paul revealed a new hope to believers of his gospel. The hope of members of the Church, the body of Christ, is resurrection and life in *heaven*. This was a *secret*. No one knew this before Paul. When a believer dies today, he does not go to the grave, to Abraham's bosom (Luke 16.22), but to heaven. Paul wrote the Corinthians:

> [6] Therefore, we are always confident, because we know that while we are at home in the body, we are absent from the Lord. [7] For we walk through faith, not through sight. [8] Now we are confident and rather wish to be absent from the body and be at home with the Lord (2 Corinthians 5.6-8).

To be present with the Lord means to be in heaven, His location until He returns (Psalm 110.1). Paul wrote that God has blessed members of His body with "all spiritual blessings" (Ephesians 1.3) and that believers have been raised with Christ (Romans 6.5; Ephesians 2.6; Colossians 1.3). Positionally, members of the Church, alive or dead, are in Christ and enjoy heavenly citizenship (Philippians 3.20). This was not known before Paul.

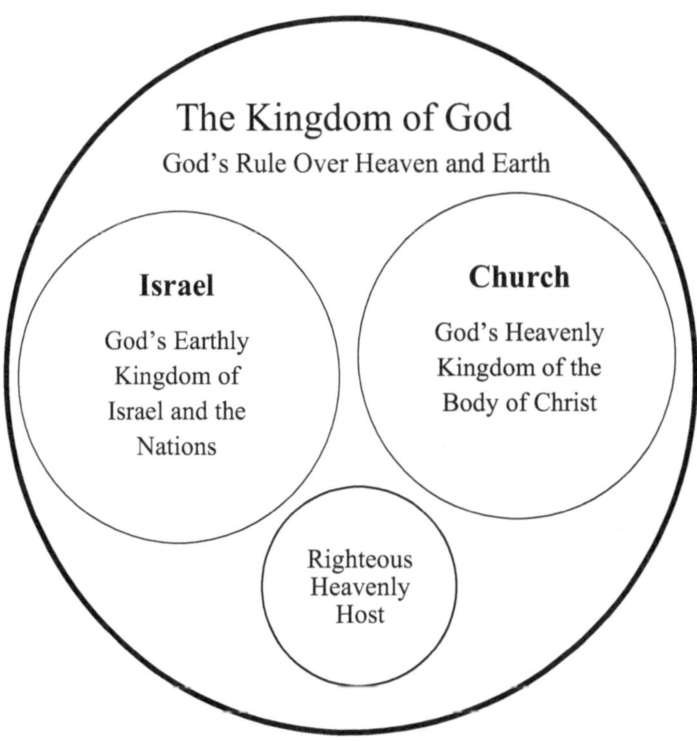

## Use of the Word "Grace"

Paul declared believers are under grace, not Law (Romans 6.14).

| Sources | Passages Using Χάρις | Frequency |
|---|---|---|
| Gospels | | |
| Luke 1.30, 2.40, 52, 4.22, 6.32, 33, 6.34, 17.9 | | 8x |
| John 1.14, 16, 17 | | 4x |
| Acts | Acts 2.47, 4.33, 7.10, 46, 11.23, 13.43, 14.3, 26, 15.11, 40, 18.27, 20.24, 32, 24.27, 25.3, 9 | 16x |
| Paul's Epistles | | |
| Romans 1.5, 7, 3.24, 4.4, 16, 5.2, 15, 17, 20, 21, 6.1, 14, 15, 17, 11.5, 6, 12.3, 12.6, 15.15, 16.20, 24 | | 25x |
| 1 Corinthians 1.3, 4, 3.10, 10.30, 15.10, 57, 16.3, 23 | | 10x |
| 2 Corinthians 1.2, 12, 15, 2.14, 4.15, 6.1, 8.1, 4, 6, 7, 9, 16, 19, 9.8, 14, 15, 12.9, 13.14; | | 18x |
| Galatians 1.3, 6, 15, 2.9, 21, 5.4, 6.18 | | 7x |
| Ephesians 1.2, 6, 7, 2.5, 7, 8, 3.2, 7, 8, 4.7, 29, 6.24 | | 12x |
| Philippians 1.2, 7, 4.23 | | 3x |
| Colossians 1.2, 6, 3.16, 4.6, 18 | | 5x |
| 1 Thessalonians 1.1, 5.28 | | 2x |
| 2 Thessalonians 1.2, 12, 2.16, 3.18 | | 4x |
| 1 Timothy 1.2, 12, 14, 6.21 | | 4x |
| 2 Timothy 1.2, 3, 9, 2.1, 4.22 | | 5x |
| Titus 1.4, 2.11, 3.7, 15 | | 4x |
| Philemon 1.3, 7, 25 | | 3x |
| Hebrews 2.9, 4.16, 10.29, 12.15, 12.28, 13.9, 25 | | 8x |
| James' Epistle | James 4.6 | 2x |
| Peter's Epistles | | |
| 1 Peter 1.2, 10, 13, 2.19, 20, 3.7, 4.10, 5.5, 10, 12 | | 10x |
| 2 Peter 1.2, 3.18 | | 2x |
| John's Epistles | | |
| 2 John 1.3 | | 1x |
| Revelation 1.4, 22.21 | | 2x |
| Jude's Epistle | Jude 1.4 | 1x |

The chart reveals χάρις is used 156 times in 147 verses in the New Testament. Paul used the word 110 times if Hebrews is included. This means Paul's writings account for 70% of its use. If one considers that Luke, Paul's constant companion, was undoubtedly influenced by Paul's teachings, and used the word 24 times, then the usage is 86%. Only the Gospels of Luke and John use χάρις and John used it only 4x.

Also, Peter wrote his letters late in life by which time he had gained more understanding of Church theology.[67] One can see why Paul is the "apostle of grace" (Romans 12.3; Ephesians 3.8). Being "under grace" rather than Law was a revolution in how believers live before God.

## Completion of the Scriptures

While most of Christendom has been taught the writings of the Apostle John were the last Scriptures written, the Bible says otherwise. Paul wrote the Colossians:

> [24] Now I rejoice in my sufferings for you and am filling up the things lacking of the afflictions of the Christ in my flesh for His body, which is the Church, [25] of which I became *a* servant according to the dispensation of the God, which was given to me for you, to complete [πληρόω] the Word of the God, [26] the secret [μυστήριον] which has been hidden from the ages and from the generations, but now was manifested to His saints, [27] to whom the God wished to make known, what *is* the glorious riches of this secret [μυστήριον] among the Gentiles, which is Christ in you, the hope of the glory (Colossians 1.24-27).

Paul reaffirmed his office as the apostle of the Gentiles and reiterated to the Colossians what he had written the Ephesians: the Church, the body of Christ, was a secret, unknown before him (Ephesians 3.1-11). Paul also stated in this passage that his stewardship included completing the Scriptures.

The KJV translation reads, "to fulfill the word of the God" (verse 25). This rendering is ambiguous. The word πληρόω means "fill up" or "complete." Paul used this word twenty-four times, each time with this sense.[68] A better rendering is, "to complete the word of the God."

The "dispensation" or "stewardship" (οἰκονομία) God gave Paul was to reveal His program of the Church, the body of Christ, and all its doctrines.[69] The Church and its doctrines was God's last program He revealed. Once revealed, the Scriptures were complete. While almost all scholars teach that John's writings were the last books of the Bible that were written, the Scriptures clearly state that Paul completed the New Testament. When the Scriptures declare something clearly,

---

[67] Shortly before his death, Peter wrote Paul's letters were Scripture but hard to understand (2 Peter 3.14-18).

[68] See Romans 1.29, 8.4, 13.8, 15.13-14, 19; 2 Corinthians 7.4, 10.6; Galatians 5.14; Ephesians 1.23, 3.19, 4.10, 5.18; Philippians 1.11, 2.2, 4.18-19; Colossians 1.9, 25, 2.10, 4.12, 17; 2 Thessalonians 1.11;2 Timothy 1.4

[69] Paul used the word οἰκονομία three other times: his stewardship of the gospel of grace (1 Corinthians 9.17), the revelation of the dispensation of the fulness of times of gathering all things in Christ (Ephesians 1.10), and his stewardship of the grace of God (Ephesians 3.2). It is a synonym for his commission to reveal God's secrets.

tradition and opinion must be abandoned. A strong scholarly case can be made that the Scriptures were completed before 70 A.D. but Paul's words of Colossians 1.25 *end* all debate—if one believes the Scriptures.[70]

## The Believer's Salvation

Paul described salvation for members of the Church, the body of Christ, in three temporal phases: past, present, and future. The believer *has been saved* from sin and death, *is being saved* from sin and death, and *will be saved* from sin and death.

These phases of salvation are usually described as justification, sanctification, and glorification. Salvation from the perspective of *past* action is known by the terms Forgiveness, Justification, Redemption,[71] and Reconciliation.

| The Believer's Salvation | | |
|---|---|---|
| Justification | Past | Deliverance from the Penalty of Sin |
| Sanctification | Present | Deliverance from the Power of Sin |
| Glorification | Future | Deliverance from the Presence of Sin |

Forgiveness is to pardon or remit from a penalty or from guilt. Paul used two words to describe this aspect of salvation: ἄφεσις (noun) and χαρίζομαι (verb). Paul wrote:

> In whom we have the redemption through His blood, the forgiveness [ἄφεσις] of the sins, according to the riches of His grace (Ephesians 1.7; cf. Colossians 1.14).
>
> But be kind, compassionate to one another, forgiving [χαρίζομαι] each other, even as the God in Christ also forgave [χαρίζομαι] you (Ephesians 4.32).
>
> And you, while you were dead in the trespasses and the uncircumcision of your flesh, He made you alive with Him, for He forgave [χαρίζομαι] all your trespasses (Colossians 2.13).

Justification is a legal term that goes beyond pardon. The guilty party is not only forgiven but *declared righteous*. Paul used the term, "justify" many times with δίκαιος (adjective), δικαιοσύνη (noun), δικαιόω (verb), δικαίωμα (noun), δικαίωσις (noun). Consider:

---

[70] See Robinson, John A. T. 1976. *Redating the New Testament*. Philadelphia: Westminster Press.

[71] Redemption also has a future aspect, the redemption of the believer's mortal body (Romans 8.23; Ephesians 1.14), usually described as "glorification."

> Who are declared righteous, [δικαιόω] freely by His grace, through the redemption that *is* in Christ Jesus (Romans 3.24).
>
> For *a* demonstration of His righteousness [δικαιοσύνη] at the present time—so He might be righteous, and the One who declares righteous [δικαιόω] the one from faithfulness of Jesus (Romans 3.26).
>
> For we reckon *a* man to be declared righteous [δικαιόω] by faith without works of Law (Romans 3.28).
>
> But to the one who does not work, but believes on the One declaring righteous [δικαιόω] the ungodly, his faith is reckoned for righteousness [δικαιοσύνη] (Romans 4.5).
>
> Who was delivered for our offences and raised for our justification [δικαίωσις] (Romans 4.25).
>
> Therefore, because we were declared righteous [δικαιόω] by faith, we have peace with the God through our Lord Jesus Christ (Romans 5.1).
>
> And the gift *is* not like *what came* through *the* one who sinned. For the judgment from one *was* for condemnation. But the gift *is* from many offences for justification. [δικαίωμα] (Romans 5.16).
>
> For just as through the disobedience of the one man, the many were rendered sinners, so also through the obedience of the One, the many will be rendered righteous [δίκαιος] (Romans 5.19).
>
> And some of you used to be these! But you were washed, but you were sanctified, but you were declared righteous, [δικαιόω] in the name of the Lord Jesus, and by the Spirit of our God. (1 Corinthians 6.11).
>
> So that, since we were declared righteous [δικαιόω]by His grace, we might become heirs according to *the* hope of eternal life (Titus 3.7).

A third description of the believer's salvation is Redemption. To redeem means to buy back something lost.

| Words Used for Redemption | |
|---|---|
| Noun | Verb |
| ἀπολύτρωσις: redeem by paying a price (Romans 3.24) | ἀγοράζω to be bought in the marketplace (1 Corinthians 6.20) |
| ἀντίλυτρον: what is given in exchange for another as the price of redemption (1 Timothy 2.6) | ἐξαγοράζω: redeem by payment of a price, to recover from another's power (Galatians 3.13) |

| λύτρωσις: a ransom, deliverance (Hebrews 9.12). | λυτρόω to redeem or liberate on receipt of ransom (Titus 2.14) |
|---|---|

> Who are declared righteous, freely by His grace, through the redemption [ἀπολύτρωσις] that *is* in Christ Jesus (Romans 3.24).
>
> [19] Or do you not know that your body is *a* temple of the Holy Spirit in you, whom you have from God? So you are not your own. [20] For you were bought [ἀγοράζω] with *a* price. So glorify the God in your body and in your spirit, which is God's (1 Corinthians 6.19-20).
>
> Christ redeemed [ἐξαγοράζω] us from the curse of the Law, when He became *a* curse for us. For it has been written: Everyone hung on *a* tree is cursed (Galatians 3.13).
>
> [5] For *there is* one God and One agent between God and men, *the* man Christ Jesus, [6] the One who gave Himself *a* ransom [ἀντίλυτρον] for all, the witness in their proper times (1 Timothy 2.5-6).
>
> Who gave Himself for us, so He might redeem [λυτρόω] us from all lawlessness and might purify to Himself *a* special people, eager for good works (Titus 2.14).
>
> Or through blood of goats and calves, but through His own blood, He entered into the holy places once, because He obtained eternal redemption [λύτρωσις] (Hebrews 9.12).

The purchase price of our redemption was Christ's blood. Christ shed His blood on our behalf as a *substitutionary transaction*—His life for ours. The price of redemption from the Law—the wages of sin is death—was Christ's death. He was cursed for (ὑπέρ) us (Galatians 3.13).

Paul told the elders in Ephesus, before sailing to Jerusalem:

> Therefore, take care among yourselves and to all the flock among which the Holy Spirit set overseers, to shepherd the church of the God, which He purchased [περιποιέω][72] through His own blood (Acts 20.28).

Finally, there is Reconciliation. God has reconciled believers and indeed, the world, to Himself. Paul implored men to "be reconciled to God" (2 Corinthians 5.20) with the words καταλλάσσω (verb), καταλλαγή (noun), and ἀποκαταλλάσσω (verb). These words were primarily used in finance for the exchange of money. Through Christ's death for our sins and His resurrection, God has exchanged His

---

[72] The verb περιποιέω is the aorist middle indicative, giving the sense of purchase or gain for oneself. We are Christ's inheritance (cf. Ephesians 1.18).

disfavor for favor. Because of this, one can exchange condemnation for salvation. One only need accept God's gift by faith.

> For if, when we were enemies, we were reconciled [καταλλάσσω] to the God through the death of His Son, much more, because we were reconciled, [καταλλάσσω] will we be saved by His life (Romans 5.10).

> How God was in Christ reconciling [καταλλάσσω] *the* world to Himself, not reckoning to them their trespasses and who put in us the word of the reconciliation [καταλλαγή] (2 Corinthians 5.19).

> 21 Even you, who were once alienated and hostile in the mind by the evil works. 22 But now He reconciled [ἀποκαταλλάσσω] *you* by His body of flesh through the death, to present you holy and spotless and blameless before Him (Colossians 1.21-22).

## Summary of God's Program of the Church

To understand Church theology, one must recognize:

**ALL** CHURCH DOCTRINE IS FOUND IN PAUL'S LETTERS

God began a new program, the Church, the body of Christ, with His salvation and commission of Paul. Two thousand years before, God began a new program, Israel, with Abraham. Later, God gave Moses the Mosaic Law and made covenant promises to the nation through the prophets. Paul combined these roles of Abraham, Moses, and the prophets for the Church. The Lord told Saul on the road to Damascus:

> 16 But get up and stand on your feet. I appeared to you for this purpose: To handpick[73] you *a* servant and *a* witness both of the things you saw from Me and of the things I will show to you, 17 by rescuing you from the people and from the Gentiles, to whom I send you, 18 to open their eyes, so they might turn from darkness to light, and from the power of Satan to the God, that they might receive forgiveness of sins and inheritance among those who have been sanctified by faith that is in Me (Acts 26.16-18).

Paul did not exaggerate when he wrote of the "superiority of revelations" (2 Corinthians 12.7) he had received from the risen Lord. As a result of the many revelations the Lord gave Paul, all Church doctrine is found in Paul's letters from Romans through Philemon. These Scriptures are TO us. The rest of the Scriptures are FOR us.

---

[73] The word προχειρίσασθαί means "handpick before." See Acts 22.14.

| Major Differences in God's Programs: Israel and Church | |
|---|---|
| Israel | Church |
| Earthly | Heavenly |
| Under Law | Under Grace |
| Established by Covenant | Established by Grace |
| Revealed through Prophecy | Revealed through Secrets |

For the Scriptures to make sense we must let them lay out as they are. When men force one area of Scripture onto another area, mix Israel and the Church, law and grace, salvation by faith alone and salvation by faith and works, the gospel of the kingdom and the gospel of the grace of God, the apostleship of the Twelve and Paul's apostleship, the prophetic plan of Israel and Paul's revelations to the Church, the body of Christ, contradiction and confusion results. God is the *same* throughout all generations. But His *methods* of dealing with men *change*. God is sovereign. He does as He pleases. He reveals different programs at different times to accomplish His will. Dealing solely with Gentiles, choosing Israel, creating the Church, returning to Israel and establishing His earthly kingdom, creating a new heavens and new earth is His prerogative. To understand the Scriptures and be obedient to God one must allow God to be God and the Scriptures to mean what they say.

| | Israel | Church |
|---|---|---|
| Vehicle | Covenants (Prophetic Theology) | Secrets (Paul's Theology) |
| Corporate Destiny | Eternal Earthly Kingdom | Eternal Heavenly Kingdom |
| Individual Destiny | Priests of God | Joint-Heirs with Christ |
| Prophetic Destiny | Day of the Lord | Rapture |
| | Kingdom on Earth | Heavenly Citizenship |

| Israel | | Church | |
|---|---|---|---|
| ABRAHAM | Founder | PAUL | Founder |
| MOSES | Under Law | | Under Grace |
| PROPHETS | Covenants | | Secrets |

# Chapter 5
# Imitate Paul

*Therefore, I urge you, become imitators of me (1 Corinthians 4.16).*

## "To Me" Application

That no other writer of Scripture wrote such "to me" statements examined above should arrest our attention. Equally striking is that Paul *commanded* believers to imitate *him,* using the nouns μιμητής and συμμιμητής and the verb μιμέομαι.[1] The nouns mean an "imitator" or "copier" and the verb "imitate." He also included τύπος, an "example" or "pattern" with the μιμ* words (Philippians 3.17, 2 Thessalonians 3.9).

| The "Imitation" Texts | |
|---|---|
| παρακαλῶ οὖν ὑμᾶς, μιμηταί μου γίνεσθε. | 1 Corinthians 4.16 |
| Therefore, I urge [present middle imperative] you, become imitators of me. | |
| μιμηταί μου γίνεσθε, καθὼς κἀγὼ Χριστοῦ. | 1 Corinthians 11.1 |
| Become [present middle imperative] imitators of me as I also *am* of Christ. | |
| Γίνεσθε ὡς ἐγώ, ὅτι κἀγὼ ὡς ὑμεῖς, ἀδελφοί, δέομαι ὑμῶν. οὐδέν με ἠδικήσατε: | Galatians 4.12 |
| Become [present middle imperative] as I *am*, because I also *became* as you brethren—I implore you. You did me no wrong! | |
| Συμμιμηταί μου γίνεσθε, ἀδελφοί, καὶ σκοπεῖτε τοὺς οὕτω περιπατοῦντας καθὼς ἔχετε τύπον ἡμᾶς. | Philippians 3.17 |
| Brethren, become [present middle imperative] imitators of me and observe [present active imperative] those who so walk, as you have us *for a* pattern [τύπον]. | |

[1] Words such as "mimeograph" come from them. Paul also used the noun μιμητής in Ephesians 5.1 to exhort believers to be imitators of God.

| | |
|---|---|
| καὶ ὑμεῖς μιμηταὶ ἡμῶν ἐγενήθητε καὶ τοῦ κυρίου, δεξάμενοιτὸν λόγον ἐν θλίψει πολλῇ μετὰ χαρᾶς πνεύματος ἁγίου, | 1 Thessalonians 1.6 |
| And you became [aorist passive indicative] imitators of us, even of the Lord, for you received the word in much affliction, with *the* joy of *the* Holy Spirit. | |
| αὐτοὶ γὰρ οἴδατε πῶς δεῖ μιμεῖσθαι ἡμᾶς, ὅτι οὐκ ἠτακτήσαμεν ἐν ὑμῖν | 2 Thessalonians 3.7 |
| For you yourselves know how you must [present middle infinitive] imitate us for we did not act disorderly among you. | |
| οὐχ ὅτι οὐκ ἔχομεν ἐξουσίαν, ἀλλ' ἵνα ἑαυτοὺς τύπον δῶμεν ὑμῖν εἰς τὸ μιμεῖσθαι ἡμᾶς. | 2 Thessalonians 3.9 |
| Not because we do have *the* authority, but that we might give ourselves as *an* example [τύπον] for you to imitate [present middle infinitive] us. | |

Throughout his letters, Paul vigorously defended his apostleship. Since he was not one of the Twelve or a follower of Christ in His earthly ministry, his apostleship came under relentless attack. Paul wrote that God separated (ἀφορίζω)[2] him from the womb to reveal Christ to him (Galatians 1.15). God also separated him from the Twelve (Galatians 1.12, 16-19) after his salvation to reveal the gospel he proclaimed. Through such separation, Paul became "the apostle of the Gentiles" and the founder of a new divine program, the Church, the body of Christ. God kept the Church a secret throughout the Old Testament, Jesus did not reveal it in His earthly ministry to Israel, and the Twelve knew nothing of it. It was *new.* As new, it had new rules and new theology. This was why Paul stated believers should copy or imitate him. He was the prototype and model of this new divine program.

---

[2] The verb ἀφορίζω combines ἀπό (away from) and ὁρίζω (to mark a boundary). God kept Paul away from the Twelve to reveal a new and different program to him. The word ὁρίζω with the α privative is how we get the word "aorist" as in aorist tense, which denotes past action without definition or boundary as to the length of time of the action, a.k.a., punctiliar, a summary or snapshot of past action.

## Doctrine and Lifestyle

### 1 Corinthians 4.16

> Therefore, I urge you, become imitators [μιμηταί] of me.

Paul wrote that he should be regarded (λογίζομαι) as a servant of Christ and a steward of the secrets of God (1 Corinthians 4.1). The word λογίζομαι was a favorite of Paul's, which he used many times, particularly in the book of Romans. It means "reckon," "count," "consider." Paul reminded the Corinthians, "For though you may have ten thousand guardians in Christ, yet not many fathers. For I fathered you in Christ Jesus through the gospel" (1 Corinthians 4.15). Paul was their father because it was through his gospel that they had become believers. Because of this, Paul commanded them to imitate him. This is no less true for us than for the Corinthians. One becomes a Christian through believing Paul's gospel. To follow Paul's doctrine and imitate his life is *what it means to be a Christian.*

In 1 Corinthians 4.17, Paul wrote he had sent Timothy to remind (ἀναμιμνήσκω–another μιμ* word) them of his ways (ὁδός) in Christ which he taught everywhere in every church. Paul's "ways" were his doctrines. The Corinthians needed to be reminded of these doctrines due to their many problems.

### 1 Corinthians 11.1

> Become imitators [μιμηταί] of me as I also *am* of Christ.

Paul commanded the Corinthians to become imitators of him as he was of Christ. Paul's main point was his *doctrine*. The next verse makes this clear.

> Now I praise you, brethren, that you have remembered everything from me and keep the doctrines [παράδοσις] as I gave you (1 Corinthians 11.2).

Paul used the word παράδοσις for Jewish traditions (Galatians 1.14), Gentile philosophical teachings (Colossians 2.8), and for his doctrines. He also used the word διδαχή (teaching, doctrine) for his doctrines (Titus 1.9). He wrote the Thessalonians:

> So then, brethren, stand fast, and hold the teachings [παράδοσις] that you were taught, whether through word or through letter from us (2 Thessalonians 2.15).

> Now we command you, brethren, in *the* name of our Lord Jesus Christ, to withdraw from every brother who walks disorderly and not according to the teaching [παράδοσις] which you received from us (2 Thessalonians 3.6).

Paul received his doctrines by direct revelation from the ascended Lord. For this reason, he *commanded* believers to follow his teachings and to *disassociate* from those did not follow them. In Romans 16.17,

Paul commanded believers to mark and avoid those who do not follow the doctrine (τὴν διδαχὴν) he taught. This was the revelations and secrets he had received from the risen Lord.

## Galatians 4.12

> Become as I *am* [Γίνεσθε ὡς ἐγώ], because I also *became* as you, brethren, I implore you. You did me no wrong!

Paul wrote the Galatians to correct their error of abandoning his doctrines of grace and placing themselves under the Law of Moses. He asked them:

> 2 I only want to learn this from you: Did you receive the
> Spirit from works of *the* Law or from *the* hearing of faith?
> 3 Are you so foolish? Since you began by *the* Spirit are you
> now being completed by *the* flesh? 4 Did you suffer so many
> things for nothing? *Was* it truly for nothing? 5 Therefore, is
> the One who supplies the Spirit to you and works miracles among you—*is it* from works of *the* Law or from *the* hearing of faith (Galatians 3.2-5)?

The Galatians had been saved by faith *alone*—believing Paul's gospel (1 Corinthians 15.1-4). Paul asked them since they received life through faith if they thought they were to live now by the Law. Could they really be that foolish? He continued his appeal in Galatians 4 and wrote that they were not slaves under the Law but sons under grace (Galatians 4.3, 5, 31, 5.1). This was the context in which Paul issued the command to the Galatians to "be as I am." He wanted them to return to what he had taught them and live Christian lives in freedom rather than place themselves in bondage. They were free! We are too!

## Philippians 3.17

> Brethren, become imitators [συμμιμηταί] of me and observe those who so walk as you have us *for* a pattern [ἔχετε τύπον ἡμᾶς].

Paul wrote the Philippians to copy him and those who walked according to his example. In the next verse, he explained his insistence.

> For many walk, of whom I used to tell you often. Now, even weeping I say: the enemies of the cross of the Christ (Philippians 3.18).

Paul stated that those who do not follow his doctrines *are enemies of the cross of the Christ*. These are strong words but every believer is responsible to obey them. Those who reject Paul are enemies of Christ's cross, the gospel of salvation. No one wrote more about the cross of Christ than Paul (1 Corinthians 1.17-18; Galatians 5.11, 6.12, 14; Ephesians 2.16; Philippians 2.8, 3.18; Colossians 1.20, 2.14). The cross of Christ was the gospel, the "power of God," (Romans 1.16), the way by which Jew and Gentile are reconciled to God.

## 1 Thessalonians 1.6

> And you became imitators [μιμηταὶ] of us, even of the Lord, for you received the word in much affliction, with *the* joy of *the* Holy Spirit.

Paul wrote that the Thessalonians, by imitating him, became imitators of the Lord. The phrase, "even of the Lord," καὶ τοῦ κυρίου, identified Paul's doctrine with the Lord. Paul's use of the conjunctive καί is likely used in its ascensive sense, "even." In the previous verse, he wrote,

> For our gospel did not come to you in word only, but also in power and in *the* Holy Spirit, and in much assurance, as you know how we acted among you for your sakes (1 Thessalonians 1.5).

How does one know he is controlled by the Holy Spirit? One is controlled by the Holy Spirit if one follows Paul's doctrines. If not, one is controlled by another spirit.

## 2 Thessalonians 3.7 and 2 Thessalonians 3.9

> For you yourselves know how you must imitate [μιμεῖσθαι] us, for we did not act disorderly [ἀτακτέω] among you.

> Not because we do not have *the* authority, but that we might give ourselves as *an* example for you to imitate [μιμεῖσθαι] us.

Paul commanded believers to withdraw from those who did not follow his teachings (2 Thessalonians 3.6; Romans 16.17; 1 Timothy 6.3-5). The two verses above focus more on personal behavior. Paul reminded them that when he was with them, he did not eat their food without paying for it (2 Thessalonians 3.8) and that he and his companions worked day and night to avoid being a financial burden (v. 8). In this vein, Paul taught if one was unwilling to work, he was not to eat (2 Thessalonians 3.10). Believers should not only follow Paul's doctrine but should imitate his personal behavior and be accountable in Christian ministry. Such behavior brings honor to Christ.

# Conclusion

Paul commanded believers to imitate him especially in doctrine and also in living the Christian life. Apart from following Paul's doctrines, sanctification, the process by which God conforms us to the image of Christ (Romans 8.29), is impossible. Only by obeying the doctrines the glorified Lord revealed to Paul can one become the person Christ has destined us to be.

# Chapter 6
# Paul on Faith

*Now without faith it is impossible to please Him, for the one who comes near to the God must believe He exists and is a rewarder to those who seek Him (Hebrews 11.6).*

## Faith: Sine Qua Non

Paul had much to say about faith. Indeed, he wrote more about faith than all other writers of Scripture combined. The words, faith, trust, and believe, mean the same. What the Bible means by faith is believing what God says, believing the Bible. God has given mankind three means of perception to obtain knowledge of the external world. They are reason, senses, and faith. Reason derives knowledge by logic and thinking. Senses gain knowledge through taste, touch, sight, smell, and hearing. Faith obtains knowledge through authority.

Consider these two propositions:

| Statement | Meaning of Statement |
|---|---|
| I believe in God | Mental Assent |
| I believe God | Personal Trust |

The first proposition in the chart is a statement of mental assent. It means one believes in God's existence. No reliance, trust, or personal engagement with God is present. The second proposition is a statement of personal trust. When one says he believes God it means he trusts God. It is personal. It means one believes what God has said. This is Biblical faith. Biblical faith is trusting what God has said.

Paul wrote that Christ died for our sins and rose from the dead (1 Corinthians 15.1-4). This is his gospel. One can believe in the historical fact that Christ died for the sins of the world and rose from the dead without trusting in this for one's salvation. Biblical faith, saving faith, is *personal.* Saving faith trusts a *person*—God. Saving faith trusts Christ died for *my* sins and rose for *my* justification. It is worlds apart from merely believing in the historical fact of Christ's death and resurrection.

## Salvation in the Old Testament

No clear statement or definition of the gospel or of salvation exists in the Old Testament. Compared to Paul's straightforward words about salvation, the Old Testament is murky. The most one can say is that in the Old Testament salvation required faith and works. Salvation by faith alone (*sola fide*) was unknown before Paul.[1]

## Salvation and the Levitical Sacrifices

Hebrews reveals the Old Testament Levitical sacrifices were typical and temporary. Animal sacrifices were pictures or shadows of the future, effective sacrifice for sin by the Lord Jesus Christ (Hebrews 10.4). They "covered" or "covered up" sin and provided a temporary propitiation (satisfaction) for sin. Looking back, they revealed God was laying the groundwork for a greater reality—the shed blood of the Messiah to remove sin.

The Jews of the Old Testament had no idea the sacrifices they offered pointed to a greater reality. For them, they *were* the reality. All they knew was that God had commanded them to offer them and that they involved the shedding of blood to deal with sin. Leviticus contains the following instructions regarding the burnt offering:

> [1] Then the Lord called to Moses and spoke to him from the tent of meeting, saying, [2] Speak to the sons of Israel and say to them, When any man of you brings an offering to the Lord, you will bring your offering of animals from the herd or the flock. [3] If his offering is a burnt offering from the herd, he will offer it, a male without defect; he will offer it at the doorway of the tent of meeting, that he may be accepted before the Lord (Leviticus 1.1-3).

A Jew who sinned was to bring an unblemished animal to the priest for a sacrifice to make himself right with God. Moses wrote:

> [4] He will lay his hand on the head of the burnt offering, that it may be accepted for him to make atonement[2] on his behalf. [5] He will slay the young bull before the Lord; and Aaron's sons the priests will offer up the blood and sprinkle the blood around on the altar that is at the doorway of the tent

---

[1] Abraham was an exception (Genesis 15.6; Romans 4.3).

[2] Most occurrences of כָּפַר involve a priest "making an atonement" (cf. Leviticus 4.20). Our word "atonement" was created in the early 1500s by combining at + one + ment. But animal sacrifices could not reconcile man to God. Only Christ's death on the cross and His resurrection could do that (Romans 5.10; 2 Corinthians 5.18-19). Animal sacrifices were a temporary measure for God to deal with Israel in a covenant relationship. The LXX translated כָּפַר with ἐξιλάσομαι, "propitiate" and ἱλάσκομαι "be merciful" in Luke 18.13 and "to propitiate" in Hebrews 2.17. Propitiation is mercy and appeasement, not reconciliation. Nouns associated with כָּפַר shed additional light: כֹּפֶר was a "ransom," and כַּפֹּרֶת was the "mercy seat," the lid of the Ark of the Covenant. כָּפַר was first used in Genesis 6.14 for covering with pitch (Noah's ark). This is where the idea of "covering sins" comes.

> of meeting. [6] He will then skin the burnt offering and cut it into its pieces (Leviticus 1.4-6).

The sinner would place his hand upon the animal's head to identify with the animal and then kill it. The priest would take the blood and sprinkle it on the brazen altar. The animal was then skinned and cut up. This sacrifice "covered" and propitiated his sin.

The Mosaic Law required animal sacrifices. Bringing an animal to a priest was a work. From the divine perspective, the sacrifice was effective for it fulfilled the Law, and therefore, God's justice. For the individual, it was effective if he believed it.[3] Thus, animal sacrifices required a work (bringing an animal sacrifice) and faith (believing the sacrifice covered the sin). Faith and work were interwoven.

## Salvation in the Gospels

How was one saved in the Gospels? Consider the following account in the Gospel of Mark (cf. Matthew 19.16-26; Luke 18.18-30):

> And as He went on the road, one ran and knelt before Him, who began asking Him, Good teacher, what must I do that I might inherit eternal life (Mark 10.17)?

The man's question was straightforward: "How do I obtain eternal life?" What was the Lord's answer? Did He tell the man to believe He would die for his sins and rise from the dead? The next verses declare:

> [18] So Jesus said to him, Why do you call Me good? No one *is* good but One, the God. [19] You know the commandments: Do not commit adultery, Do not murder, Do not steal, Do not give false testimony, Do not defraud, Honor your father and mother. (Mark 10.18-19).

The man responded:

> Then he began saying to Him, Teacher, all these I kept from my youth (Mark 10.20).

The conversation concluded in the following manner:

> [21] Now when Jesus He looked at him, He loved him. And He said to him, You lack one thing. Go, sell whatever you have and give to the poor and you will have treasure in heaven. And come, follow Me, by taking up the cross. [22] And he became sad at this response and left grieving. For he had many possessions. [23] And after Jesus looked around, He said to His disciples, How hard will it be for those who have

---

[3] Hebrews expressed this thought: "For we also had good news proclaimed, even as they, but the word which they heard did not benefit their hearing, because it was not joined [συγκεράννυμι] with the faith by those who heard" (Hebrews 4.2).

> riches to enter into the kingdom of the God. [24] And the disciples were astonished at His words. But Jesus, when He again replied, said to them, Children, how hard it is to enter the kingdom of the God *for* those who trust in riches! [25] It is easier *for a* camel to pass through the eye of the needle than *for a* rich man to enter into the kingdom of the God. [26] Now they kept being exceedingly astonished, saying among themselves, So who can be saved? [27] And when Jesus looked at them, He said, With men, *it is* impossible. But not with God. For all things *are* possible with the God (Mark 10.21-27).

Jesus told the man to gain eternal life required keeping the commandments (Matthew 19.17)—works. When the man responded he had kept them, Jesus told him to do another work: sell his possessions, give them to the poor, and follow Him. Did Jesus teach salvation by works? Yes, He did.

Now, consider the following passage:

> [17] And it happened on one of the days when He was teaching and Pharisees and teachers of the Law were sitting (who came from every village of Galilee, and Judea, and Jerusalem) and *the* power of *the* Lord was present for Him to heal. [18] And behold, men who carried *a* man on *a* stretcher, who was paralyzed, kept looking for Him so they could bring him in and put *him* before Him. [19] And when they could not find *a* way to bring him in because of the crowd, they went on the roof and lowered him through the tiles with the stretcher, right before Jesus. [20] And when He saw their faith, He said to him,[4] Man, your sins have been forgiven you. [21] And the scribes and the Pharisees began to deliberate, saying, Who is this that speaks blasphemies? Who can forgive sins except the God alone? [22] Now because Jesus knew their thinking, when He replied, He said to them, Why are you thinking so in your hearts? [23] Which is easier: To say, Your sins have been forgiven you? Or, to say, Get up and walk? [24] But, so you may know that the Son of the Man has authority on the earth to forgive sins (He said to the one who was paralyzed) I tell you, Get up! And after you pick up your stretcher, go into your house (Luke 5.17-24).

Jesus saw the men's faith and told the paralytic his sins were forgiven. Did Jesus teach salvation by faith? Yes, He did.

What are we to make of these two passages? Did Jesus teach contradictory things? The obvious, unequivocal answer is that in the Jewish economy, faith *and* works were required for salvation.

---

[4] Some manuscripts do not have "to him," αὐτῷ.

## The Gospel of the Kingdom

John the Baptist came as the herald of the King and proclaimed the gospel of the kingdom (Matthew 3.1-2) and Jesus continued this joyous announcement (Matthew 4.17, 9.35). Water baptism was intrinsic to this salvation message. Water baptism is a *work*. During Jesus' earthly ministry and in the preaching of the Twelve, water baptism was *required* for salvation. How do we know this? We know it because the Bible says so. Consider the following verses:

> [4] John, the one who baptized in the wilderness and proclaimed *the* baptism of repentance for forgiveness of sins, came [5] and all the region of Judea and those of Jerusalem began going to him. And everyone used to be baptized by him in the Jordan river, when they confessed their sins (Mark 1.4-5).

> [15] Then He said to them, When you go into all the world, proclaim the gospel to all the creation. [16] The one who believes and is baptized will be saved. But the one who does not believe will be condemned (Mark 16.15-16).

Jesus told Nicodemus the same thing:

> [4] Nicodemus said to him, How can *a* man be born when he is old? Can he enter the womb of his mother *a* second time and be born? [5] Jesus replied, Truly, truly, I tell you, Unless one is born of water and of Spirit, he cannot enter into the kingdom of the God (John 3.4-5).

What were Peter's words to the Jews on the day of Pentecost?

> [36] Assuredly, therefore, let all *the* house of Israel know: The God made Him both Lord and Christ—this Jesus whom you crucified. [37] Now when they heard, they were pierced to the heart. Then they said to Peter and the other apostles, What should we do, men, brethren? [38] Then Peter said to them, Repent and be baptized, every one of you, in the name of Jesus Christ, for forgiveness of your sins and you will receive the gift of the Holy Spirit (Acts 2.36-38).

Paul was saved under the gospel of the kingdom and water baptism was required for his salvation. Luke wrote:

> [12] Then Ananias, *a* devout man according to the Law, who was attested to by all the Jews who lived *there*, [13] when he came and stood by me, he said to me, Brother Saul, receive you sight. And at that moment I saw him. [14] Then he said, The God of our fathers previously handpicked you to know His will and to see the Righteous One and to hear *the* voice from His mouth. [15] For you will be His witness to all men of what you have seen and heard. [16] So why delay? When you

> get up, be baptized and wash away your sins after you call on the name of the Lord (Acts 22.12-16).

What did Ananias tell Saul? He told him to be baptized and wash away his sins. Did Ananias understand salvation under the gospel of the kingdom? Absolutely.

These passages should convince anyone willing to believe the Scriptures that the gospel of the kingdom required water baptism for salvation. Under that gospel, *works* were required for salvation.

## Faith During the Ministry of Jesus

Faith *and* works were necessary for salvation under the Jewish economy and in the Gospels. What was the *content* of this faith? What were they to believe? Consider the following passages:

> 13 Now after Jesus came to the area of Caesarea Philippi, He
> began to question His disciples, saying, Who do men say
> that the Son of the Man is? 14 Then they said, Some, John the
> Baptist. But others, Elijah. And others, Jeremiah, or one of
> the prophets. 15 He said to them, But you, who do you say I
> am? 16 And when Simon Peter answered, he said, You are
> the Christ, the Son of the living God. 17 Now when Jesus
> replied, He said to him, You are blessed Simon Bar-Jona!
> For flesh and blood did not reveal *this* to you, but My Father,
> the One in the heavens (Matthew 16.13-17).

What did Peter believe? He believed in the *identity* of Christ—He was the Messiah, the Son of God. That was his salvation.

Consider these passages from John's Gospel:

> 43 On the next day, He wished to go to Galilee. And He found
> Philip and said to him, Follow Me. 44 Now Philip was from
> Bethsaida, from the city of Andrew and Peter. 45 Philip
> found Nathanael and said to him, We have found *him* of
> whom Moses wrote in the Law, also the Prophets, Jesus, the
> son of Joseph, who *is* from Nazareth. 46 Then Nathanael said
> to him, Can anything good be from Nazareth? Philip said to
> him, Come and see. 47 As Jesus saw Nathanael coming to
> him and He said about him, Look! Truly *an* Israelite in
> whom is no deceit. 48 Nathanael said to Him, How do you
> know me? Jesus replied and said to him, Before Philip called
> you, I saw you when you were under the fig tree. 49
> Nathanael replied and said to Him, Rabbi, you are the Son
> of the God. You are the King of Israel. 50 Jesus replied and
> said to him, Because I said to you, I saw you under the fig
> tree, you believe? You will see greater things than these! 51
> Then He said to him, Truly, truly, I tell you all, from now
> on, you will see the heaven opened and the angels of the God

> ascending and descending on the Son of the Man. (John 1.43-51).
>
> [23] Jesus said to her, Your brother will rise again. [24] Martha said to Him, I know that he will rise again at the resurrection on the last day. [25] Jesus said to her, I am the resurrection and the life. The one who believes in Me, even if he should die, will live. [26] And everyone who lives and believes in Me will never die—forever. Do you believe this? [27] She said to him, Yes, Lord. I believe that you are the Christ, the Son of the God, the One who comes into the world. (John 11.23-27).

Nathaniel believed in the *identity* of Christ. Martha believed in the *identity* of Christ: He was the Messiah, the Son of God. That was their faith for salvation.

Saul's testimony was the same:

> [3] Now while he traveled, it happened as he neared Damascus, suddenly, light from the heaven enveloped him. [4] And after he fell on the ground, he heard *a* voice say to him, Saul, Saul, why do you persecute Me? [5] Then he said, Who are you, Lord? Then the Lord said, I am Jesus whom you are persecuting. *It is* hard for you to kick against the goads. [6] And while he trembled and was astonished, he said, Lord, what do you want me to do? And the Lord said to him, Get up and go into the city. And it will be told to you what you must do (Acts 9.3-6).

Saul believed in the *identity* of Christ. He was the Messiah, the Son of God. That was his salvation. That was what he preached immediately following his salvation:

> [19] And after he received food, he became strengthened. Now Saul was with the disciples for some days in Damascus. [20] And immediately, he began preaching Jesus in the synagogues—that He is the Son of the God (Acts 9.19-20).

This truth is confirmed in the following passages: John 3.18; Acts 2.21, 38, 3.6, 16, 4.7, 10, 12, 17, 18, 30, 5.28, 40-41, 8.12, 16, 9.14-15, 21, 27, 10.43, 48, 19.5, 22.16, 26.9.

## Faith and Works and the Jerusalem Council

The faith component of the gospel of the kingdom focused on the *identity* of Christ. The focus of Paul's gospel is the *work* of Christ—His dying for our sins and rising from the dead (1 Corinthians 15.1-4). Paul received his gospel directly from the risen Lord (Galatians 1.11-12) and this gospel was a "secret" (Romans 2.16, 16.25; 1 Corinthians 9.17; 1 Timothy 1.11; Ephesians 6.19). Paul's gospel was faith + 0. One need only believe Christ died for one's sins and rose from the dead.

Luke's account of the Council of Jerusalem (Acts 15), held in 51 A.D., reveals how different Paul's gospel was from the gospel proclaimed by believing Jews at Jerusalem. Because of the conflict between Jerusalem and Paul over Gentile salvation, a council was required to settle the matter. Luke gave the human reason for the meeting: the church at Antioch decided Paul should go to Jerusalem to meet with its leaders (Acts 14.25-15.2). Paul gave the divine reason for his going: he went "by revelation" (κατὰ ἀποκάλυψιν), the risen Christ ordered him to go:

> [1] Then, after fourteen years, I went up again to Jerusalem with Barnabas and also took Titus. [2] Now I went up by revelation, and explained to them the gospel that I proclaim among the Gentiles, but privately to those who were recognized, so I should not run or did run in vain (Galatians 2.1-2).

Luke laid out the conflict between Jerusalem and Paul:

> [1] And certain men, when they came down from Judea, began teaching the brethren: If you are not circumcised after the custom of Moses, you cannot be saved. [2] Now since this created great debate and arguing with Paul and Barnabas with them, they arranged for Paul and Barnabas, and certain others from them, to go up to the apostles and elders in Jerusalem about this matter. [3] Therefore, after they were sent out by the church, they began traveling through both Phoenicia and Samaria and describing in detail the conversion of the Gentiles. And they kept bringing great joy to all the brethren. [4] Now when they came to Jerusalem, after they were welcomed by the congregation, and the apostles, and the elders, they related all the things the God did with them. [5] Then, some of those from the party of the Pharisees who believed, got up and said, They must be circumcised and commanded to keep the law of Moses (Acts 15.1-5).

The Jerusalem leaders maintained (rightly, according to the Old Testament and the gospel of the kingdom) that salvation required faith *and* works. Because of this, some of them had been going to Paul's converts and telling them they were not saved unless they were circumcised and kept the Mosaic Law (Acts 15.1, 5).

Paul wrote he "explained" (ἀνεθέμην, aorist middle indicative) his gospel to the believers at Jerusalem (Galatians 2.2). The verb ἀνατίθημι means "set forth," "communicate," "explain." It is found one other place, Acts 25.14, where Festus explained (ἀνατίθημι) Paul's case to Agrippa. Why would Paul need to explain his gospel if they were proclaiming the same gospel? The answer is obvious. They were *not* proclaiming the same gospel. Had they been, there would have been no need for Paul to explain his gospel. Furthermore, there would have been no need for a council.

The meeting was contentious (Acts 15.7; Galatians 2.5). Neither side would give an inch. Why should they? Both the gospel of the kingdom and Paul's gospel were valid! Both were from God. The gospel of the kingdom required repentance, belief that Jesus was the Messiah, the Son of God, and works.[5] Paul's gospel required faith alone—trust in Christ's death on the cross for our sins and His resurrection. These gospels were different. The Twelve *did not know* Paul's gospel.

After much argument, Peter, who had been silent during the debate made a remarkable statement.[6] Luke recorded this event:

> [7] Now after great argument took place, Peter got up and said to them, Men, brethren, you know that *a* long time ago, the God chose among us, through my mouth, for the Gentiles to hear the word of the gospel and to believe. [8] And the God who knows the hearts, witnessed to them when He gave the Holy Spirit, just as also to us and he made no distinction between us and them, because He cleansed their hearts by the faith. [10] Now, therefore, why do you test the God, to put *a* yoke on the neck of the disciples, which neither our fathers or we were strong enough to bear? [11] But, through the grace of *the* Lord Jesus Christ, we believe we are to be saved in the same way as they. (Acts 15.7-11).

At the critical moment, God the Holy Spirit moved Peter to recall his visit, many years before, to the house of Cornelius, a Gentile, a Roman centurion (Acts 10.1-48).[7] After he remembered this experience, Peter rose to Paul's defense. He stated that in that remarkable visit, Cornelius and his family were saved without circumcision or keeping the Mosaic Law. Peter reminded the Jewish believers in Jerusalem that Gentiles, by his mouth, were saved by faith alone. He then made a transformational statement:

> But, through the grace of *the* Lord Jesus Christ, we believe we are to be saved in the same way as they (Acts 15.11).

What? Peter's statement was stunning. Jews must now to be saved like Gentiles? Peter's statement overturned two millennia of Jewish theology. For 2,000 years, Jews had occupied God's favored position.

---

[5] The fact that water baptism was not listed as a requirement for salvation is interesting since it was required for salvation in the gospel of the kingdom. This indicated it was no longer being practiced.

[6] It is significant that Peter was not in charge of the Council. Peter's authority had been supplanted by James, the Lord's half-brother (Galatians 1.19). In the years since Pentecost, Peter lost his position of leadership.

[7] Peter went to Cornelius' house under duress (Acts 10.9-16). When he arrived, he told Cornelius it was prohibited (ἀθέμιτος) for a Jew to associate with a Gentile (Acts 10.28) but that God had permitted his visit. When Peter returned to Jerusalem, the Jewish believers rebuked him for going. Their reaction proves the Twelve had no ministry to Gentiles (cf. Acts 11.19).

Gentiles had to come to God through Israel's rulebook for salvation. Gentiles were saved like Jews. But *now*, Peter recognized God was doing something entirely new and different through Paul. He declared that from now on *Jews had to be saved like Gentiles*—by faith *alone* believing *Paul's gospel*.[8] Peter's statement ended the gospel of the kingdom.[9] From this point, only one gospel now existed: Paul's gospel.

Paul wrote these strong words to the Galatians:

> [8] But even if we or *an* angel from heaven should proclaim *a* gospel to you contrary to what we proclaimed to you, Let him be accursed! [9] As we have said before, and now I say again, If anyone proclaims *a* gospel to you contrary to what you received, Let him be accursed (Galatians 1.8-9)!

Paul could not have written such a statement prior to the decision at the Council of Jerusalem. Before this meeting, the gospel of the kingdom and Paul's gospel were valid salvation messages. After Peter's declaration, only Paul's gospel was valid. Now, anyone who proclaims a gospel other than Paul's is under a divine curse.

| Timetable of the Gospel Messages | | | | | |
|---|---|---|---|---|---|
| Valid Gospels | John the Baptist | Paul | Council of Jerusalem | Rapture | Tribulation |
| Kingdom Gospel | x | x | x | | x |
| Grace Gospel | | x | x | x | |

| | |
|---|---|
| Gospel of the Kingdom | John the Baptist until the Council of Jerusalem (Matthew 3.1-2; Acts 15.11) |
| Gospel of Grace | Paul's return from Arabia/Damascus until Rapture (Galatians 1.15-18) |
| Gospel of the Kingdom | Rapture until 2nd Advent (Matthew 24.14) |

---

[8] Did Peter have the authority to do this? Yes. Peter had lost much of his authority in the Jewish assembly but the Lord had given him the keys of the kingdom and told him that what he bound on earth would be bound in heaven (Matthew 16.19, 18.18). Peter exercised this authority in his pronouncement.

[9] Paul's gospel will continue until the completion of the Church, the body of Christ. After this, the gospel of the kingdom will return. It will be the gospel that saves until Christ's 2nd Advent (Matthew 24.14). In Revelation 2-3, Jesus revealed what will be required for salvation during the Tribulation.

## Faith Alone

Salvation by faith *alone* was a new revelation Paul received from the risen Lord. He wrote many passages stating one is saved by faith alone:

> For I am not ashamed of the gospel of the Christ for it is *the* power of God for salvation to everyone who believes: to Jew first and to Greek (Romans 1.16).

The gospel Paul had received from Christ was the power of God to salvation, for everyone who *believes*. No hint of works, circumcision, keeping the Law, water baptism, etc. is present.

In Romans chapter 3, Paul declared:

> 21 But now, apart from Law, God's righteousness has been
> manifested, being witnessed by the Law and the prophets: 22
> Now, God's righteousness through faithfulness of Jesus Christ *is* for all and on all who believe—for there is no difference (Romans 3.21-22).

Paul's νυνὶ δὲ, "but now," was his favorite expression to denote contrast. What was contrasted? Before Paul, salvation required keeping the Law. This was what the believers in Jerusalem declared (Acts 15.1, 5). They were right. They knew their Bible and they knew what Jesus taught in His earthly ministry. *But now*, Paul declared God's righteousness was for all who *believe*. This was *new*.

Paul used Abraham to make his case of salvation by faith alone:

> 1 What, therefore, will we say Abraham, our father
> according to *the* flesh, to have found? 2 For if Abraham was
> declared righteous by works, he has *a* boast—but not
> towards God. 3 For what does the Scripture say? Then Abraham believed the God and it was reckoned to him for righteousness (Romans 4.1-3).

Abraham was saved by believing what God had revealed to him—that he would be the father of innumerable children (Genesis 15.2-6). He was saved by faith alone. Paul hammered this point in the next verses:

> 4 Now to the one who works, the reward is not reckoned
> according to grace, but according to debt. 5 But to the one
> who does not work, but believes on the One declaring righteous the ungodly, his faith is reckoned for righteousness (Romans 4.4-5).

Could words be clearer? Salvation is to the who *does not work*. It is to the one who *believes*—his faith is counted for righteousness. Paul concluded his dissertation on Abraham with the words:

> 23 Now it was not written for him only that it was reckoned
> to him, 24 but for us also, to whom it is about to be reckoned,
> to the ones who believe on the One who raised Jesus our

> Lord from the dead, [25] who was delivered for our offences and raised for our justification (Romans 4.23-25).

Salvation by faith alone was not just for Abraham but for all who believe. What is to be believed? It is Paul's gospel: Christ died for our sins and rose from the dead.[10] Paul wrote the Corinthians:

> For since in the wisdom of the God, the world did not know the God through its wisdom, the God was pleased through the foolishness of the preaching to save those who believe (1 Corinthians 1.21).

Again, salvation under Paul's gospel is to save those who *believe.*

The clearest statement of Paul's gospel is 1 Corinthians 15.1-4:

> [1] Now I declare to you, brethren, the gospel that I proclaimed to you, which you also received, by which also you stand, [2] through which also you are saved, if you possess[11] that message I proclaimed to you, unless you believed in vain. [3] For I delivered to you first what I also received: Christ died for our sins, according to the Scriptures, [4] and that He was buried, and that He has been raised on the third day, according to the Scriptures (1 Corinthians 15.1-4).

Paul wrote the Galatians:

> So the Law has become our tutor[12] to Christ, so we might be declared righteous by faith (Galatians 3.24).

Paul stated that justification is to those who *believe*. Notice in all these passages, there is no believe *and.* It is just believe.

To the Ephesians, Paul wrote:

> In whom you too, when you heard the word of the truth, the gospel of your salvation, in whom, when you too believed,

---

[10] Some read Paul's statements in Romans 4 and try to apply them to the Old Testament or to Jesus' earthly ministry to prove salvation has always been by faith alone. To do this, one must revoke numerous passages which state the contrary. Abraham was an exception. Paul used him to make his case for salvation by faith alone for Gentiles, who are the "children of Abraham." This subject will be explored in detail in the chapter, Paul on Israel.

[11] The word κατέχετε has been translated poorly. The KJV, "keep is memory," the NIV, NET "hold firmly," the NASB, ESV "hold fast," imply salvation may be lost unless one "hangs on." The best rendering of κατέχετε is "possess" and agrees with the rest of the verse, "unless you believed in vain (εἰκῇ), did not truly believe. One who truly believes Paul's gospel is eternally secure.

[12] The word translated "tutor," παιδαγωγός, was a guardian employed by upper-class Roman families who supervised young men in their life and morals until manhood.

> you were sealed[13] with the promised Holy Spirit (Ephesians 1.13).

When the Ephesians heard the gospel, they responded and believed. The "gospel of your salvation" is a genitive of apposition, i.e., "the gospel which is salvation." By believing Paul's gospel one is saved. This verse describes the human part of salvation—believing—and the divine part—the sealing with the Holy Spirit. The word "sealed" (σφραγίζω) is an aorist passive indicative. The aorist indicates past action, the passive voice means the subject, the believer, receives the action, and the indicative mood is the mood of reality.

A few verses later, Paul wrote:

> And what *is* the surpassing greatness of His power for us who believe, according to the working[14] of the strength of His might (Ephesians 1.19).

God's salvation is for those who *believe.* Paul wrote the Thessalonians:

> For if we believe that Jesus died and rose, so also, the God will bring with Him those who fell asleep through Jesus (1 Thessalonians 4.14).

Here again is Paul's gospel: Christ died and rose from the dead. Anyone who believes it, God will resurrect when He returns for the Church. Other verses could be examined but these provide sufficient witness that Paul taught salvation by faith alone—believing Christ died for one's sins and rose from the dead.

## "The Faith"

Paul used the word "faith," πίστις, 142 times in his thirteen letters and thirty-two times in Hebrews. Sometimes he included the definite article with the noun and sometimes he did not. The noun with the definite article reads "the faith."[15]

The Scriptures reveal that faith, believing God, has *always* been required for salvation. Hebrews 11.6 states it is impossible to please God apart from faith. But one word can make a vast difference in the meaning of a passage. In the following cases, that one word is the definite article, "the."

The noun, πίστις, "faith," has three basic meanings: 1) the act of believing, 2) what is believed, and 3) faithfulness. Unfortunately, the

---

[13] Seal, σφραγίζω , was to mark, secure, authenticate, cf. Ephesians 4.30.

[14] "Working," ἐνέργεια, only used by Paul and always for superhuman power (Ephesians 1.19, 3.7, 4.16; Philippians 3.21; Colossians 1.29, 2.12; 2 Thessalonians 2.9, 11).

[15] Greek has a definite article (the) but no indefinite article (a, an). A noun can be definite *with* or *without* the definite article but when the definite article *is* present, the noun is *always* definite.

translations are inconsistent. In almost all cases, when Paul included the definite article with the noun, he meant faith in the sense of "what is believed." The following examples demonstrate the issue.

## "The Faith" With the Personal Pronoun

Several times Paul wrote of the faith of believers.[16]

| But if Christ has not been raised, then our preaching is worthless and your faith is worthless (1 Corinthians 15.14). |
|---|
| εἰ δὲ Χριστὸς οὐκ ἐγήγερται κενὸν ἄρα τὸ κήρυγμα ἡμῶν κενὴ δὲ καὶ ἡ πίστις ὑμῶν. |

The verse above has "the faith" with the second person plural personal pronoun. Literally, it reads, "the faith of you." The translators did not render the verse in this manner for stylistic reasons. This is true also for the third person singular personal pronoun, "his," (Romans 4.5), "the faith of him," the third person plural verb "they have cast off their first faith" (1 Timothy 5.12), "the first faith of them," and the first-person personal pronoun (2 Timothy 3.10), "the faith of me."

What did Paul mean by the expression "your faith?" Two possibilities exist: 1) their act of believing or 2) what they believed. In these cases, Paul included the definite article with the noun for what they had believed, i.e., the content of their faith. *What* they had believed was spoken of throughout the world, not the fact that they had believed.

## Faith as Faithfulness

The noun πίστις can also mean "faithfulness" and may or may not include the definite article. The following examples show where some translations have rendered πίστις as "faith" but should be "faithfulness."

| Now what if some did not believe? Will their unbelief abrogate God's **faithfulness** (Romans 3.3)? |
|---|
| τί γὰρ εἰ ἠπίστησάν τινες μὴ ἡ ἀπιστία αὐτῶν τὴν πίστιν τοῦ θεοῦ καταργήσει |
| But we know that a man is not declared righteous except through the **faithfulness** of Jesus Christ, not from works of the Law. And we believed in Christ Jesus so we might be declared righteous from *the* faithfulness of Christ and not by works from the Law. For no flesh will be declared righteous from the works of the Law (Galatians 2.16). |

[16] Other examples of this rendering are 1 Corinthians 2.5, 15.14; 2 Corinthians 1.24, 10.15; Ephesians 1.15; 1 Thessalonians 1.8, 3.2, 5, 7, 10; 2 Thessalonians 1.3; Philemon 1.5-6.

| εἰδότες ὅτι οὐ δικαιοῦται ἄνθρωπος ἐξ ἔργων νόμου ἐὰν μὴ διὰ πίστεως Ἰησοῦ Χριστοῦ καὶ ἡμεῖς εἰς Χριστὸν Ἰησοῦν ἐπιστεύσαμεν ἵνα δικαιωθῶμεν ἐκ πίστεως Χριστοῦ καὶ οὐκ ἐξ ἔργων νόμου διότι οὐ δικαιωθήσεται ἐξ ἔργων νόμου πᾶσα σάρξ |
|---|
| I have been crucified with Christ. Now I no longer live. But Christ lives in me. Now what *life* I now live in *the* flesh, I live by the **faithfulness** of the Son of God, the One who loved me and gave himself for me (Galatians 2.20). |
| Χριστῷ συνεσταύρωμαι ζῶ δὲ οὐκέτι ἐγώ ζῇ δὲ ἐν ἐμοὶ Χριστός ὃ δὲ νῦν ζῶ ἐν σαρκί ἐν πίστει ζῶ τῇ τοῦ υἱοῦ τοῦ θεοῦ τοῦ ἀγαπήσαντός με καὶ παραδόντος ἑαυτὸν ὑπὲρ ἐμοῦ |
| And might be found in Him—not having my righteousness, which *is* from Law, but the righteousness from God which *is* through *the* **faithfulness** of Christ, by the faith (Philippians 3.9). |
| καὶ εὑρεθῶ ἐν αὐτῷ μὴ ἔχων ἐμὴν δικαιοσύνην τὴν ἐκ νόμου ἀλλὰ τὴν διὰ πίστεως Χριστοῦ τὴν ἐκ θεοῦ δικαιοσύνην ἐπὶ τῇ πίστει |
| For we were buried with him in the baptism, in which you were also raised through God's **faithful** working, who raised him from the dead (Colossians 2.12). |
| συνταφέντες αὐτῷ ἐν τῷ βαπτίσματι ἐν ᾧ καὶ συνηγέρθητε διὰ τῆς πίστεως τῆς ἐνεργείας τοῦ θεοῦ τοῦ ἐγείραντος αὐτὸν ἐκ τῶν νεκρῶν |

In these cases, Paul meant the faithfulness of God and the faithfulness of Christ. The focus of Paul's words was upon God's faithful work on behalf of mankind. Other examples of πίστις used as "faithfulness" may include 1 Thessalonians 1.8, 3.6-7.

## "The Faith" vs. "Faith"

Translations render πίστις inconsistently. As a result, one cannot tell whether πίστις means the *act of believing* or *what is believed*. To show this, the chart first lists the KJV translation, then the Greek text, and lastly, my translation.

| Do we then make void the law through faith? God forbid: yes, we establish the law (Romans 3.31). |
|---|
| νόμον οὖν καταργοῦμεν **διὰ τῆς πίστεως** μὴ γένοιτο ἀλλὰ νόμον ἱστῶμεν. |
| Therefore, do we abolish Law through the faith? Never! Rather, we establish Law. |

Failure to include the definite article in the KJV translation can lead one to think Paul was writing about faith as the *act* of believing. But this is *not* what the grammar indicates. The text reads, "through the faith." Read this way, it means *what* is believed. Thus, Paul meant, "Do we make void Law through "the faith?" "The faith" was Paul's gospel. Thus, the sense of the passage is, "do we abolish Law through the faith," i.e., through the gospel?

In Romans 4.5 Paul wrote:

| Comes this blessedness then upon the circumcision only, or upon the uncircumcision also? for we say that faith was reckoned to Abraham for righteousness. (Romans 4.9). |
|---|
| ὁ μακαρισμὸς οὖν οὗτος ἐπὶ τὴν περιτομὴν ἢ καὶ ἐπὶ τὴν ἀκροβυστίαν λέγομεν γάρ ὅτι ἐλογίσθη τῷ Ἀβραὰμ **ἡ πίστις** εἰς δικαιοσύνην. |
| Therefore, *is* this happiness on the circumcision or also on the uncircumcision? For we say the faith was reckoned to Abraham for righteousness. |

Did Paul mean Abraham's act of believing or what he believed reckoned righteousness to Abraham? The Genesis text is clear.

> [5] And he brought him forth abroad, and said, Look now toward heaven, and tell the stars, if you be able to number them: and he said to him, So shall your seed be. [6] And he believed in the Lord; and he counted it to him for righteousness (Genesis 15.5-6).

God showed Abraham the night sky and asked if he could number the stars. He told him his descendants would be as innumerable as the stars. The text states, Abraham "believed in the Lord." Abraham believed what God told him—his descendants would be as countless as the stars. Because Abraham believed *what* God told him, God declared him righteous. Commenting on this to the Galatians, Paul wrote:

| That the blessing of Abraham might come on the Gentiles through Jesus Christ; that we might receive the promise of the Spirit through faith (Galatians 3.14). |
|---|
| ἵνα εἰς τὰ ἔθνη ἡ εὐλογία τοῦ Ἀβραὰμ γένηται ἐν Χριστῷ Ἰησοῦ ἵνα τὴν ἐπαγγελίαν τοῦ πνεύματος λάβωμεν **διὰ τῆς πίστεως**. |
| so the blessing of Abraham might come to the Gentiles in Christ Jesus, so we might receive the promise of the Spirit through the faith. |

Gentiles are heirs of Abraham and have received the Holy Spirit, not through faith, as translated, but through the faith. Like Abraham, who believed God and obtained salvation, believers today receive the gift of the Holy Spirit by believing *what* God has revealed: Paul's gospel.

Paul continued the point in Romans 4.11-13 and wrote the following in Romans 4.14:

| For if they which are of the law be heirs, faith is made void, and the promise made of none effect (Romans 4.14).[17] |
|---|
| εἰ γὰρ οἱ ἐκ νόμου κληρονόμοι κεκένωται **ἡ πίστις** καὶ κατήργηται ἡ ἐπαγγελία. |
| For if those of the Law are heirs, the faith has been voided and the promise has been rendered useless. |

The KJV translators rendered ἡ πίστις as "faith" rather than "the faith." *What* is believed is in view, *not* the act of believing. Paul wrote:

| By whom also we have access by faith into this grace wherein we stand, and rejoice in hope of the glory of God (Romans 5.2). |
|---|
| δι᾽ οὗ καὶ τὴν προσαγωγὴν ἐσχήκαμεν **τῇ πίστει** εἰς τὴν χάριν ταύτην ἐν ᾗ ἑστήκαμεν καὶ καυχώμεθα ἐπ᾽ ἐλπίδι τῆς δόξης τοῦ θεοῦ. |
| Through whom we also have the access by the faith into this grace in which we stand. And we boast on the basis of hope of God's glory. |

Paul's point is that we have access to God's grace, not by faith, the act of believing, but by the faith, i.e., what is believed. What is believed? Paul's gospel. In Romans 10.8 Paul wrote:

| But what says it? The word is nigh you, even in your mouth, and in your heart: that is, the word of faith, which we preach (Romans 10.8). |
|---|
| ἀλλὰ τί λέγει Ἐγγύς σου τὸ ῥῆμά ἐστιν ἐν τῷ στόματί σου καὶ ἐν τῇ καρδίᾳ σου τοῦτ᾽ ἔστιν τὸ ῥῆμα **τῆς πίστεως** ὃ κηρύσσομεν. |
| But what does it say? The word is near you, in your mouth and in your heart. This is the word of the faith, which we proclaim: |

Paul proclaimed "the word of the faith," not "the word of faith." The expression, "the word of the faith" is a genitive of apposition and means, "the word, which is the faith," or "the word, namely faith." Paul declared "the word," i.e., his message, his gospel, was "the faith." In Paul's great dissertation of the olive tree, he wrote:

| Well, because of unbelief they were broken off, and you stand by faith. Be not high-minded, but fear: (Romans 11.20). |
|---|
| καλῶς τῇ ἀπιστίᾳ ἐξεκλάσθησαν σὺ δὲ **τῇ πίστει** ἕστηκας μὴ ὑψηλοφρόνει ἀλλὰ φοβοῦ. |
| Right! They were broken off by the unbelief. So, you stand by the faith. Do not be high-minded, but be afraid. |

---

[17] In Romans 4.13, Paul wrote, ἀλλὰ διὰ δικαιοσύνης πίστεως, "but through righteousness of faith." He did *not* include the definite article and *could* have meant the act of believing. But since a noun can be definite even without the definite article it is likely Paul meant *what* was believed based on Romans 4.14.

The text reads, “you stand by the faith,” not “you stand by faith.” Paul’s point is that a believer’s standing before God is based on *what* he has believed, not by the act of believing. Obedience is believing what God has said.

The following passage reveals how inconsistent the translators were:

| 23 But before faith came, we were kept under the law, shut up unto the faith which should afterward be revealed. 24 Wherefore the law was our schoolmaster to bring us unto Christ, that we might be justified by faith. 25 But after that faith is come, we are no longer under a schoolmaster. 26 For you are all the children of God by faith in Christ Jesus (Galatians 3.23-26). |
|---|
| 23 Πρὸ τοῦ δὲ ἐλθεῖν **τὴν πίστιν** ὑπὸ νόμον ἐφρουρούμεθα συγκλειόμενοι εἰς **τὴν** μέλλουσαν **πίστιν** ἀποκαλυφθῆναι. 24 ὥστε ὁ νόμος παιδαγωγὸς ἡμῶν γέγονεν εἰς Χριστόν, ἵνα ἐκ **πίστεως** δικαιωθῶμεν· 25 ἐλθούσης δὲ **τῆς πίστεως** οὐκέτι ὑπὸ παιδαγωγόν ἐσμεν. 26 πάντες γὰρ υἱοὶ θεοῦ ἐστε διὰ **τῆς πίστεως** ἐν Χριστῷ Ἰησοῦ. |
| 23 Now before the faith came, we were in custody under the Law, being imprisoned until the faith which was about to be revealed. 24 So the Law has become our tutor to Christ, so we might be declared righteous by faith. 25 Now, since the faith arrived, we are no longer under a tutor. 26 For you are all sons of God through the faith in Christ Jesus. |

In verse 23, the first occurrence of πίστις is translated “faith,” but the second, “the faith.” Why? Both have the definite article. The most reasonable explanation is the KJV translators did not understand Paul’s meaning.[18] A clearer translation is in the third row of the table. In verse 24, which reads ἐκ πίστεως, Paul most likely meant the *act* of believing or faith in general since it does not include the definite article.[19] Verse 25 concludes the thought, “*after* the faith came.” Again, “the faith” was Paul’s gospel and Paul’s revelations concerning the Church. Lastly, in verse 26, Paul stated, “you are all sons of God through the faith in Jesus Christ.” His meaning of “the faith,” was his gospel. Paul closed his letter to the Galatians:

| As we have therefore opportunity, let us do good unto all men, especially unto them who are of the household of faith (Galatians 6.10). |
|---|
| ἄρα οὖν ὡς καιρὸν ἔχομεν ἐργαζώμεθα τὸ ἀγαθὸν πρὸς πάντας μάλιστα δὲ πρὸς τοὺς οἰκείους **τῆς πίστεως**. |
| So then, as we have opportunity, we should work the good to all, especially those of the household of the faith. |

---

[18] Modern translations are no better.

[19] More will be said about ἐκ πίστεως later in the chapter.

It is not "the household of faith" but "the household of the faith." The "household of the faith" is those who have believed Paul's gospel and doctrines.

The well-known verse of Ephesians 2.8 is another example in which the translators erred.[20] The KJV reads:

| For by grace are you saved through faith; and that not of yourselves: it is the gift of God (Ephesians 2.8). |
|---|
| **τῇ** γὰρ **χάριτί** ἐστε σεσῳσμένοι διὰ **τῆς πίστεως** καὶ τοῦτο οὐκ ἐξ ὑμῶν θεοῦ τὸ δῶρον. |
| For by the grace you have been saved through the faith and this is not from yourselves: it is the gift of God |

It is *not* "by grace" and "through faith" that one is saved. Rather, it is "by the grace" and "through the faith" that one is saved. Paul's inclusion of the definite article identified a specific grace and a specific faith through which salvation comes. This was the grace and the faith that the risen Lord revealed to him as "the apostle of the Gentiles." The grammatical construction ἐστε σεσῳσμένοι is the present tense of εἰμί with the perfect passive periphrastic participle of σῴζω. Literally, it reads, "you are having been saved." The sense is, "you have been saved and continue in this status."[21]

Ephesians 3.17 provides further support for the article's inclusion with πίστις in the Ephesians 2.8 passage. It reads:

| That Christ may dwell in your hearts by faith; that you, being rooted and grounded in love (Ephesians 3.17). |
|---|
| κατοικῆσαι τὸν Χριστὸν διὰ **τῆς πίστεως** ἐν ταῖς καρδίαις ὑμῶν ἐν ἀγάπῃ ἐρρίζωμένοι καὶ τεθεμελιωμένοι. |
| so Christ might dwell through the faith in your hearts, since you have been rooted and established in love, |

---

[20] The critical text does not include the article τῆς while the majority text does. The article's absence is supported by ℵ, B, D, F, G, P. 6, 33, 104, 1175, 1739, 2464, 2495, and a few Coptic versions. The witnesses with the article are A, D2, Ψ, 1881 and the great majority of the manuscripts. In almost all cases, Paul included the definite article with διὰ πίστεως when it referred to what was believed. He did not include it in certain expressions which referred to Christ's faithfulness (Romans 3.22; Galatians 2.16; Philippians 3.9). The presence of the definite article with χάρις (τῇ γὰρ χάριτί ) lends further weight to it inclusion with πίστις. Paul was specifying "the grace" given to Gentiles according to "the faith," his gospel (1 Corinthians 3.10, 15.10; 2 Corinthians 6.1, etc.).

[21] See Moule, C F. D. *Idiom Book of New Testament Greek*. Cambridge: Cambridge University Press, 1979, p. 18-19.

Christ comes to dwell in the believer's hearts through *the* faith—Paul's gospel.[22] *What* we believe, *not our believing,* creates this happy state.

In the familiar passage on Christian warfare, Paul wrote:

| Above all, taking the shield of faith, wherewith you shall be able to quench all the fiery darts of the wicked (Ephesians 6.16). |
|---|
| ἐπὶ πᾶσιν ἀναλαβόντες τὸν θυρεὸν **τῆς πίστεως** ἐν ᾧ δυνήσεσθε πάντα τὰ βέλη τοῦ πονηροῦ τὰ πεπυρωμένα σβέσαι. |
| In everything, take up the shield of the faith, by which you can extinguish all the flaming arrows of the evil one. |

Paul did not tell us to take up the "shield of faith" but to take up "the shield of the faith." This is another genitive of apposition—"the shield, which is the faith," or "the shield, namely the faith." The shield of the faith is Paul's gospel and doctrines.

Paul's letter to the Philippians is a tome of joy. Though Paul was incarcerated in Rome, he rejoiced in this condition because God was using it to spread the gospel (Philippians 1.12). He wrote:

| And having this confidence, I know that I shall abide and continue with you all for your furtherance and joy of faith (Philippians 1.25). |
|---|
| καὶ τοῦτο πεποιθὼς οἶδα ὅτι μενῶ καὶ συμπαραμενῶ πᾶσιν ὑμῖν εἰς τὴν ὑμῶν προκοπὴν καὶ χαρὰν **τῆς πίστεως**. |
| And since I am confident of this, I know that I will stay and continue with you all, for your progress and joy of the faith, |

The joy of which Paul wrote in verse 25 was not "joy of faith," but "joy of the faith." The "joy of the faith" is Paul's gospel, the wonderful news Christ died for our sins and rose from the dead.

| Only let your conversation be as it becomes the gospel of Christ: that whether I come and see you, or else be absent, I may hear of your affairs, that you stand fast in one spirit, with one mind striving together for[23] the faith of the gospel (Philippians 1.27). |
|---|
| Μόνον ἀξίως τοῦ εὐαγγελίου τοῦ Χριστοῦ πολιτεύεσθε ἵνα εἴτε ἐλθὼν καὶ ἰδὼν ὑμᾶς εἴτε ἀπὼν ἀκούσω τὰ περὶ ὑμῶν ὅτι στήκετε ἐν ἑνὶ πνεύματι μιᾷ ψυχῇ συναθλοῦντες **τῇ πίστει** τοῦ εὐαγγελίου. |
| Only live worthily of the gospel of the Christ, so whether I come and see you, or whether I am absent, I may hear these things about you: that you stand fast in one spirit, with one soul, striving together in the faith of the gospel. |

---

[22] The preposition διά is better rendered "through" rather than "by."

[23] The preposition τῇ πίστει is a dative and better rendered, "in," or "by" the faith rather than "for the faith."

Verse 27 reveals that "the faith" is "the gospel." The text reads, "in the faith of the gospel," another genitive of apposition meaning, "the faith which is the gospel," or "the faith, namely, the gospel."

Paul concluded his second letter to the Thessalonians with a prayer request:

| And that we may be delivered from unreasonable and wicked men: for all men have not faith (2 Thessalonians 3.2). |
|---|
| καὶ ἵνα ῥυσθῶμεν ἀπὸ τῶν ἀτόπων καὶ πονηρῶν ἀνθρώπων οὐ γὰρ πάντων **ἡ πίστις**. |
| and that we might be delivered from the perverse and evil men. For not all have the faith. |

Paul was not talking about men who did not *believe* but men who did not *believe his gospel*. Thus, not all men have the faith—Paul's gospel.

1 Timothy 1.19 is another clear illustration of the difference between "faith" and "the faith." It reads:

| Holding faith, and a good conscience; which some having put away concerning faith have made shipwreck: (1 Timothy 1.19). |
|---|
| ἔχων **πίστιν** καὶ ἀγαθὴν συνείδησιν ἥν τινες ἀπωσάμενοι περὶ **τὴν πίστιν** ἐναυάγησαν. |
| by holding faith and a good conscience, which some, who have rejected the faith, became shipwrecked, |

The first use of "faith," does not have the definite article and means either the act of believing or faithfulness. The verb in "ἔχων πίστιν," a present active indicative means "holding," "having," "maintaining." Paul was urging believers to continue to believe or remain faithful. In the latter part of the verse, Paul wrote τὴν πίστιν, "the faith"—what was believed—that some had perverted the faith—his gospel.[24]

1 Timothy 4.6 is another example of rendering "the faith" as "faith."

| If you, you shall be a good minister of Jesus Christ, nourished up in the words of faith and of good doctrine, whereunto you have attained (1 Timothy 4.6). |
|---|
| Ταῦτα ὑποτιθέμενος τοῖς ἀδελφοῖς καλὸς ἔσῃ διάκονος Ἰησοῦ Χριστοῦ ἐντρεφόμενος τοῖς λόγοις **τῆς πίστεως** καὶ τῆς καλῆς διδασκαλίας ᾗ παρηκολούθηκας.[25] |
| By pointing out these things to the brethren you will be an honorable servant of Jesus Christ, since you are being nourished by the words of the faith and of the correct doctrine, which you have followed. |

[24] Paul identified these as Hymenaeus and Alexander in 1 Timothy 1.20.
[25] Paul used the verb παρακολουθέω twice—here and in 2 Timothy 3.10 (see below). It means to "follow," "follow after," "adhere to."

Paul warned Timothy that in latter times some would depart from "the faith" (τῆς πίστεως) and revealed the nature of their false teaching (1 Timothy 4.1-3). He exhorted him to "put the brethren in remembrance of these things"—his doctrines—to combat this threat. In the above passage, Paul wrote believers were to be nourished "in the words of the faith" (τοῖς λόγοις τῆς πίστεως) even "of the good doctrines" (τῆς καλῆς διδασκαλίας) which they had attained (cf. 2 Timothy 3.10). The "words of the faith" and "the good doctrines" mean the same. Paul used the ascensive sense "even" for the conjunction καί to convey this truth. Both nouns, "faith" and "doctrines" have the definite article—omitted by the KJV translators.

Paul concluded his first letter to Timothy with this exhortation:

| Fight the good fight of faith, lay hold on eternal life, whereunto you are also called, and have professed a good profession before many witnesses (1 Timothy 6.12). |
|---|
| ἀγωνίζου τὸν καλὸν ἀγῶνα **τῆς πίστεως** ἐπιλαβοῦ τῆς αἰωνίου ζωῆς εἰς ἣν καὶ ἐκλήθης καὶ ὡμολόγησας τὴν καλὴν ὁμολογίαν ἐνώπιον πολλῶν μαρτύρων. |
| Fight the good fight of the faith. Take hold of the eternal life to which you were called and confessed the good confession before many witnesses. |

Some translations rendered the passage, "fight the good fight of faith" and this leads one to conclude the exhortation is to "keep believing." That was not what Paul meant. The text reads, "fight the good fight of the faith," Paul's doctrines. The word ἀγωνίζου is an imperative. We are under orders to *fight* for Paul's doctrines. How few do!

In his second letter to Timothy Paul wrote:

| But you have fully known my doctrine, manner of life, purpose, faith, longsuffering, charity, patience, (2 Timothy 3.10). |
|---|
| Σὺ δὲ παρηκολούθηκάς μου τῇ διδασκαλίᾳ τῇ ἀγωγῇ τῇ προθέσει **τῇ πίστει** τῇ μακροθυμίᾳ τῇ ἀγάπῃ τῇ ὑπομονῇ. |
| But you followed my teaching: in the conduct, in the purpose, in the faith, in the patience, in the love, in the endurance, |

This passage reads, "But you have followed in the doctrine, in the conduct, in the purpose, in the faith, in the perseverance, in the love, in the patience of me." The definite article occurs with each of the nouns to emphasize Paul's specific beliefs, attitudes, and behaviors. Paul cited these to encourage Timothy to remain strong in his own life with Paul as his example, i.e., "imitate me." Thus, he wrote in verse 14, "But continue in the things which you have learned and have been assured of, knowing of whom you have learned them.

Paul wrote Titus similar words:

| That the aged men be sober, grave, temperate, sound in faith, in charity, in patience (Titus 2.2). |
|---|
| πρεσβύτας νηφαλίους εἶναι σεμνούς σώφρονας ὑγιαίνοντας **τῇ πίστει** τῇ ἀγάπῃ τῇ ὑπομονῇ. |
| Older men are to be temperate, dignified, self-controlled, sound in the faith, in the love, in the endurance. |

This passage reads, "That the aged men be temperate, honorable, sound in the faith, in the love, in the patience." Each noun has the definite article. The "soundness" of which Paul wrote concerned "the faith," and "the love," and "the patience" he taught.

Lastly, Paul wrote Timothy concerning deacons:

| 8 Likewise must the deacons be grave, not double-tongued, not given to much wine, not greedy of filthy lucre; 9 Holding the secret [μυστήριον] of the faith in a pure conscience (1 Timothy 3.8-9). |
|---|
| 8 Διακόνους ὡσαύτως σεμνούς μὴ διλόγους μὴ οἴνῳ πολλῷ προσέχοντας μὴ αἰσχροκερδεῖς 9 ἔχοντας τὸ μυστήριον **τῆς πίστεως** ἐν καθαρᾷ συνειδήσει. |
| 8 Likewise, deacons must be dignified, not double-tongued, not given to excessive drinking, not greedy for dishonest gain, 9 who hold the secret of the faith with a pure conscience. |

Paul included the definite article with "faith" and with "secret" (τὸ μυστήριον τῆς πίστεως), "the secret of the faith." This genitive of apposition means, "the secret which is the faith." Faith was no secret. But Paul's gospel was a secret. This echoes "the secret of the gospel" in Ephesians 6.19 and Philippians 1.27, τῇ πίστει τοῦ εὐαγγελίου (in the faith of the gospel), i.e., "in the faith, which is the gospel."

Paul's inclusion of the definite article with πίστις is highly significant. When he included the definite article, he meant *what* he taught and what was believed, the *body of truth he had received from the risen Lord.* Omission of the definite article in the translations is a serious error and leads to misunderstandings and confusion.

## Romans 3.30: ἐκ πίστεως vs. διὰ τῆς πίστεως

Romans 3.31 was discussed above but verse 3.30 was omitted. It requires attention. Together these verses read:

| 30 Since there is One God who will declare righteous *the* circumcision by faith and *the* uncircumcision through the faith (Romans 3.30).[26] |
|---|
| 30 ἐπείπερ εἷς ὁ θεός ὃς δικαιώσει περιτομὴν ἐκ πίστεως (by faith) καὶ ἀκροβυστίαν διὰ τῆς πίστεως (through the faith) |

[26] The text is translated with the definite article where it occurs, not as the KJV translators, who omitted it.

Paul's language in Romans 3.30 is both intriguing and informative. If his point was that Jews and Gentiles are justified the same way, why did he use different language for each? He used the expression ἐκ πίστεως for Jews and διὰ τῆς πίστεως for Gentiles. Why use separate expressions when he could have included both groups in one: "Since there is One God who will declare righteous circumcision and uncircumcision by faith (ἐκ πίστεως)?"

This change in wording of ἐκ πίστεως and διὰ τῆς πίστεως has not gone unnoticed.[27] The vast majority of commentators, as far back as Augustine, dismiss any significance to this wording and state Paul's change of language was merely stylistic. While some have seen more to Paul's language than mere style, attempts to explain the significance of ἐκ πίστεως for Jews and διὰ τῆς πίστεως for Gentiles have fallen short. It is time to remedy this.

Examining Paul's use of ἐκ πίστεως shows he used this prepositional expression for both Jews and Gentiles to express salvation by faith.[28] The sense of this expression is of salvation by faith in a general or source sense for both Jew and Gentile. Thus, Paul wrote the Romans:

| Therefore, because we were declared righteous **by faith**, we have peace with the God through our Lord Jesus Christ (Romans 5.1). |
|---|
| Δικαιωθέντες οὖν **ἐκ πίστεως** εἰρήνην ἔχομεν πρὸς τὸν θεὸν διὰ τοῦ κυρίου ἡμῶν Ἰησοῦ Χριστοῦ. |

But Paul associated the expression διὰ τῆς πίστεως, "through the faith," with respect to his gospel and with Gentiles. This is seen in his letter to the Galatians:

| So the blessing of Abraham might come to the Gentiles in Christ Jesus, so we might receive the promise of the Spirit **through the faith** (Galatians 3.14). |
|---|
| ἵνα εἰς τὰ ἔθνη ἡ εὐλογία τοῦ Ἀβραὰμ γένηται ἐν Χριστῷ Ἰησοῦ ἵνα τὴν ἐπαγγελίαν τοῦ πνεύματος λάβωμεν **διὰ τῆς πίστεως** |

Paul's "we" in this verse indicated he wrote from his office as "the apostle of the Gentiles." Why did he differentiate salvation of Jews with ἐκ πίστεως but διὰ τῆς πίστεως for the salvation of Gentiles?

Insight about how and why Paul used the propositions ἐκ and διά with the genitive may be seen in his discussion of women's head coverings.

---

[27] Stowers, Stanley K. 1989. "ἐκ πίστεως and διὰ τῆς πίστεως in Romans 3:30." *Journal of Biblical Literature*. 108 (4): 665-674. Origen (184-253 A.D.) and Theodore of Mopsuestia (350-428 A.D.) argued Paul's language was significant.

[28] See Romans 1.17, 4.16, 5.1, 9.30, 32, 10.6, 14.23; Galatians 3.7, 8, 9, 11, 24 for examples of Paul's use of ἐκ πίστεως. Romans 1.17, Galatians 3.11, and Hebrews 10.38 quote Habakkuk 2.4.

Paul wrote the Corinthians:

| For as the woman is from the man, so also, the man is through the woman, but all the things *are* from the God (1 Corinthians 11.12). |
|---|
| ὥσπερ γὰρ ἡ γυνὴ **ἐκ τοῦ ἀνδρός (from the man)** οὕτως καὶ ὁ ἀνὴρ **διὰ τῆς γυναικός (through the woman)** τὰ δὲ πάντα **ἐκ τοῦ θεοῦ (from the God)**. |

Paul wrote that the woman is "from the man," ἐκ τοῦ ἀνδρός, a genitive of source. Man is the source of woman in the original creation but man is "through the woman," διὰ τῆς γυναικός, a genitive of means or instrument, afterwards. Adam was a direct creation of God. The woman was "in Adam" (Genesis 1.27, 2.21-23) but God fashioned her from the man.[29] Thus, God was the "source" of Adam and Adam was the "source" of the woman. But after Adam, all men (and women) come *through* the woman, i.e., by childbirth. Paul ended the verse with another genitive of source and stated all things are "from the God," ἐκ τοῦ θεοῦ, i.e., God is the source of both man and woman.

At the *source* or *origin* level, both Jews and Gentiles are justified by faith (ἐκ πίστεως).[30] At the *means* level, Gentiles are justified "through the faith" (διὰ τῆς πίστεως), i.e., through Paul's gospel. Put another way, ἐκ is a kind of "parent" of διά.

Paul used ἐκ πίστεως for the salvation of both Jews and Gentiles in several verses. But in Romans 3.30, he used it just of Jews. This rendering was shorthand for the Abrahamic Covenant. By that covenant, Jews, God's covenant people, became the source of Gentile blessing. Jesus told the Samaritan woman at the well, σωτηρία ἐκ τῶν Ἰουδαίων ἐστίν, "salvation is from the Jews" (John 4.22 cf. Romans 15.27). Note the preposition ἐκ. Like the woman in Genesis 2, who came from the man, Gentiles are saved *through* the Jews. Paul, as proxy Israel, served in this role. God gave him a new gospel to accomplish this task: διὰ τῆς πίστεως—through the faith—his gospel (1 Corinthians 15.1-4).

But aren't Jews saved the same as Gentiles when they believe Paul's gospel? Yes. But under Paul's apostleship, Gentiles are the major beneficiaries since they now occupy the place of God's favor in the olive tree (Romans 11). Gentiles are blessed through Paul's

---

[29] According to Genesis, woman was in man (Genesis 1.27) and God "built" בָּנָה her from Adam (Genesis 2.21-22). Adam was the "source of woman." When he saw her, he said, "This is now bone of my bones, and flesh of my flesh: she will be called Woman, because she was taken out of Man." The LXX reads, τοῦτο νῦν ὀστοῦν **ἐκ τῶν ὀστέων μου** καὶ **σὰρξ ἐκ τῆς σαρκός μου** αὕτη κληθήσεται γυνή ὅτι **ἐκ τοῦ ἀνδρὸς αὐτῆς** ἐλήμφθη αὕτη. These prepositional phrases have the preposition ἐκ and are genitives of source. The LXX translators rightly used used ἐκ instead of διά.

[30] This is seen in Romans 5.1, "Therefore being justified by faith **(ἐκ πίστεως)**, we have peace with God through our Lord Jesus Christ."

apostleship and gospel (διὰ τῆς πίστεως). This truth can also be understood from the following passage:

> [4] But when the fullness of the time came, the God sent His
> Son, born of *a* woman, born under the Law, [5] so He might
> redeem those under *the* Law, so we might receive the
> adoption as sons (Galatians 4.4-5).

Notice the passage states that God redeemed Jews so that Gentiles might receive the adoption of sons. This was a new order of blessing that God established with the Abrahamic Covenant. Jews became the *source* of Gentile blessing. Thus, God redeemed the Jews (those under the Law) so "we," Gentiles might receive "the adoption as sons." Paul became the agent of God's blessing to Gentiles through his gospel and doctrines.

The following chart compares the distinction between the prepositions ἐκ and διά in Romans 3.30 and 1 Corinthians 11.12. As the woman was "from the man" and then man is "through the woman," salvation is "from God" and "from the Jews" as a source and Gentiles are saved "through the faith," that Paul, as a Jew, as the apostle of the Gentiles, proclaimed to Gentiles.

<table>
<tr><th>Faith: Genitive of Source and of Means</th><th>Creation: Genitive of Source and of Means</th></tr>
<tr><td>Salvation by faith—<br>ἐκ πίστεως: Genitive of source<br>↓</td><td>Woman is from the man—<br>ἐκ τοῦ ἀνδρός: Genitive of source<br>↓</td></tr>
<tr><td rowspan="2">Salvation through the faith—<br>διὰ τῆς πίστεως:<br>Genitive of means</td><td>Man is through the woman—<br>διὰ τῆς γυναικός:<br>Genitive of means</td></tr>
<tr><td>Man and woman are from God—<br>ἐκ τοῦ θεοῦ<br>Genitive of source</td></tr>
</table>

# Chapter 7

# Paul and the Law

*For sin will not rule over you. For you are not under Law, but under grace (Romans 6.14).*

## Introduction to the Law

The Mosaic Law was a large subject for Paul. And why not? God gave the Law to Moses and it had governed Israel's life for 1,500 years. As a Pharisee, Paul knew the Law inside and out. But as "the apostle of the Gentiles" (Romans 11.13), the risen Lord revealed to him many things about the Law he did not learn at the feet of Gamaliel.

The Mosaic Law was a package. It governed all aspects of Israel's moral, civil, and ceremonial life. Paul wrote that the primary purpose of the Law was to *reveal sin.*

> [19] Now we know that whatever the Law says, it says to those under the Law, so every mouth might be shut and all the world might become accountable to the God. [20] Therefore, from works of Law, no flesh will be declared righteous before Him. For through Law *is* knowledge of sin (Romans 3.19-20).

Paul wrote to Timothy:

> [8] Now we know that the Law *is* good if one uses it lawfully—[9] when one realizes this: that law is not intended for *the* righteous but for lawless and insubordinate, ungodly and sinful, unholy and worldly, murderers of fathers and murderers of mothers, murderers, [10] sexually immoral, homosexuals, kidnappers, liars, perjurers, and anything else opposed to what is the sound doctrine, [11] according to the gospel of the glory of the blessed God with which I was entrusted. (1 Timothy 1.8-11).

Most in Christendom believe God gave the Mosaic Law to make one better. Many churches teach the Church, the body of Christ, is under the governance of the Mosaic Law in some form or fashion. Paul taught the exact opposite.

Anyone who spends time with Paul understands he was adamant that believers are not under the administration of the Mosaic Law. The great apostle's teachings are completely contrary to such thought. Paul taught the Church has *nothing* to do with the Mosaic Law. The Church, the body of Christ, is under totally new and different management.

## Paul's Use of Νόμος

Paul used the word "law," νόμος, 136 times in his fourteen letters. Most of them are in Romans (75), Galatians (32), and Hebrews (14) which constitute 89% of the uses. The Mosaic Law revealed sin, first to the Jew, to whom God gave it, but also to Gentiles. Thus, he wrote:

> Now we know that whatever the Law says, it says to those under the Law, so every mouth might be shut and all the world might become accountable to the God (Romans 3.20).

Those "under the Law" were the Jews (Ephesians 11-12). But whomever the Law encountered it condemned: "so every mouth may be shut and all the world might become accountable to the God." The Law revealed that all of mankind was guilty of sin. Paul summed the matter in Romans 3.23:

> For all sinned and fall short of the glory of the God.

A person could not be justified by God solely by keeping the Law. No matter how hard one tried, one broke the Law. The Law revealed sin and the Levitical sacrifices were the Law's provision for sin.

Paul taught that the revelations he received from the risen Lord created a whole new relationship with God by which one is saved and sanctified. He wrote:

> 21 But now, [νυνὶ δὲ] apart from Law, God's righteousness has been manifested, being witnessed by the Law and the prophets: 22 Now, God's righteousness through faithfulness of Jesus Christ *is* for all and on all[1] who believe—for there is no difference (Romans 3.21-22).

Paul's "but now" (νυνὶ δὲ) denoted contrast—what was entirely new and different. What was new and different was that righteousness was available to mankind through the faithfulness of Jesus Christ (His dying for our sins and resurrection), for all who *believe*. What did this mean? It meant works were no longer involved in salvation—no animal sacrifices, no keeping the Law, no baptism, no circumcision, etc. Righteousness was based on faith *alone* in Paul's gospel.

## The Law and the Christian Life

Paul settled the issue of salvation by faith alone and not by works or keeping the Mosaic Law in Romans 1-5 and Galatians 1-2. He wrote:

> But we know that *a* man is not declared righteous except through *the* faithfulness of Jesus Christ, not from works of *the* Law. And we believed in Christ Jesus so we might be declared righteous from *the* faithfulness of Christ and not by

---

[1] Some manuscripts do not have "and on all," καὶ ἐπὶ πάντας.

> works from *the* Law. For no flesh will be declared righteous from *the* works of *the* Law (Galatians 2.16).

Because of Christ's faithfulness—His death and resurrection—one is saved by faith alone. But how was one to live the Christian life? Was it under the administration of the Mosaic Law or by some other way?

Paul wrote the Romans:

> For sin will not rule over you. For you are not under Law, but under grace (Romans 6.14).

A normal, but erroneous, human reaction to such a statement is to conclude that if one is not under Law, one is free to sin. Paul anticipated this reaction:

> What therefore? Should we sin because we are not under Law but under grace? Never (Romans 6.15)!

Paul continued his thought and concluded:

> 22 But now, because you were set free from the sin, because you now became servants to the God, you have your fruit for sanctification. Now, the result *is* eternal life. 23 For the wages of the sin *is* death. But the gift of the God *is* eternal life in Christ Jesus our Lord (Romans 6.22-23).

God did not save believers to continue in sin. What would be the point in saving us from sin only so we would continue in it? That would be madness. Sin leads to death. True freedom is the freedom from sin. Jesus told the Pharisees that whoever commits sin is a slave of the sin (John 8.34). Sin is a domineering tyrant. Paul wrote, "you used to be servants of the sin," (Romans 6.17) and "you became servants to the righteousness (Romans 6.18). God has delivered the believer from slavery—the slavery of sin to serve righteousness.

## The "How To"

Paul addressed how the believer is to live a godly life in Romans 6:

> 11 So you too. Reckon yourselves to be dead to the sin but alive to the God in Jesus Christ our Lord. 12 Therefore, do not let the sin rule in your mortal body to obey its desires. 13 Neither present your members *as* weapons of unrighteousness to the sin. But present yourselves to the God as alive from the dead and your members, weapons of righteousness to the God (Romans 6.11-13).

The way to live a righteous life is by "reckoning." "Reckoning" is an act of faith. Paul wrote that believers are to "reckon" or "consider" (present, middle, imperative of λογίζομαι, "do the math") themselves dead to sin and alive to God. Why can the believer do this? Paul answered this question at the beginning of Romans 6. He wrote:

> [3] Or do you not know that as many as were baptized into Christ Jesus, were baptized into His death? [4] Therefore, we were buried with Him through the baptism into the death, so that just as Christ was raised from *the* dead through the glory of the Father, so we also might walk in newness of life. [5] For if we have become united in the likeness of His death, we will also be *in the likeness* of *His* resurrection. [6] For we know this: our old man was crucified with *Him* so that the body of the sin may be rendered inactive, so that we are no longer enslaved by the sin. [7] For the one who died, has been set free from the sin (Romans 6.3-7).

God sees the believer as having died with Christ, “baptized into His death.” God also sees the believer as being identified in His resurrection. Our “old man,” our fallen nature, has been crucified with Christ. Thus, “the one who died, has been set free from sin.” What is dead does not sin. Believers are to consider themselves dead to sin. This is *faith*. The secret to living the Christian life is *faith*. It begins with faith and it continues with faith.

The Godward part of living by faith is that God begins to change our “want to.” As we mature in Christ, God changes our desires. People think if they have to give up certain sins they will be unhappy. But to the contrary, God replaces sinful desires with better, more *enjoyable* desires. When God removes something, He replaces it with something better. Paul wrote the Corinthians, “the love of Christ constrains us” (2 Corinthians 5.14). The “how to,” living by faith, becomes the believer’s “want to.” We *want* to obey Christ, we *want* to please Him, we *want* to obey the moral law. All this comes as a result of living by faith through the guidance of the Holy Spirit.

> But now, [νυνὶ δὲ] we were released from the Law, because we died to what we used to be bound, so we might serve in newness of *the* Spirit and not in oldness of *the* letter (Romans 7.6).

Here again is Paul’s favorite expression of contrast “but now” (νυνὶ δὲ) to denote something new. God has delivered the believer from the Law. Why? Because the Law condemned us and agitated sin. The new “governor” is God the Holy Spirit, who indwells us. God the Holy Spirit reveals sin but does not condemn as the Law did. Paul wrote:

> [1] Therefore, no condemnation now *exists* to those in Christ Jesus.[2] [2] For the law of the Spirit of the life in Christ Jesus set me free from the law of the sin and of the death. [3] Because the Law was powerless, in that it was continually weak through the flesh, the God sent His own Son in *the*

---

[2] The KJV includes, “who walk not after the flesh, but after the Spirit.” This is a variant reading and it is unlikely the expression was in both verse 1 and verse 4. It properly belongs in verse 4.

> likeness of sinful flesh, and concerning sin—condemned the sin in the flesh, [4] so that the Law's righteousness might be fulfilled in us, who do not walk after *the* flesh but after *the* Spirit (Romans 8.1-4).

Paul began his discussion in Romans 6 of how the Christian life is to be lived—through faith. The believer is to consider himself dead to sin. This is the human side of sanctification. Paul wrote the Galatians:

> [24] Now those of the Christ have crucified the flesh with its passions and its desires. [25] If we live by *the* Spirit, we should also walk by *the* Spirit (Galatians 5.24-25).

The divine side of sanctification comes through the work of the Holy Spirit. As we allow the Holy Spirit to control us, He changes us into the image of Christ. Paul wrote the Corinthians:

> [17] Now the Lord is the Spirit. Where the Spirit of the Lord *is*, *is* freedom. [18] Now we all, with unveiled face, as we view the glory of the Lord as in *a* mirror, we are transformed to the same image, from glory to glory, even as from *the* Lord, *the* Spirit (2 Corinthians 3.17-18).

Paul wrote the Romans:

> [29] Because whom He foreknew, He also predestined *to be* conformed to the image of His Son, so He might be Firstborn among many brethren.[30] Now whom He predestined, these also He called. And whom He called, these He also declared righteous. And whom He declared righteous, these He also glorified (Romans 8.29-30).

The destiny of believers is to be conformed to the image of Christ. That is what predestination (προορίζω) means. Predestination is a *destiny*—the believer's position and inheritance in Christ (Romans 8.29-30; Ephesians 1.5, 11). The work of the Holy Spirit in the believer's life produces an experiential sanctification in anticipation of the believer's glorification, his resurrection, at the Rapture.

Paul wrote he was the minister of the *new* covenant. The New Covenant is empowered by the indwelling Holy Spirit. Paul wrote:

> [6] Who also qualified us *as* ministers of *a* new covenant, not of *the* letter, but of *the* Spirit. For the letter kills, but the Spirit gives life. [7] Now if the ministry of the death, which was engraved in letters on stones, came with glory, so that the sons of Israel could not continue to look at the face of Moses because of the glory of his face, because it faded away, [8] how will the ministry of the Spirit not be more glorious? [9] For if in the ministry of the condemnation there was glory, the ministry of the righteousness abounds in much greater glory! [10] Also, for even what has been glorious, has no glory in this respect, due to the glory surpassing it.

> [11] For if what is being abolished *came* through glory, much more glorious *is* what remains (2 Corinthians 3.6-11)!

The Mosaic Law was "glorious" since it came from God, but was a "ministration of death." Its purpose was to reveal sin. The "ministration of the Spirit" has greater glory. Its administration is life and is the new governor for members of the Church, the body of Christ. Paul wrote the Ephesians:

> So do not be drunk with wine, in which is dissipation, but be filled with the Spirit (Ephesians 5.18).

This is a command. Believers are not to be drunk (μεθύσκεσθε, present passive imperative) with wine, i.e., under the control of wine, but filled (πληροῦσθε, present passive imperative), controlled by the Holy Spirit. To the Thessalonians, Paul gave the command:

> Do not quench the Spirit (1 Thessalonians 5.19).

The word "quench" is σβέννυτε (present active imperative) and is used for quenching a fire or metaphorically for suppressing the influence of the Holy Spirit. When we allow our old nature to control us the Holy Spirit is quenched.

Paul wrote the Thessalonians:

> [13] Now we ought to thank the God always for you, brethren, beloved by *the* Lord, that the God chose you from the beginning for salvation, by *the* sanctification of *the* Spirit and by faith in *the* truth [ἐν ἁγιασμῷ πνεύματος καὶ πίστει ἀληθείας]. [14] For which He also called you through our gospel for possession of *the* glory of our Lord Jesus Christ. (2 Thessalonians 2.13-14).

"Sanctification of the Spirit" is the Godward side of salvation and "belief in the truth"—Paul's gospel, is the manward side.

## Dead to the Law

Paul taught that the believer is dead to the Law. He illustrated this with the example of a spouse who has died.

> [1] Or are you ignorant, brethren, for I am speaking to those who know *the* law—the law rules over the man as long *a* time *as* he lives? [2] For the married woman has been bound by law to the living husband. But if the husband should die, she has been released from the law of the husband. (Romans 7.1-2).

The "husband" in Paul's illustration is our old nature and is viewed as having died on the cross. The believer, viewed as the surviving wife, is now free to marry another—Christ.[3] Paul wrote the Romans:

> So then my brethren, you also were put to death to the Law through the body of the Christ, so you might become to another, to the One who was raised from *the* dead, so we might produce fruit to the God (Romans 7.4).

Paul wrote we have been delivered from the Law:

> But now, [νυνὶ δὲ] we were released from the Law, because we died to what we used to be bound, so we might serve in newness of *the* Spirit and not in oldness of *the* letter (Romans 7.6).

By virtue of Christ's death for us, we have been delivered from the Law. Why? The answer is not so we can sin, but so we can live righteously by faith through the Holy Spirit. Paul expressed this reality to the Galatians with these words:

> I have been crucified with Christ. Now I no longer live. But Christ lives in me. Now what *life* I now live in *the* flesh, I live by the faithfulness of the Son of God, the One who loved me and gave Himself for me (Galatians 2.20).

We are to "reckon" the Adamic nature as crucified with Christ and our new nature as alive to the indwelling Christ.

<table>
<tr><th colspan="3">Victory in Christian Living</th></tr>
<tr><th>Constitution</th><th colspan="2">The Result of Believing the Gospel</th></tr>
<tr><td>Body</td><td colspan="2">Will be raised to new life</td></tr>
<tr><td rowspan="2">Soul</td><td>New nature<br>(τὸν καινὸν ἄνθρωπον)</td><td>Old nature<br>(τὸν παλαιὸν ἄνθρωπον)</td></tr>
<tr><td>Live by faith under the control of the indwelling Holy Spirit</td><td>Reckon the old nature as dead, crucified with Christ</td></tr>
<tr><td>Spirit</td><td colspan="2">Made alive</td></tr>
</table>

## A Challenge to Christian Living

One of the greatest challenges to Christian living is from those who teach that Christians are to live under the Mosaic Law. Paul wrote the book of Galatians to combat this error. In Paul's day, Jewish leaders

---

[3] This passage does not teach the Church is the "bride of Christ." It illustrates the believer's new relationship to the Law and to Christ. Paul taught the Church is the "body of Christ," not the bride of Christ.

went to the Galatians and taught they were to live under the authority of the Mosaic Law. Paul addressed this deceit:

> [1] O foolish Galatians! Who bewitched you to not obey the truth, before whose eyes Jesus Christ was openly displayed when He was crucified? [2] I only want to learn this from you: Did you receive the Spirit from works of *the* Law or from *the* hearing of faith? [3] Are you so foolish? Since you began by *the* Spirit are you now being completed by *the* flesh (Galatians 3.1-3)?

Does one live the Christian life by faith or not? Is the Law of faith? Paul wrote it was not:

> But the Law is not from faith, but, The one who does these things will live by them (Galatians 3.12).
>
> [25] Now, since the faith arrived, we are no longer under *a* tutor.[26] For you are all sons of God through the faith in Christ Jesus (Galatians 3.25-26).

Paul explained this further:

> [1] Now I say, for as long *a* time as the heir is *a* child, he is no different from *a* servant *though* he is master of all, [2] but is under guardians and trustees until the time appointed by his father. [3] So we too, when we were children, used to be held in bondage under the ruling forces of the world. [4] But when the fullness of the time came, the God sent His Son, born of *a* woman, born under the Law, [5] so He might redeem those under *the* Law, so we might receive the adoption as sons (Galatians 4.1-5).

Paul declared that at the appointed time (the fullness of the time) Christ came to redeem those under the Law (the Jews). What was the result? Gentiles could receive the adoption of sons.

The Jews who came in after Paul threatened the freedom Paul's Galatians had in Christ. Paul asked them:

> [8] But then, when you did not know God, you were enslaved to those who by nature are not gods. [9] But now, since you now know God, rather are known by God, how do you again return to the weak and destitute ruling forces to which you wish to be enslaved again from above? [10] You observe *religious* days and months and seasons and years. [11] I am afraid for you, lest I have perhaps labored in vain for you (Galatians 4.8-11).

The Galatian church was composed of Jews and Gentiles. The threat to both groups was to return to the "weak and destitute ruling forces" by observing "days, months, seasons, and years." The temptation was to exchange the freedom of living by faith through the power of the

Holy Spirit for the weakness of pagan religion or the weakness of the Mosaic Law. Paul wrote similarly to the Colossians:

> Be careful so no one will captivate you through the philosophy and empty deceit, after the tradition of mankind, after the ruling forces of the world, and not after Christ (Colossians 2.8).
>
> [20] Therefore, if you died with the Christ from the ruling forces of the world, why do you submit to decrees as if you live in *the* world? [21] Do not handle! Do not taste! Do not touch!—[22] all which are destined to perish with the use, based on the commands and teachings of mankind, [23] which have *an* appearance of wisdom with self-imposed worship, and humility, and harsh treatment of the body, but *have* no value against fleshly indulgence (Colossians 2.20-23).

The word στοιχεῖον means the fundamental principles or basics of something. It was used for letters of the alphabet, heavenly bodies, primary elements or principles. Paul gave the phrase τὰ στοιχεῖα τοῦ κόσμου a technical sense for the cosmic powers against God who seek to control and deceive mankind (cf. Galatians 4.8, 9; Ephesians 6.11-12; Colossians 2.8, 20). In essence these "ruling forces of the world" are Babylon, Satan's theater of deceit, his alternate, false reality. Paul described this deceit as "commands and teachings of mankind," which included rules about touching religious items, eating certain foods, keeping certain days, asceticism, etc. In other words, "religion." Paul taught Christ' work has freed believers from all this.

Paul asked the Galatians, "Tell me, those who wish to be under *the* Law, do you not hear the Law" (Galatians 4.21)? He then gave an illustration of the two sons of Abraham, one from the bondwoman, Hagar, and the other from Abraham's wife, Sarah. Paul wrote:

> [28] Now we, brethren, as Isaac, are children of promise. [29] But as then, the one born by human intervention used to persecute the one *born* according to the Spirit. [30] But what says the Scripture? Cast out the bondwoman and her son. For the son of the bondwoman will not inherit with the son of the free woman. [31] So then, brethren, we are not children of *the* bondwoman but of the free (Galatians 4.28-31).

Those of faith are "children of promise." Those not of faith (the Law) persecute those of faith. The Judaizers were attempting to bring the Galatians under the Law—into bondage. Paul instructed them that as Sarah cast out Hagar and her son, believers are to cast out the Law. Why? Christ has freed members of the Church, the body of Christ, from the Law according to Paul's gospel.

Religion always seeks to control it adherents. Inevitably, those in positions of power in religious systems wish to control those who are in their religion. The believer in Christ has been freed from the Law and freed from religion. The believer lives by faith through the Spirit.

## The Effect of the Law

The Law's purpose was to reveal sin. It did its job extremely well. Paul used himself as an example of the effect of the Law upon the old nature and wrote that with regard to righteousness which is from the Law, that he was blameless (Philippians 3.6).[4] But Paul also revealed in Romans 7 that he had not really understood the Law:

> 8 But the sin, since it took advantage through the commandment, produced in me every kind of lust. For apart from *the* Law sin *is* dead. 9 Now I was once alive apart from Law. But when the commandment came, the sin revived. Then I died. 10 And the commandment that *was* for life, I found *to be* death! 11 For the sin, which took advantage through the commandment, deceived me, and through it, killed *me*. 12 So, *the* Law *is* holy, and the commandment *is* holy, and righteous, and good (Romans 7.8-12).

Paul *thought* he was righteous according to his understanding of the Law through Pharisaic Judaism. This was what he meant by, "I was once alive apart from Law," i.e., before understanding the true effect of the Law. But "when the commandment came, the sin revived." The Law stirred up his fallen nature, "the sin." Paul wrote the commandment was "holy, righteous, and good" (Romans 7.12) and asked,

> Therefore, did the good become death to me? Never! But the sin, so that it might be shown to be sin through the good, produced death to me, so the sin might become extremely sinful through the commandment (Romans 7.13).

The problem was not the Law but Paul. The Law was perfect. But when it confronted his fallen nature, it rebelled against it. No one likes to be told they are guilty, that they are a sinner. That is what the Law does. That is its *job*. Human nature rebels against this. That is why Paul asked "did the good become death to me?"

Earlier, Paul wrote:

> For when we were in the flesh, the passions of the sins that *were* through the Law, kept working in our members to produce fruit to the death (Romans 7.5).

The "flesh," our fallen nature, rebels against the Law because the Law condemns us. The result is "the passions of the sins, that were through

---

[4] See the chapter on Paul and the Nature of Man for a fuller discussion of our constitution.

the Law, kept working in our members to produce fruit to the death." The Law could not *remedy* sin. It could reveal sin and *excite* sin. Thus:

> [21] So, I find the law: [5] when I want to do the good, that the evil is present in me. [22] For I delight in God's Law according to the inner man. [23] But I see another law in my members which wages war[6] against the law of my mind and takes me captive to the law of the sin that is in my members (Romans 7.21-23).

The "inward man," the new nature, delights in the Law because it wishes to please and obey God. But the old nature is at war with the new nature and desires to rebel against God and to sin. Believers are engaged in a constant internal warfare. Paul expressed this truth to the Galatians:

> For the flesh desires against the Spirit, and the Spirit against the flesh. For these oppose one another, so you may not do the things you may wish (Galatians 5.17).

The verb translated "desires," ἐπιθυμέω, means "desire" or "covet." It is a present active indicative which means it is an ongoing action. The believer has two natures, a nature inherited from Adam Paul called "the flesh" (cf. Romans 6.19, 7.5, 18, 25, 8.1, 3-5, 8-9, 12-13, etc.) and a new nature from God, governed by the Holy Spirit. Paul identified what comes from the old nature:

> [19] Now the works of the flesh are evident, which are: sexual immorality, impurity, [20] idolatry, sorcery, enmities, strife, jealousy, angry outbursts, rivalries, dissensions, factions, [21] envying, murders, drunkenness, carousing, and things like these, which I forewarn you, even as I warned before, that those who practice such things will not inherit *the* kingdom of God (Galatians 5.19-21).

Verses 22-23 describe what the new nature produces:

> [22] But the fruit of the Spirit is love, joy, peace, patience, kindness, goodness, faithfulness, [23] gentleness, self-control: against such things there is no Law (Galatians 5.19-23).

Notice Paul's words: "against such things there is no Law." The production, "the fruit of the Spirit," does not come from the Law but from the Holy Spirit's working in the new nature.

Similarly, Paul wrote the Ephesians:

> [8] Once, you used to be darkness. But now, light in *the* Lord. Walk as children of light. [9] For the fruit of the Spirit *is* in

---

[5] This is another occasion in which Paul used the word "law," νόμος, as "principle."

[6] The word, "warring against," ἀντιστρατεύομαι means to fight an enemy.

every goodness, and righteousness, and truth, [10] for it discerns what is pleasing to the Lord (Ephesians 5.8-10).

Before believing Paul's gospel, each of us is in darkness, blinded by the god of this world (2 Corinthians 4.3-4). After believing the gospel, one is in the light. Having received light, we are to live righteously, proving (δοκιμάζω)[7] what is pleasing or acceptable (εὐάρεστος)[8] to the Lord.

## Paul and the Decalogue

Paul taught that Christ has freed members of the Church, the body of Christ, from the Mosaic Law. This does not mean believers are not to keep the moral law. The moral law reflects God's character and existed long before God gave Moses the Law.

| The Decalogue | | |
|---|---|---|
| 1 | You will have no other gods before Me. | 1 Thessalonians 1.9 |
| 2 | You will not make for yourself an idol, or any likeness of what is in heaven above or on the earth beneath or in the water under the earth. | 1 Corinthians 5.11, 6.9-10, 10.7, 14; 2 Corinthians 6.16; Galatians 5.19-20; Ephesians 5.5; Colossians 3.5; 1 Thessalonians 1.9 |
| 3 | You will not take the name of the LORD your God in vain, for the LORD will not leave him unpunished who takes His name in vain. | Ephesians 4.31; Colossians 3.8; 1 Timothy 1.20 |
| 4 | Remember the sabbath day, to keep it holy. Six days you will labor and do all your work, but the seventh day is a sabbath of the LORD your God. | Colossians 2.16-17; Romans 14.5-6. |
| 5 | Honor your father and your mother, that your days may be prolonged in the land which the LORD your God gives you. | Ephesians 6.1-3; Colossians 3.20 |
| 6 | You will not murder. | Romans 13.9 |
| 7 | You will not commit adultery. | Romans 13.9; 1 Corinthians 5.11, 6.9-10, 18, 10.8; Galatians 5.19; Ephesians 5.5 |

[7] The verb δοκιμάζω means to test or examine and was used for assaying metals to see if they were genuine. Paul used the word 23 of the 28 times it occurs in the New Testament.

[8] The adjective εὐάρεστος is used 10x in the New Testament, all by Paul in his 13 letters and Hebrews (Hebrews 13.21; Romans 12.1, 2, 14.18; 2 Corinthians 5.9; Ephesians 5.10; Philippians 4.18; Colossians 3.20; Titus 2.9).

| | | |
|---|---|---|
| 8 | You will not steal. | Romans 13.9; 1 Corinthians 6.10; Ephesians 4.28 |
| 9 | You will not bear false witness against your neighbor. | Romans 13.9; Ephesians 4.25; Colossians 3.9 |
| 10 | You will not covet your neighbor's house; you will not covet your neighbor's wife or his male servant or his female servant or his ox or his donkey or anything that belongs to your neighbor. | Romans 13.9; 1 Corinthians 6.10, 10.6; Ephesians 5.5; Colossians 3.5; 1 Thessalonians 2.5 |

Paul taught believers are to keep the moral law found in the Mosaic Law. How does one to keep it? Paul taught that believers are not under the governance of the Mosaic Law. Rather, believers keep the moral law of the Mosaic Law through faith and the power of the Holy Spirit. Thus, Paul wrote the Galatians:

> For through *the* Law, I died—so I might live to God (Galatians 2.19).

The believer of Paul's gospel "died through the Law" to "live to God."

> [14] For the love of the Christ constrains us, for we have concluded this: that One died for all, therefore all died. [15] And He died for all, so that those who live, should no longer live for themselves but for the One who died for them and was raised (2 Corinthians 5.14-15).

## Paul and the Sabbath

Paul repeated every commandment in the Decalogue *except* the Sabbath and taught that believers are not under Sabbath requirements. God established the Sabbatic covenant with Israel, not the Church (Exodus 31:12-18). The sabbath, which means "rest" was the last day of the week, based on the revelation that God "rested," שָׁבַת, on the seventh day from His work (Genesis 2.2). Sunday is the first day of the week. The idea that Sunday is the "new Sabbath" is not Scriptural. Christians celebrate the *first* day of the week (Sunday) for it was the day Christ rose from the dead. For Christians, *every* day should be considered resurrection day.

# Chapter 8
# Paul on Israel

*I tell the truth in Christ. I am not lying because my conscience testifies to me by the Holy Spirit, because I have great sorrow and unceasing pain in my heart. For I kept wishing that I myself might be a curse, separated from the Christ for my brethren, my kindred according to the flesh, who are Israelites, whose is the adoption, and the glory, and the covenants, and the law-giving, and the service, and the promises—whose are the fathers and from whom is the Christ, after the flesh, the God who is over all, blessed forever. Amen. (Romans 9.1-5).*

## Introduction

Much of Christendom has been taught that the Church, the body of Christ, has replaced Israel. This view has various names, "replacement theology," "supersessionism," "fulfillment theology," etc. Most who adhere to this view identify themselves with "covenant theology" or "reformed theology." Whatever the association, the essence of this theology is 1) the church has replaced Israel in the sense that God's promises to national Israel are fulfilled in the Church and 2) the prophesied blessings of Israel's restoration to the land are allegorized as God's blessings to the church.

Those who hold to "replacement theology" argue Israel was a "type" which has been fulfilled by the Church. In other words, the Church is the fulfillment of what began as Israel. They do not see Israel and the Church as two distinct and separate programs, each with its own promises and destiny. To hold this theological theory, one must accept the following: 1) The prophets, Jesus, and the Twelve misunderstood the theology of the Old Testament, the covenants, and the kingdom promises and 2) "Israel" does not *always* mean the offspring of Jacob.

The theory that the Church had replaced Israel began early in Church history[1] and continues to predominate most of Christendom.[2] What did Paul teach about this important subject?

---

[1] Vlach, Michael J. "Rejection Then Hope: The Church's Doctrine of Israel in the Patristic Era." *Master's Seminary Journal*. 19, no. 1. (Spring 2008) 51-70. See https://doctrine.org/wp-content/uploads/2022/07/tmsj19c.pdf. Vlach has an excellent analysis of how the early Church regarded Israel.

[2] In 2002, Knox Theological Seminary published "An Open Letter to Evangelical and Other Interested Parties: The People of God, the Land of Israel, and the Impartiality of the Gospel" (https://doctrine.org/wp-content/uploads/2018/08/Open-Letter-To-Evangelicals-2002.pdf). Signed by

## Romans 9

Romans 9-11 are Paul's primary teachings concerning national Israel. Paul began his dissertation with the following words:

> [1] I tell the truth in Christ. I am not lying because my conscience testifies to me by the Holy Spirit, [2] because I have great sorrow and unceasing pain in my heart. [3] For I kept wishing that I myself might be a curse, separated from the Christ for my brethren, my kindred according to the flesh, [4] who are Israelites, whose is the adoption, and the glory, and the covenants, and the law-giving, and the service, and the promises—[5] whose are the fathers and from whom is the Christ, after the flesh, the God who is over all, blessed forever. Amen (Romans 9.1-5).

This passage reveals Paul wrote about the *physical offspring of Jacob*—Paul's "kindred according to the flesh." To them, Israelites, God gave "the adoption, and the glory, and the covenants, and the law-giving, and the service of God, and the promises."

Paul also taught that within the physical offspring of Abraham, Isaac, and Jacob was another Israel, *spiritual* Israel. He wrote:

> [6] Now *it is* not as though the word of the God has failed: for not all who *are* from Israel *are* Israel. [7] Not because they *are the* descendants of Abraham *are* all children. Rather, In Isaac your descendants will be called. [8] That is, the children of the flesh, these *are* not *the* children of the God. Rather, the children of the promise are reckoned for descendants (Romans 9.6-8).

Paul taught that "spiritual Israel," *believing Israel,* existed within "physical Israel." When God established the Abrahamic Covenant, He placed Israel, the entire race or nation, into a position of favor. But not every Jew knew God, i.e., "not all Israel are of Israel." Only Jews who believed God were "the children of the promise."

Paul confirmed and expanded this idea in his discussion of a "remnant."[3] He wrote:

> [25] As also He says in Hosea: I will call what *is* not My people, My people and her not having been loved, having

---

over 150 educators, pastors, and others, it declared the Abrahamic Covenant does not apply to Israel but to the Church, the Church is Israel, Jews (Israel) have no right to or hope for a Promised Land, and that there will be no kingdom of God on earth. Paul commanded believers to withdraw from such apostates (Romans 16.17; 2 Thessalonians 3.6; 1 Timothy 6.3-5).

[3] Many commentators apply verses 25-26 to Gentiles but the Old Testament teaches otherwise: Israel, whom God have given a "bill of divorcement" (Isaiah 50.1; Jeremiah 3.8), will become God's reconciled wife.

> been loved. 26 And it will be in the place where it was said to
> them: You *are* not My people, there they will be called sons
> of *the* living God. 27 Now Isaiah shouts for Israel: Though
> the number of the sons of Israel should be as the sand of the
> sea, the remnant will be saved. 28 For He completes the word
> and cuts *it* short[4] in righteousness for *the* Lord will do *a* short
> word on the earth (Romans 9.25-28).

While "all Israel was not Israel," God would preserve and save a remnant. This was Israel's hope. Paul grieved that the Jews had rejected their Messiah, but wrote that God would preserve a remnant and fulfill His promises to them. He concluded the chapter with the following verses:

> 31 But Israel, because they pursue *a* law of righteousness, did
> not attain to *the* Law. 32 Why? Because *it was* not from faith,
> but from works of Law. They tripped on the stumbling
> block. 33 As it has been written: Behold, I place in Zion *a*
> stumbling block and *an* offending rock. But the one who
> believes on Him will never be ashamed (Romans 9.31-33).

Israel's problem was it thought it could obtain righteousness solely by works of the Mosaic Law. What was missing? Faith. The nation stumbled because they refused to believe Jesus of Nazareth was the Messiah. He was their stumbling block and rock of offense even as Isaiah had prophesied (Isaiah 8.14; cf. 1 Peter 2.6-8).

## Who is Israel?

The above verses provide enough information to define "Israel." The term, "Israel" is technical. It *always* means the physical descendants of Jacob.[5] An Israelite might be a believer or an unbeliever. But Israel always referred to Jews,[6] to the physical offspring of Jacob.

After the nation split after Solomon, ten of the tribes became known as "Israel" and the other tribes were called "Judah." In that context, Israel meant the northern tribes.[7] At other times, Israel referred to the entire nation (Acts 2.36).

---

[4] Wordplay with συντελέω "complete" and συντέμνω "cut short." This "cutting short" is what Jesus stated in Matthew 24.22 and Mark 13.20 though there, the Lord used the word κολοβόω.

[5] The term "Gentile" is one who is not a Jew. The term "Church" in Paul's letters is one who has believed his gospel. When one believes Paul's gospel he becomes a member of the Church, the body of Christ. Paul defined the world into three groups: Jew, Gentile, and Church in 1 Corinthians 10.32.

[6] The word "Jew," יְהוּדִי, originally meant a member of the tribe of Judah. By the time of the Babylonian Captivity, anyone from Israel's tribes was known as a Jew (Mark 7.3; Luke 23.3; John 2.6, 13, 18, 20).

[7] The northern kingdom was also called Ephraim and Samaria.

The lexical evidence that "Israel" *always* and *only* refers to the physical offspring of Jacob is overwhelming. *No* lexical evidence exists that "Israel" means anything other than ethnic Jews, the offspring of Jacob. In the New Testament, the term "Israel" occurs seventy-one times and the term "Israelite," four times. In *every case*, they mean ethnic Jews. *No* exceptions exist.

Luke wrote in his Gospel:

> [30] And the angel said to her, Do not fear, Mary. For you found favor with the God. [31] And behold, you will conceive in *the* womb and will give birth to *a* son. And you will call His name Jesus. [32] He will be great and will be called Son of the Highest. And the Lord God will give Him the throne of His father, David. [33] And He will rule over the house of Jacob forever. And His kingdom will never end (Luke 1.30-33).

The angel promised Mary she would have a son named Jesus who would occupy the throne of David and reign over the house of Jacob, i.e., Israel, forever. This one passage puts a knife in the heart of "replacement" or "covenant" theology since it maintains Jesus is now reigning from heaven on the throne of David. *David's* throne was on earth in Jerusalem. *Every* Jew understood this. Israel's earthly kingdom was the essence of Jewish hope.

## Romans 10

In Romans 10, Paul appealed to Israel to be saved through faith:

> [13] For all who would call upon the name of *the* Lord will be saved. [14] How then could they call on *Him* whom they did not believe? But how could they believe of whom they did not hear? And how could they hear apart from one who preaches? [15] And how could they preach if they should not be sent? Just as it has been written: How beautiful *are* the feet of those who proclaim peace, of those who proclaim the good things! [16] But not all heeded the gospel. For Isaiah says: Lord, who believed our report? [17] So, the faith *is* from hearing but the hearing *is* through *the* word of God (Romans 10.13-17).

Paul understood the rejection of his message and the role of faith. The state of Israel in Paul's day was no different than in Isaiah's. Isaiah wrote, "who has believed our report?" Paul's appeal was for the nation to believe, just as had Isaiah.

## Romans 11

Romans 11 concludes Paul's argument. National Israel is in unbelief but that condition is temporary. Anticipating the question of Israel's future, Paul asked:

> [1] So I say, Did the God reject His people? Never! For I too am *an* Israelite, from *the* stock of Abraham, of *the* tribe of Benjamin. [2] The God did not reject His people whom He foreknew. Or do you not know, in Elijah, what the Scripture says, how he pleads with the God against Israel, saying: [3] Lord, they killed your prophets. They demolished your altars. And I alone was left, and they seek my life. [4] But what says the divine answer to him? I reserved to Myself seven thousand men who did not bow *a* knee to Baal. [5] So then, also in the present time, a remnant has come to be according to *the* choice of grace (Romans 11.1-5).

Paul returned to his earlier subject of a remnant. Israel's hardness of heart was not new. Elijah thought he was the only believer in Israel. But God told him he was not alone, that 7,000 had not worshipped Baal. While this was an encouragement, it also showed the dearth of believers. In Elijah's day, Israel's population was about seven million. This meant the number of believers was one-tenth of one percent—1 in 1,000. Despite such low numbers, Paul adamantly declared God had not cast away His people. God had preserved a remnant.

Paul continued with another question:

> [11] So I say, Did they stumble that they might fall? Never! But by their misstep, the salvation *is* to the Gentiles, to make them jealous. [12] Now if their misstep *is* riches of *the* world, and their failure *is* riches of *the* Gentiles, how much more their fullness (Romans 11.11-12)!

Israel had tripped but not fallen as indicated by Paul's second use of μὴ γένοιτο (verse 11). What occurred from Israel's stumble? Gentile salvation. Isn't that amazing? Gentiles were supposed to have been saved through Israel's *obedience*. But God in His great mercy and love had a plan in which Gentiles could be saved by Israel's *disobedience*. Israel did exactly the wrong thing. But God is greater than sin (Romans 5.20). Who but God can do this? He is the Alpha and Omega, the God of glory. Nothing is impossible for Him. Thus, Paul stated in verse 15:

> For if their rejection *is the* reconciliation of *the* world, what *will be* their acceptance—except life from *the* dead (Romans 11.15)?

Israel's present state of unbelief is temporary. As "the apostle of the Gentiles," he explained how God's program was working for Gentiles and how it would work out for Israel in his illustration of the olive tree.

## The Olive Tree

The olive tree represents the place of God's favor, His place of blessing—the Abrahamic Covenant (Genesis 12.1-3). To his Gentile readers, Paul wrote:

> [17] Now if some of the branches were broken off, and you, being *a* wild olive tree, were grafted in among them, and became *a* partner of the rich root of the olive tree, [18] do not boast against the branches. But if you do boast, *remember*, you do not support the root, but the root you (Romans 11.17-18)!

Paul continued his discourse with a warning to Gentiles:

> [19] You will then say, *The* branches were broken off so I might be engrafted. [20] Right! They were broken off by the unbelief. So, you stand by the faith. Do not be high-minded, but be afraid. [21] For if the God did not spare the natural branches, He will not spare you. [22] Behold, therefore, *the* gentleness and severity of God. On those who fell, severity. But on you, God's gentleness—if you should remain in the gentleness. Otherwise, you too will be cut off. [23] So they too, if they should not remain in the unbelief they will be engrafted. For the God can graft them in again (Romans 11.19-23).

It is human nature to boast. Paul warned Gentiles that Israel had been removed from its place of blessing due to unbelief and warned that if God did not spare the natural branches (Israel) this fate could happen to the wild branches (Gentiles).[8] His phrase, "if you should remain in the gentleness" means faith--believing God. Paul anticipated God's restoration of national Israel to its place of blessing—"if they should not remain in the unbelief." Thus, he wrote:

> [24] For if you were cut from *a* wild olive tree by nature and engrafted against nature into *a* cultivated olive tree, how much more will these natural *branches* be grafted back into their own olive tree? [25] For I do not wish you to be ignorant brethren of this secret—so you may not be wise in yourselves—partial hardening has happened to Israel, until the completion of the Gentiles might enter in. [26] And so, all Israel will be saved. As it has been written: The Rescuer will come from Zion. He will remove ungodliness from Jacob. [27] And this *is* My covenant with them when I should take away their sins (Romans 11.24-27).

Paul wrote that Gentiles were cut from a "wild olive tree." What did he mean? A wild olive tree is untended and uncultivated. Israel, on the other hand, was a cultivated olive tree. It had "the adoption, and the glory, and the covenants, and the giving of the law, and the service of God, and the promises" (Romans 9.4). Gentiles had none of these. If God grafted "wild olive branches" (Gentiles) into the cultivated tree

---

[8] Paul was not speaking of individuals but *programs*: Israel and Gentiles, specifically, the Church. This passage has nothing to do with a believer's security in Christ.

how much more willing will He be to re-graft the natural branches back into their own tree? Paul then revealed a secret (μυστήριον): temporary, partial hardening has afflicted national Israel. That dullness will continue "until the completion of the Gentiles might enter in," the completion of the Church, the body of Christ.[9]

After God has completed the Church, "all Israel will be saved" (verse 26). Paul quoted Isaiah 59.20-21 as the prophetic confirmation of this hope. Who is "all Israel?" It is not every Jew who has ever lived but every Jew who is alive at the return of Christ. Every Jew will become "true Israel," believing Israel at Christ's return. This was what the gospel of the kingdom required. The Lord told the nation shortly before He was crucified:

> [37] Jerusalem, Jerusalem, the one who kills the prophets and stones the ones who have been sent to her! How often I wished to gather your children, as *a* hen gathers her chicks under her wings, and you would not! [38] Behold, your house is left to you desolate! [39] For I tell you, you should never see Me from now until you should say, Blessed *is* the One who comes in *the* name of *the* Lord (Matthew 23.37-39).

Jesus told the nation He would not return until they said, "Blessed is the One who comes in the name of the Lord." These are words of repentance. Peter reiterated this condition on the Day of Pentecost:

> [36] Assuredly, therefore, let all *the* house of Israel know: The God made Him both Lord and Christ—this Jesus whom you crucified. [37] Now when they heard, they were pierced to the heart. Then they said to Peter and the other apostles, What should we do, men, brethren? [38] Then Peter said to them, Repent and be baptized, every one of you, in the name of Jesus Christ, for forgiveness of your sins and you will receive the gift of the Holy Spirit. [39] For to you is the promise, and to your children, and to all those far away, as many as the Lord our God will call (Acts 2.36-39).

The Lord Jesus Christ will not return until Israel nationally repents. Peter told the nation, "Repent and be baptized *every one of you.*"[10]

The same thing occurred at the Temple after Peter and John healed the lame man. Peter told the Jews:

> [19] Therefore, repent and return so your sins might be wiped out, [20] so that the season of refreshment might come from the presence of the Lord and He might send the One chosen for

---

[9] The Church, the body of Christ, is composed of both Jew and Gentile but the vast majority of its members are Gentiles.

[10] Peter did not tell them to believe Christ died for their sins and rose from the dead. He did not tell them this because he did not know this. This was Paul's gospel, a secret, to which Peter was not privy.

> you, Christ Jesus, [21] whom heaven must receive until *the* times of restoration of all things, of which the God spoke through the mouth of all His holy prophets, from long ago (Acts 3.19-21).
>
> [25] You are the sons of the prophets and of the covenant that the God made with your fathers when He said to Abraham: And by your descendants, all the families of the earth will be blessed. [26] To you first, the God, since He raised up His servant, Jesus, sent Him by blessing you, in turning each one from your iniquities (Acts 3.25-26).

As at Pentecost, Peter told the Jewish people to repent (verse 19) and this meant every Jew (verse 26). If they did, God would forgive their sins, bring in "the season of refreshment," and send Jesus Christ back to earth. This would constitute the "restoration of all things," the earthly kingdom, in which God would return the earth to its Edenic splendor.[11]

Zechariah wrote concerning this future remnant who will believe and usher in the Lord's return:

> [9] And it will come to pass in that day, that I will seek to destroy all the nations that come against Jerusalem. [10] And I will pour on the house of David, and on the inhabitants of Jerusalem, the spirit of grace and of supplications: and they will look on me whom they have pierced, and they will mourn for him, as one mourns for his only son, and will be in bitterness for him, as one that is in bitterness for his firstborn (Zechariah 12.9-10).
>
> [6] And one will say to him, What are these wounds in your hands? Then he will answer, Those with which I was wounded in the house of my friends. [7] Awake, O sword, against my shepherd, and against the man that is my fellow, says the Lord of hosts: smite the shepherd, and the sheep will be scattered: and I will turn mine hand on the little ones. [8] And it will come to pass, that in all the land, says the LORD, two parts therein will be cut off and die; but the third will be left therein. [9] And I will bring the third part through the fire, and will refine them as silver is refined, and will try them as gold is tried: they will call on my name, and I will hear them:

---

[11] Peter's language, "the season of refreshment," and "restoration of all things" referred to God's establishment of His kingdom on earth. Jesus told his disciples when He was transfigured that Elijah was coming and would "restore (ἀποκαθίστημι) all things" (Matthew 17.11). The disciples asked Jesus right before his ascension if He was now going to "restore again the kingdom to Israel" (Acts 1.6). God's earthly kingdom was Israel's great national hope.

> I will say, It is my people: and they will say, The LORD is my God (Zechariah 13.8-9).

These prophecies will be fulfilled when Jerusalem is surrounded by the nations of the world (Isaiah 34.2-3; Zechariah 12.3, 14.2; Luke 21.20).[12] As He returns, the Jews will see the wounds of their Messiah, Jesus of Nazareth, and repent. Two-thirds will die but one-third will survive—the remnant, "all Israel." Israel will no longer be, "not my people" but "my people" (Hosea 1.9-10, 2.23; Zechariah 8.8, 13.9).

Paul concluded his illustration of the olive tree with these words:

> 27 And this *is* My covenant with them when I should take away their sins. 28 As far as the gospel is concerned, *they are* enemies for your sakes. But as far as the election, *they are* beloved because of the fathers. 29 For the gifts and the calling of the God *are* irrevocable. 30 For just as you were once disobedient to the God but now obtained mercy by their disobedience, 31 so also these are disobedient now, so they might obtain mercy by your mercy. 32 For the God enclosed all in disobedience, so He might show mercy to all (Romans 11.27-32).

Verses 26- 27 refer to Isaiah 59.20-21.[13] Paul's statement, "for the gifts and calling of the God are irrevocable" (ἀμεταμέλητα γὰρ τὰ χαρίσματα καὶ ἡ κλῆσις τοῦ θεοῦ) explicitly declares God has not forgotten or forsaken national Israel.[14] Paul summed up his illustration by saying Gentiles have obtained mercy through Israel's unbelief but that Jews could obtain mercy through Gentiles.[15]

Throughout the Scriptures, the prophets reiterated God's faithfulness to the nation of Israel. Paul knew these Scriptures and must have considered passages such as the following in writing about Israel:

> 18 Who is a God like to you, that pardons iniquity, and passes by the transgression of the remnant of his heritage? he retains not his anger forever, because he delights in mercy.

---

[12] Israel has never been surrounded by "all nations." At the end of the Tribulation, the Beast will assemble all nations and armies against Israel. It will be Satan's final attempt to destroy the Jews. Once again, he will fail.

[13] The covenant of the Isaiah passage is the Abrahamic Covenant, the source of God's blessing to Israel.

[14] The sense of ἀμεταμέλητα is that God will not change His mind. His gifts and election of Israel is irrevocable. See Hebrews 7.21 for this sense.

[15] Jews are blessed through Gentiles, specifically through Paul's gospel in his office as "the apostle of the Gentiles" (Romans 11.13). A Jew who believes Paul's gospel becomes "Church," a member of the body of Christ. Everyone who names the name of Christ should recognize God's ongoing relationship with ethnic Israel. Christians should be Israel's greatest ally and friend. The Abrahamic Covenant remains in effect: God will bless those who bless Israel and curse the one who curses Israel (Genesis 12.3).

> [19] He will turn again, he will have compassion on us; he will subdue our iniquities; and you will cast all their sins into the depths of the sea. [20] You will perform the truth to Jacob, and the mercy to Abraham, which you have sworn uo our fathers from the days of old (Micah 718-20).

Paul concluded his dissertation on Israel's future and God's blessings to Gentiles with this paean:

> [33] O *the* depth of riches, both of wisdom and knowledge of God! How unsearchable *are* His judgments and incomprehensible His ways! [34] For who knew *the* mind of the Lord? Or who became His adviser? [35] Or who first gave to Him so he will be repaid? [36] For from Him, and through Him, and to Him, *are* all the things. To Him *be* the glory forever. Amen (Romans 11.33-36).

The revealed prophetic plan was that God would bless Gentiles *through* Israel. God had revealed *no plan* to bless Gentiles *apart from Israel.* If one had asked a Jew how God could bless Gentiles apart from Israel, they would have answered that this was impossible. But with God, nothing is impossible. God found a way to bless Gentiles despite Israel's national disobedience. He chose Paul to be proxy Israel. Is it any wonder Paul broke out in praise of God's wisdom and knowledge?

## Children of Abraham

The terms "Israel" and "Abraham's children" are not synonymous. As noted above, "Israel" *always* refers to the offspring of Jacob whether believers or unbelievers. But Abraham's "seed" (σπέρμα Ἀβραάμ) includes *more* than racial Jews. It has three senses and context determines meaning:

| Children of Abraham |
|---|
| 1. Ethnic Israel (all Jews), descendants of Jacob (John 8.37; Acts 3.25; Romans 11.1; 2 Corinthians 11.22). |
| 2. Believing Israel, ethnic Jews who have believed God (Romans 2.28-29, 9.6-7). |
| 3. Gentiles saved like Abraham, through faith alone (Romans 4.16; Galatians 3.7-8, 29). |

With regard to *ethnic* Israel, Jesus told the Jews:

> I know that you are Abraham's descendants. But you seek to kill Me, because My word has no place in you (John 8.37).

Jesus distinguished these Jews from *believing* Israel:

> They answered and said to Him, Abraham is our father. Jesus said to them, If you were children of Abraham, you would do the works of Abraham (John 8.39).

These Jews were "Abraham's descendants," the physical progeny of Abraham. But they were *not* his spiritual children. They were unbelievers. Paul expressed this truth to the Romans:

> [28] For one is not *a* Jew outwardly, nor is circumcision outwardly, in *the* flesh. [29] Rather, one *is a* Jew inwardly. And circumcision *is* of heart, in spirit, not in letter—of whom the praise *is* not from men but from the God (Roman 2.28-29).

A "true Jew" was not a Jew who had been circumcised in the flesh but one who had been circumcised in heart: a Jew who believed God.

Paul wrote that those who believe in Christ are the children of Abraham. Does this mean Paul taught that Gentiles or the Church was Israel? Quite the contrary. Paul kept Jew, Gentile, and the Church distinct. He wrote the Corinthians:

> Do not offend Jews, or Greeks, or the Church of the God (1 Corinthians 10.32).

Beginning with Paul, God divided the world into three distinct groups: Jews, Gentiles, and Church.[16] The Church is neither Jew nor Gentile (Galatians 3.28). One who believes the gospel becomes, "Church." Thus, Paul wrote:

> Therefore, if anyone *is* in Christ: *a* new creation. The old things passed away. Behold, new things have come into existence (2 Corinthians 5.17).

When one believes Paul's gospel one becomes Church—a new creation, neither Jew or Gentile. Paul wrote the Corinthians:

> [13] So *as a* fair exchange, as to children I say, open your hearts to us also! [14] Do not become unequally yoked with unbelievers. For what partnership *is* righteousness and lawlessness? Or what fellowship *is* light with darkness? [15] Now what harmony is Christ with Belial? Or what does *a* believer share with *an* unbeliever? [16] Now what agreement is in *the* Temple of God with idols? For you are *the* temple of *the* living God, as the God said: I will live in them and will walk among *them.* And I will be their God and they will be My people. [17] Therefore, come out from among them and be separate says *the* Lord and do not touch anything unclean and I will receive you. [18] And I will be to you for *a* Father and you will be to Me for sons and daughters, says *the* Lord Almighty (2 Corinthians 6.13-18).

---

[16] God divided the world into *two* distinct peoples: Jews and Gentiles, by the Abrahamic Covenant. When God established the Church, the body of Christ, the world became *three* distinct peoples: Jews, Gentiles, and Church (1 Corinthians 10.32).

In verses 16-17, Paul quoted Leviticus 26.12, Isaiah 52.11, and Ezekiel 20 and *applied* them to Gentile believers. Did he mean the Church is part of Israel? Do such statements indicate the Church has replaced or fulfilled Israel? Not at all. These passages deal with righteous living. The moral law applies to the Jew, the Gentile, and the Church.

Believers of Paul's gospel become "children of Abraham" *by faith*. Paul explained this in his letter to the Galatians:

> [7] Then recognize that those from faith, these are sons of Abraham. [8] Now the Scripture, when it saw in advance that the God would declare the Gentiles righteous from faith, declared in advance the gospel to Abraham: All the Gentiles will be blessed in you. [9] So then, those from faith are blessed with believing Abraham (Galatians 3.7-9).

The Abrahamic covenant anticipated God blessing Gentiles. Paul's point in applying prophetic passages to Gentiles was to show that the Abrahamic Covenant was being fulfilled through him in revealing God's salvation by the grace through the faith alone (Ephesians 2.8). Abraham was the prototype of salvation by faith alone (Romans 4.1-5) and members of the Church, the body of Christ, become Abraham's children because they are saved in the same manner as Abraham.

God promised Abraham two kinds of offspring: earthly and heavenly. God described Abraham's earthly descendants as dust or sand:

> [14] The LORD said to Abram, after Lot had separated from him, Now lift up your eyes and look from the place where you are, northward and southward and eastward and westward; [15] for all the land which you see, I will give it to you and to your descendants forever. [16] I will make your descendants as the dust of the earth, so that if anyone can number the dust of the earth, then your descendants can also be numbered (Genesis 13.14-16).

God promised the Jews, His covenant people, land. They are Abraham's earthly progeny. A second metaphor revealed Abraham's heavenly progeny:

> [4] Then behold, the word of the Lord came to him, saying, This man will not be your heir; but one who will come forth from your own body, he will be your heir. [5] And He took him outside and said, Now look toward the heavens, and count the stars, if you are able to count them. And He said to him, So shall your descendants be. [6] Then he believed in the LORD; and He reckoned it to him as righteousness (Genesis 15.4-6).

Note that Abraham's heavenly progeny (stars) were identified with *faith*. The Church, the body of Christ, is Abraham's heavenly progeny. Those who become members of the Church obtain salvation by faith alone.

Genesis 22.17 brought both progeny, sand and stars, together:

> Indeed, I will greatly bless you, and I will greatly multiply your seed as the stars of the heavens and as the sand which is on the seashore; and your seed will possess the gate of their enemies.

Abraham was to have two types of children. One was earthly and the other was heavenly. God repeated this promise to Isaac (Genesis 26.3-5) and Jacob (Genesis 28.13-14).

The Church did *not* replace Israel nor is it a "fulfillment" of Israel. Nor is Israel a "type," prefiguring the Church. On the contrary, from Genesis through the teachings of Paul, Israel is revealed as one program (earthly) and the Church as another (heavenly) program.

The Scriptures always keep heaven and earth separate and distinct. Genesis 1.1 does not read, "In the beginning, God created the universe" but "In the beginning, God created the heavens and the earth." This is the way the Bible begins and this is the way it ends. The last book, Revelation, reveals God will create a new heaven and a new earth. John echoed Moses: "Then I saw a new heaven and a new earth; for the first heaven and the first earth passed away" (Revelation 21.1). Heaven and earth remain separate throughout eternity.

Abraham's "sand/dust" progeny aligns with the land promise God gave him which national Israel will experience. The line of Jacob will obtain God's covenant promises in the Messianic kingdom when the Lord rules the earth (Zechariah 14.9; Matthew 6.10). The Abrahamic, Mosaic, Sabbatic, and Davidic covenants are *physical* blessings. Israel also receives *spiritual* blessing with the New Covenant—forgiveness of sins and the indwelling Holy Spirit.

Abraham's "stars" progeny aligns with faith (Genesis 15.6) and with (primarily) Gentiles. Paul wrote that the Church is Abraham's heavenly progeny (Romans 4; Galatians 3). The terms "sand/dust" and "stars" are metonymies for two separate divine programs: Israel and the Church. These two entities retain their identities throughout eternity, even as heaven and earth remain separate. Members of the Church are "children of Abraham" by faith alone, separate from Israel. Thus, again,

> [7] Then recognize that those from faith, these are sons of Abraham. [8] Now the Scripture, when it saw in advance that the God would declare the Gentiles righteous from faith, declared in advance the gospel to Abraham: All the Gentiles will be blessed in you. [9] So then, those from faith are blessed with believing Abraham (Galatians 3.7-9).

Jews operated under an entirely different program than the Church—under Mosaic Law and saved by faith *and* works. Members of the Church, the body of Christ, are not under the Law but under grace (Romans 6.14), saved by faith alone—by believing Paul's gospel.

Paul used Abraham as an example to teach that in this age, Abraham's experience of salvation was the pattern for salvation after Paul's gospel: "Abraham believed the God and it was reckoned to him for righteousness" (Romans 4.3). No works were required. Abraham believed what God told him—he would be the father of many nations, etc. (Genesis 15.3-6) and was saved.

## A Problem Passage: Galatians 6.16

Perhaps the strongest "proof" text of those who teach the Church is Israel is Galatians 6.16. It reads:

| And as many as will walk by this rule, peace be on them, and mercy [and] [even] on the Israel of the God (Galatians 6.16). |
|---|
| καὶ ὅσοι τῷ κανόνι τούτῳ στοιχήσουσιν, εἰρήνη ἐπ' αὐτοὺς καὶ ἔλεος, καὶ ἐπὶ τὸν Ἰσραὴλ τοῦ θεοῦ. |

Two issues need to be resolved in this verse: 1) was Paul addressing one group or two? 2) If one group, what was it? If two groups, what were they? Those who maintain the Church is Israel argue Paul addressed one group, i.e., the Church which they claim is the Israel of God. Such a view requires the conjunction καί to be read with its ascensive sense, "even" rather than the more frequent connective sense "and." Thus, the passage would read, "and as many as who will walk by this rule, peace on them and mercy, **even** on the Israel of God."

If the passage is read with καί having its more frequent conjunctive sense two groups are in view: *those/them* and *the Israel of God*. The support for the reading of two groups is the following:

1. The connective sense "and" is found more frequently than its ascensive use, "even" and should be accepted unless context favors the ascensive use.
2. Syntactically, Paul repeated ἐπὶ "on": "on them" and "on the Israel of God."

| Καί in the Connective (and) Sense | |
|---|---|
| ἐπ' αὐτοὺς | One Group |
| ἐπὶ τὸν Ἰσραὴλ τοῦ θεοῦ | Another Group (Israel of God) |

or

| Καί in the Ascensive (even) Sense | |
|---|---|
| ἐπ' αὐτοὺς = ἐπὶ τὸν Ἰσραὴλ τοῦ θεοῦ | One Group |

Regarding Paul's phrase, "**And as many as will walk by this rule**," the "rule" of which Paul spoke was what he had written in Galatians about his gospel, living under grace, by faith, guided by the Holy Spirit, apart from being under the governance of the Mosaic Law. Thus, verse 15 reads, "For in Christ Jesus neither circumcision nor uncircumcision avails anything: Instead, a new creation" (cf. 2 Corinthians 5.17).

It seems slightly more likely Paul wrote of two groups given the fact he mentions the uncircumcision and the circumcision in verse 15 and because of the way he structured verse 16. But Paul could be addressing one group: the "those/them" being the "Israel of God." If this is the case, "Israel of God" is certainly not the Church, the body of Christ, but Jews saved under the gospel of the kingdom.

Paul's opponents in Galatians were Jews. They had caused problems in the matter of the salvation of Gentiles which had led to the Jerusalem Council (Acts 15, Galatians 2). Now, coming to Galatia, they were teaching believers had to live under the authority of the Mosaic Law, not for salvation, but to live the Christian life. Thus, Paul could have been targeting these believing Jews as "the Israel of God" and wished them peace *if they ceased creating discord among the Galatians and fell in line with his doctrines of grace.*

To make a case that the Church is Israel the Scriptures have to be massively twisted and contorted. No Scriptural support exists for such a view. Those who teach this make a garment out of whole cloth. They are apostates. At the end of the day, whether one takes καί in its ascensive or in its conjunctive sense and whether one gives weight to the repetition of ἐπί in both clauses is almost irrelevant. What determines the meaning of "Israel" in this verse is the same as what determines its meaning in every other Scripture. "Israel" *always*, without exception, means a *racial* descendant of Jacob. Lexically and theologically, it is *impossible* to interpret the Church as Israel.[17]

---

[17] That the term "Israel" *always* refers to the physical offspring of Jacob in both the Old Testament and the New Testament is seen from the following passages: Matthew 2.6, 20, 21; 8.10; 9.33; 10.6, 23; 15.24, 31; 19.28; 27.9, 42 Mark 12.29; 15.32; Luke 1.16, 54, 68, 80; 2.25, 32, 34; 4.25, 27; 7.9; 22.30; 24.21; John 1.31, 1.47, 49; 3.10; 12.13; Acts 1.6; 2.22, 36; 3.12; 4.10, 4.27; 5.21, 31, 35; 7.23, 37, 42; 9.15; 10.36; 13.16, 17; 13.23, 24; 21.28; 28.20; Romans 9.4, 6, 27, 31; 10.19, 21; 11.1, 2, 7, 25, 26; 1 Corinthians 10.18; 2 Corinthians 3.7; 3.13; 11.22; Galatians 6.16; Ephesians 2.12; Philippians 3.5; Hebrews 8.8, 10; 11.22; Revelation 2.14; 7.4; 21.12. The term "Israel" occurs 2,493 times in the Old Testament. As in the New Testament, it *always* refers to the physical offspring of Jacob.

# Chapter 9
# Paul and Hebrews

*And consider the patience of our Lord is salvation, even as also our beloved brother Paul, according to the wisdom given to him wrote to you, as also in all the epistles, when he speaks in them about these things, in which are some things difficult to understand, which the untaught and unstable distort, as also the other Scriptures to their own destruction (2 Peter 3.15-16).*

## Why Was Hebrews Written?

The epistle of Hebrews was written to instruct the Jews that as great as the Mosaic Law, Temple, and Levitical sacrifices were, Christ was superior (Hebrews 1.1-3, 4-2.18, 3.1-4.13, 4.14-10.18, 10.19-12.29). It revealed that reality, in the person and work of Christ, had replaced the shadows, symbols, and types of the Law. The Messiah had come and finished the work of salvation to which the Law and Prophets pointed (John 19.30). Salvation was possible only through Jesus of Nazareth. The choice was Christ or nothing.

## Authorship

A controversial but tantalizing question throughout church history has been the letter's authorship. Several persons have been named as possible authors: Barnabas, Apollos, Silas, Luke, James, Clement of Rome, Aquila, Priscilla, and Paul. For most of church history, Paul was the leading contender. But Paul has fallen into disfavor. Modern scholarship has all but dismissed him as the book's author. Anyone but Paul has become *de rigueur* and *chic* among professional theologians.

## Arguments Against Pauline Authorship

Five major objections are leveled against Paul's authoring Hebrews:[1]

1. The letter is anonymous, contrary to Paul's practice in his other letters.
2. The writing style is different and better than Paul.

---

[1] Dan Wallace wrote in "Hebrews: Introduction, Argument, and Outline," (https://goo.gl/a3iiBe) "the arguments against Pauline authorship, however, are conclusive" and that the authorship of Hebrews was "explicitly denied by Origen." But, as will be seen, Origen expressed *uncertainty*, not denial. Wallace also stated, "All in all, the external evidence counts for very little. The fact that it [Hebrews] finds a place in $P^{46}$, the earliest MS of the corpus Paulinum (c. 200 CE), ought not to be considered weighty." Wallace's statements are scholarly embarrassments.

3. The logical development is more tightly woven than is Paul's.
4. Spiritual eyewitnesses are appealed to (Hebrews 2.3) while Paul insisted on no intermediaries for his gospel (Galatians 1.12).
5. Timothy's imprisonment (Hebrews 13.23) does not seem to fit within Paul's lifetime since he is mentioned in Acts and Paul's letters as a free man.

## Consideration of Pauline Objections

### 1a. Anonymity

Paul's practice was to identify himself by name in his letters but Hebrews does not contain his name. As "the apostle of the Gentiles" (Romans 11.13), Paul's primary audience in his epistles were Gentiles. The audience of Hebrews were Jews. But throughout Acts, Paul's practice was to go first to Jews and then turn to Gentiles after they rejected Christ (Acts 13, 18, 28). The Lord had revealed to Paul that the Jews would not receive his message (Acts 22.17-18). But Paul continued to evangelize them because he loved them.[2]

Paul had a strong personality. This is clear from the record of Acts as well as his letters. His personality did not change when he was saved and God channeled his zeal for His purposes. Paul must have asked himself a thousand times how he, with all his brilliance and education, could have missed the One to whom the Law and the prophets pointed. He had been taught by one of Israel's greatest rabbis and was a "rising star" among the Pharisees. Despite this, he failed miserably. This must have shaken him tremendously. Paul thought if he, who had been so blind, could be changed, his nation could also. This motivated him in evangelizing Jews.

But the Jews steadfastly rebuffed Paul's message of salvation, even trying to kill him. Paul's efforts ended with his imprisonment in Rome. Due to the intense Jewish opposition against him, it is reasonable Paul would not identify himself as the letter's author. Clement of Alexandria (c. 150-215 A.D.) recognized such an explanation in an account written by Eusebius (c. 263-339 A.D.):

> 1. To sum up briefly, he has given in the *Hypotyposes* abridged accounts of all canonical Scripture, not omitting the disputed books,—I refer to Jude and the other Catholic epistles, and Barnabas and the so-called Apocalypse of Peter. 2. He says that the Epistle to the Hebrews is the work

---

[2] Jewish evangelism was included in Paul's commission. The Lord told Ananias, "Go. For this man is a chosen vessel to Me, to carry My name before the Gentiles, and kings, and the sons of Israel" (Acts 9.15).

> of Paul, and that it was written to the Hebrews in the Hebrew language; but that Luke translated it carefully and published it for the Greeks, and hence the same style of expression is found in this epistle and in the Acts. 3. But he says that the words, Paul the Apostle, were probably not prefixed, because, in sending it to the Hebrews, who were prejudiced and suspicious of him, he wisely did not wish to repel them at the very beginning by giving his name. 4. Farther on he says: But now, as the blessed presbyter said, since the Lord being the apostle of the Almighty, was sent to the Hebrews, Paul, as sent to the Gentiles, on account of his modesty did not subscribe himself an apostle of the Hebrews, through respect for the Lord, and because being a herald and apostle of the Gentiles he wrote to the Hebrews out of his superabundance (Eusebius, *Church History* 6.14.1-4).

Eta Linnemann, responding to Donald Guthrie's argument that anonymity did not conform to Pauline style, wrote: "*The truth is, anonymity is not a question of style but of necessity. Whoever writes anonymously has grounds for so doing*" (her italics). She also noted that no one who denies Hebrews to Paul has provided a reason why other proposed authors wrote it anonymously.[3]

The reality is that the letter's anonymity strongly argues *in favor of* Pauline authorship. Acts reveals the suspicion and hatred of the Jews towards Paul and Paul did not wish to handicap the letter's argument by attaching his name. Luke revealed how volatile an effect a word could have upon the Jews:

> [21] Then He said to me, Go! For I will send you far away to *the* Gentiles.[22] Now they kept listening to him until this word.[4] Then they raised their voice, saying, Away from the earth with such! He is not fit to live (Acts 22.21-22)!

Who besides Paul would wish to remain anonymous?

## 1b. Placement of Hebrews

Hebrews is *always* found in the body of Paul's letters in the manuscripts.[5] The four oldest manuscript codices are the following:

---

[3] Eta Linnemann, "A Call for a Retrial in the Case of the Epistle to the Hebrews," *Faith and Mission*, vol. 19.2, 2002, p. 37. Linnemann takes to task several arguments against Pauline authorship and demolishes them. See also Ben Witherington's article, "The Influence of Galatians on Hebrews," *New Testament Studies*, vol. 37, no. 1, January 1991, 146-152 which addresses literary and theological similarities between Galatians and Hebrews.

[4] This "word" was "Gentiles" and shows the animosity of Jews to the idea that God would send a Jew to Gentiles.

[5] William H. P. Hatch, "The Position of Hebrews in the Canon of the New Testament," *The Harvard Theological Review*, Vol. 29, No. 2 (Apr., 1936),

1. Codex Alexandrinus (02, A), written in the 5th century A.D., contains all Paul's letters. In the British Museum.
2. Codex Ephraemi Rescriptus (04, C), written in the 5th century A.D., is a palimpsest which originally contained Old and New Testaments. It contains 145 of the original 238 pages of the New Testament, except 2 John and 2 Thessalonians. No book is complete. In the Bibliothèque Nationale.
3. Codex Sinaiticus (01, א), probably written in the 4th century A.D. Only one of the four codices that contains all the books of the New Testament. In the British Museum.
4. Codex Vaticanus (03, B), written in the 4th century A.D. contains all books except 1 and 2 Timothy, Titus, Philemon, and Revelation. In the Vatican Library.

Paul's letters in these manuscripts follow the four Gospels, Acts and the general letters. In all the manuscripts there are fourteen Pauline letters and their sequence is uniform:

| | |
|---|---|
| Romans | 1 Thessalonians |
| 1 Corinthians | 2 Thessalonians |
| 2 Corinthians | Hebrews |
| Galatians | 1 Timothy |
| Ephesians | 2 Timothy |
| Philippians | Titus |
| Colossians | Philemon |

Hebrews follows 2 Thessalonians in these codices.[6] Those who produced the codices arranged the New Testament into five units:

1. The Four Gospels (Matthew, Mark, Luke, John)
2. The Acts of the Apostles
3. The General Epistles (James, Peter, John, Jude)
4. The Pauline Epistles
5. The Apocalypse

The order of these five groups differs in some manuscripts and the Pauline Epistles vary in their position with respect to the other four groups but Acts is always combined with the general letters. Some manuscripts start with Paul's letters followed by Acts and general letters, some start with the Gospels followed by the letters of Paul,

---

pp. 133. Professor Hatch made the definitive study of this subject. The Chester Beatty collection of manuscripts is the oldest known surviving copy of the Pauline letters (dated end of the 2nd century A.D.) and includes Hebrews among the Pauline writings (F.F. Bruce, *Paul: Apostle of the Heart Set Free.* Grand Rapids: Eerdmans, 2000, p. 466).

[6] Later manuscripts placed Hebrews at the end of the Pauline corpus.

followed by Acts and the general letters, and some contain Acts and general letters only. Manuscripts which combine Gospels and Acts only or the general letters without Acts are extremely rare. Thus, Acts essentially functions as an introduction to the general epistles. The reason for this is because Luke wrote Acts to explain to Jews why the kingdom of God was not established on earth. The kingdom program concerns *Israel*, the audience of the Gospels and the letters of James, Peter, John, and Jude. Only much later did editors and revisers move Paul's letters between Acts and general epistles.

Thus, the four oldest existing manuscripts of the New Testament reveal that Hebrews was regarded as a letter of Paul and followed 2 Thessalonians.[7] The title "To the Hebrews," Πρὸς Ἑβραίους, conforms to the nomenclature of Paul's letters to particular audiences, e.g., "To the Romans," "To the Galatians," etc. In contrast, the general epistles are named after their authors, e.g., James, 1 Peter, 1 John, Jude, etc.

## 2. Writing Style

Scholars recognized early in Church history the writing style of Hebrews was different from Paul's epistles. Origen (c. 184-253 A.D.) wrote, "Whoever wrote the epistle, God only knows for sure." Opponents of Pauline authorship have used this statement to support their case. Removed from its context, his declaration is a half-truth. Eusebius preserved Origen's complete pronouncement:

> 11. In addition he makes the following statements in regard to the Epistle to the Hebrews in his Homilies upon it: That the verbal style of the epistle entitled 'To the Hebrews,' is not rude like the language of the apostle, who acknowledged himself 'rude in speech' (2 Corinthians 11:6) that is, in expression; but that its diction is purer Greek, anyone who has the power to discern differences of phraseology will acknowledge. 12. Moreover, that the thoughts of the epistle are admirable, and not inferior to the acknowledged apostolic writings, anyone who carefully examines the apostolic text will admit. 13. Farther on he adds: If I gave my opinion, I should say that the thoughts are those of the apostle, but the diction and phraseology are those of someone who remembered the apostolic teachings and wrote down at his leisure what had been said by his teacher. Therefore, if any church holds that this epistle is by Paul, let it be commended for this. For not without reason have the ancients handed it down as Paul's. 14. But who wrote the epistle, in truth, God knows. The statement of some who have gone before us is that Clement, bishop of the Romans, wrote the epistle, and of others that Luke, the author of the

---

[7] 1 and 2 Thessalonians were the first letters Paul wrote. More will be said about this in the discussion on the date of Hebrews.

> Gospel and the Acts, wrote it. But let this suffice on these matters. (Eusebius, *Church History*, 6.25.11-14).

Origen believed Paul *authored* Hebrews but that it was *written* by another. The nature of Origen's doubt concerned style and composition, not substance. In his other writings, Origen ascribed authorship of Hebrews to Paul, e.g., *De Principiis*, *Against Celsus*, *To Africanus*.[8]

Eusebius himself wrote:

> Paul's fourteen epistles are well known and undisputed. It is not indeed right to overlook the fact that some have rejected the Epistle to the Hebrews, saying that it is disputed by the church of Rome, on the ground that it was not written by Paul. But what has been said concerning this epistle by those who lived before our time I shall quote in the proper place. In regard to the so-called Acts of Paul, I have not found them among the undisputed writings. (Eusebius, *Church History* 3.3.5)
>
> For as Paul had addressed the Hebrews in the language of his country; some say that the evangelist Luke, others that Clement, translated the epistle. (Eusebius, *Church History* 3.38.2-3)

Paul's letters of Romans to Philemon number thirteen. Hebrews makes fourteen. Could Luke have collaborated with Paul in writing Hebrews? It is reasonable since he 1) was Paul's constant traveling companion, 2) was familiar with Paul's messages to the Jews (serving as Paul's personal historian and physician), 3) was Jewish, 4) was with Paul during his imprisonment in Rome, and 5) was Paul's sole companion shortly before his execution (2 Timothy 4.11).[9]

## 3. Logical Development

The objection, "the logical development is more tightly woven than is Paul's" is baffling. The primary issues of any writing involve purpose and audience. Paul's letters of Romans through Philemon addressed mainly Gentile congregations while Hebrews addressed Jews.

For this objection to stand against Pauline authorship one must demonstrate a book such as Romans is inferior in logical development to Hebrews and show that Paul could not construct a tightly woven

---

[8] See Benno Zuiddam. "What Origen Really Taught About the Authorship of Hebrews." https://tinyurl.com/ye228z7m.

[9] For recent arguments about Pauline authorship of Hebrews see: David L. Allen, *Lukan Authorship of Hebrews*, B & H Academic, 2010.; Dave Black, *Origen on the Authorship of Hebrews* (2004); Andrew W. Pitts and Joshua F. Walker, *The Authorship of Hebrews: A Further Development in the Luke-Paul Relationship* (2013).

logical argument. This is a weighty burden. Paul was learned—taught and trained by the greatest Pharisaic rabbi of his day, Gamaliel. Paul had many encounters with the Jews during his ministry, preaching and reasoning with them. These afforded him many opportunities to consider their objections and refine his arguments. Shortly after Paul arrived in Rome he met with the Jewish leaders and Luke wrote, "he expounded and testified the kingdom of God, persuading them concerning Jesus, both out of the law of Moses, and out of the prophets, from morning till evening" (Acts 28.23). Consider Paul's words at the synagogue in Pisidia Antioch during his first missionary journey:

> 16 So Paul got up and after he signaled with his hand, said, Men, Israelites, and those who fear the God, listen. 17 The God of this people of Israel chose our fathers and exalted the people in their sojourn in the land of Egypt. And He brought them out of it with *a* raised arm. 18 And for *a* period of about forty years, He endured them in the wilderness. 19 And after He destroyed seven nations in the land of Canaan, He divided their land to them. 20 And after these things, about four hundred and fifty years, He gave *them* judges, until Samuel the prophet. 21 Then they asked for *a* king and God gave them Saul, son of Kish, *a* man of the tribe of Benjamin, for forty years. 22 And when He removed him, He raised up David for them as king, to whom also He said when He testified, I found David, the *son* of Jesse, *a* man after My heart, who will do all My will. 23 From this man's descendants, the God, according to promise, raised to Israel *the* Savior, Jesus, 24 whom John proclaimed before His coming, *a* baptism of repentance to all the people of Israel. 25 Now as John was accomplishing his mission, he kept saying, Whom do you think I am? I am not *He*. But behold, One comes after me of whom I am not worthy to untie the sandal of His feet. 26 Men, brethren, sons of *the* family of Abraham, and those among you who fear the God, the word of this salvation was sent to you. 27 For those who live in Jerusalem and their rulers, since they did not recognize Him and the voices of the prophets that are read every Sabbath, they fulfilled *them* when they condemned *Him*. 28 And while they found no cause for death, they insisted Pilate execute Him. 29 Now when they finished all the things written about Him, after they took *Him* down from the tree, they placed *Him* in *a* tomb. 30 But the God raised Him from the dead, 31 who appeared for many days to those who came up with Him from Galilee to Jerusalem, who are now His witnesses to the people. 32 And we proclaim to you good news—the promise made to the fathers, 33 that the God has fulfilled this to us, their children, by raising up Jesus, even as it has been written in the second Psalm, You are My Son, today I have begotten you. 34 Now because He raised Him from *the* dead,

> no more to return to decay, He spoke thus, I will give you
> the holy and sure *blessings* of David. 35 Therefore, also in
> another *psalm*, He said, You will not allow your Holy One
> to see decay. 36 For David, after he served God's purpose in
> his own generation, fell asleep and was placed with his
> fathers, and saw decay. 37 But the One the God raised up did
> not see decay. 38 Therefore, let it be known to you, men,
> brethren, that through this One, forgiveness of sins is
> proclaimed to you. 39 And from everything from which you
> could not be declared righteous by *the* Law of Moses,
> everyone who believes in Him is declared righteous.
> 40 Watch out, therefore, that it might not come upon you
> what has been spoken in the prophets: 41 Behold, scoffers,
> wonder, and perish. For I work *a* work in your days, *a* work
> that you would never believe, even if someone should tell
> you. (Acts 13.16-43).

Is this a tightly woven, logical argument? Particular attention should be paid to verses 38-41. Is this not the essential argument of Hebrews?

## 4. Spiritual Eyewitnesses

Another argument against Pauline authorship has been Hebrews 2.3:

> 1 Because of this, we must pay closer attention to the things
> we heard, lest we should drift away. 2 For if the word which
> was spoken through angels became steadfast and every
> transgression and disobedience received *a* just penalty,
> 3 how will we escape, if we disregard such *a* great salvation,
> which at the first began to be spoken through the Lord, and
> was confirmed to us by those who heard, 4 since God
> testified with signs, and wonders, and by various miracles
> and allocations of the Holy Spirit according to His will
> (Hebrews 2.1-4)?

Those who make this argument assert the phrase in verse 3, "confirmed to us" means the writer learned the gospel from those who heard Jesus and that this statement is contrary to Paul's declaration that he received the gospel directly from the ascended Lord (Galatians 1.11-12; Ephesians 3.3). Thus, Paul Ellingworth wrote:

> The single most striking piece of internal evidence against Pauline authorship of Hebrews is the author's explicit statement that the message which began with Jesus ὑπὸ τῶν ἀκουσάντων εἰς ἡμᾶς ἐβεβαιώθη (2:3); in other words, that the author and his readers received the gospel indirectly.[10]

[10] Paul Ellingworth, *The Epistle to the Hebrews: A Commentary on the Greek Text*, Eerdmans, 1993, p. 7.

Three major problems exist with this objection. The first concerns what the passage says. The verb βεβαιόω means "confirmed." It does *not* mean "learned" or "received." It is used 8 times in the New Testament (Mark 16.20; Romans 15.8, 1 Corinthians 1.6, 8; 2 Corinthians 1.21; Colossians 2.7; Hebrews 2.3, 13.9).

The second problem is that those who think Hebrews 2.3 is evidence against Pauline authorship think the gospel the Twelve proclaimed was the same gospel as what Paul proclaimed. It was not. The Twelve preached the "gospel of the kingdom" and faith focused upon the *identity* of Christ, who He was, the Messiah, the Son of God (Matthew 16.15-17; John 1.49, 11.25-27; Acts 8.37, 9.20). Paul proclaimed the "gospel of the grace of God" in which the focus of faith was on the *work* of Christ—He died for our sins and rose from the dead (1 Corinthians 15.1-4). These were entirely different gospel messages.

Lastly, the personal pronouns, "we" and "us" referred to Jews, not to Paul: "How shall we (Jews) escape, if we (Jews) neglect so great salvation; which at the first began to be spoken by the Lord, and was confirmed unto us (Jews) by them that heard." The verse has *nothing* to do with Paul as an individual. It has to do with Israel.

### 5. Timothy's Imprisonment

Hebrews 13.22-23 reads:

> [22] Now I urge you brethren, endure the message of the exhortation, for I wrote to you with few words. [23] You know our brother Timothy has been freed, with whom I will see you if he should come soon.

This objection to Pauline authorship is that Timothy's imprisonment does not seem able to fit within Paul's lifetime since Timothy is not mentioned in Acts or in Paul's letters as being imprisoned. Therefore, it is reasoned, the writer was not Paul.

The word translated "has been freed" is ἀπολελυμένον, the present passive participle of ἀπολύω. Some have thought this meant "freed from confinement." Others have thought it meant "sent away on some message to some other place." Paul did not use ἀπολύω in his letters but Luke used it frequently, twenty-nine times in his gospel and Acts. If the meaning is release from confinement, the lack of evidence of Timothy's imprisonment is not a strong objection. Paul wrote Aristarchus was his fellow prisoner (Colossians 4.10) as with Epaphras (Philemon 23) but no other record exists of their imprisonment.

## Audience and Date of the Letter

Consider the following statement by Peter:

> [15] And consider the patience of our Lord *is* salvation, even as also our beloved brother Paul, according to the wisdom given to him wrote to you, [16] as also in all the epistles, when

> he speaks in them about these things, in which are some things difficult to understand, which the untaught and unstable distort, as also the other Scriptures to their own destruction (2 Peter 3.15-16).

Peter wrote "to the chosen resident foreigners of *the* Dispersion of Pontus, Galatia, Cappadocia, Asia, and Bithynia" (1 Peter 1.1). His second letter addressed the same audience (2 Peter 3.1) and stated Paul wrote these same Jews.[11] Thus, the audience to whom Paul wrote Hebrews were Jews in Asia Minor. Paul's statement in 2 Timothy 1.15 sheds additional light on this matter. He wrote Timothy:

> You know this: everyone in Asia deserted me—among whom are Phygellus and Hermogenes.

Paul wrote Galatians to combat the teaching of the Judaizers who were trying to bring the Galatians under the Mosaic Law. These Jews were of "the party of the circumcision." The message of Hebrews is that Christ was superior to all that went before in Judaism and had fulfilled the Law.

Most who think Paul wrote Hebrews think he wrote it late in his ministry.[12] But why would Paul write such a letter so late in his ministry when his practice was to address Jews first and then turn to Gentiles? Why wait to write Hebrews only a few years before the destruction of the Temple and shortly before his death (2 Timothy 4.6)? The issue of the place of the Mosaic Law regarding salvation had been a subject at the Jerusalem Council in 51 A.D. (Acts 15.5-7) as well as afterward, concerning Christian living, e.g., his letter to the Galatians.

More likely is that Paul wrote Hebrews *early* in his ministry, probably during the eighteen months he was in Corinth teaching among the Jews (Acts 18.11). Such a conclusion is supported by the position Hebrews occupies in the oldest codices, Sinaiticus (א), Alexandrinus (A), Vaticanus (B), and Ephraemi (C), where Hebrews is found after 2 Thessalonians.[13] 1 and 2 Thessalonians were probably written in 51-52 A.D., shortly after the Jerusalem Council. Given the placement of Hebrews after 2 Thessalonians in the oldest codices, it is likely

---

[11] If Hebrews was not that letter, what letter did Paul write to Jews? Critics of Pauline authorship of Hebrews have no answer.

[12] Internal evidence eliminates the possibility Hebrews was written after 70 A.D. since the Temple and its operations were clearly continuing. Had the Temple been destroyed, it could not have escaped mention. See John A.T. Robinson, *Redating the New Testament*, London, SCM Press, 1976 for an analysis of the evidence in dating New Testament texts. Robinson, a liberal scholar, stunned the scholarly community by dating all New Testament books before 70 A.D.—earlier than most conservative scholars.

[13] The critical editions of Lachmann, Tischendorf, and Tregelles have Hebrews after 2 Thessalonians. See http://goo.gl/96YBqa.

Hebrews was written about 53 A.D. In his first missionary journey, Paul made oral arguments to the Jews regarding the Messiah (Acts 13). A formal, written text was needed to support these arguments to the Jews "zealous of the Law." But to attach his name to such a treatise would have compromised his purpose. In addition, Hebrews 10.25 supports an early date.

Finally, most commentators believe Hebrews was written from Italy based on Hebrews 13.24 which reads:

> Greet all those leading you and all the saints. Those from Italy [οἱ ἀπὸ τῆς Ἰταλίας] greet you.

This is possible, but unlikely. Another explanation is more felicitous. The text, οἱ ἀπὸ τῆς Ἰταλίας, "those from Italy" probably referred to Aquila and Priscilla who had fled Rome due to Claudius' decree against the Jews (Acts 18.2).[14] Such a view is grammatically supported by the use of the preposition ἀπό which denotes separation. What was more natural than to convey their greetings to fellow Jewish believers scattered throughout Asia? Paul had become acquainted with Aquila and Priscilla in Corinth. Being tentmakers like Paul, they spent many hours discussing the Scriptures and the Law while sewing (Acts 18.3).[15] During this time, Paul spoke in the synagogue every sabbath (Acts 18.4). These exchanges allowed him to hone his arguments to the Jews.

Paul sailed to Caesarea and then went to Antioch in Syria, where he stayed a while (Acts 18.23). He then traveled to Galatia and then Phrygia (Acts 18.23). It is possible Paul delivered his letter to the Hebrews in this visit. These factors favor Paul's writing Hebrews early, around 53 A.D.

## Literary Similarities

Paul wrote the Thessalonians:

> [17] The greeting *is* in my own hand, Paul, which is *my* identifier in every letter. Thus, I write: [18] The grace of our Lord Jesus Christ *be* with you all![16] Amen (2 Thessalonians 3.17-18).

---

[14] The inference of the place from οἱ ἀπὸ τῆς Ἰταλίας (Hebrews 13.24), is uncertain. In the epistolary style it may imply the writer was at that time out of Italy or in Italy. This would be more distinctly expressed by ἐν Ἰταλίᾳ or οἱ ἐξ. The brethren may have been fugitives from Italy (so Bleek). The latter view seems more natural and is defended by Theodoret, who knew Greek as his mother tongue (Schaff, Philip. *History of the Christian Church*. 3rd rev. Vol. 1, p. 817 fn. Scribner, New York, 1889.

[15] Aquila and Priscilla were faithful and vital co-workers with Paul in his ministry (Acts 18.1-4; Romans 16.3; 1 Corinthians 16.19; 2 Timothy 4.19).

[16] Paul's grace salutation in his own hand was his authentication of his letters.

Paul wrote the above because the Thessalonians had received a letter purportedly from him that the Day of the Lord (the Tribulation) had come (2 Thessalonians 2.1-2). This upset them because he had taught that Christ would deliver them from the Tribulation (1 Thessalonians 1.9-10, 4.13-18, 5.9-11). Paul normally dictated his letters but included a "grace" statement in his handwriting for a "sign" (σημεῖον) of his authorship (cf. 1 Corinthians 16.21; Colossians 4.18) to foil further forgeries. Paul's "grace" salutations are found in all 14 letters.

| "Grace" Salutations | |
|---|---|
| Romans 1.7, 16.20, 24 | 1 Thessalonians 1.1, 5.28 |
| 1 Corinthians 1.3, 16.23 | 2 Thessalonians 1.2, 3.18 |
| 2 Corinthians 1.2, 13.14 | 1 Timothy 1.2, 6.21 |
| Galatians 1.13 2 | 2 Timothy 1.2, 4.22 |
| Ephesians 1.2, 6.24, 6.18 | Titus 1.4, 3.15 |
| Philippians 1.2, 4.23 | Philemon 1.3, 1.25 |
| Colossians 1.2, 4.18 | Hebrews 13.25 |

Other literary indicators of Pauline authorship include his usage of Habakkuk 2.4, quoted three times in the New Testament: Romans 1.17, Galatians 3.11, and Hebrews 10.38 and accord with Paul's great emphasis on faith (Romans 3.26-30, 4.3-5, 5.1; Galatians 2.16, Ephesians 2.8-9, et. al. cf. Hebrews 4.2, 6.1, 12, 10.22, 38-39, 11.1-9, 11, 13, 17, 20-24, 27-31, 33, 39, 12.2, 13.7). Paul exalted Christ over all created beings (Ephesians 1.10, 20, 4.10; Philippians 2.9-10; Colossians 1.14-21; 2 Thessalonians 1.7 cf. Hebrews 1.1-14, 4.14, 7.26, 8.1). Another Pauline subject expounded in Hebrews is a heavenly calling (1 Corinthians 15.49; 2 Corinthians 5.1-2; Ephesians 1.3, 2.6; Philippians 3.20; 2 Timothy 4.18 cf. Hebrews 3.1, 11.16, 12.22. The expression "but now" (νυν[ὶ] δὲ) are found throughout Paul's writings and in Hebrews (Hebrews 2.8, 8.6, 9.26, 11.16, 12.26.14).[17] Paul also is the only writer who used ἐνίστημι (Romans 8.38; 1 Corinthians 3.22, 7.26; Galatians 1.4; 2 Thessalonians 2.2; 2 Timothy 3.1; Hebrews 9.9).

One example of interest is the word ἱλαστήριον. It is used twice in the New Testament. Paul used it in Romans 3.25, "Whom God hath set forth to be a propitiation (ἱλαστήριον) through faith in his blood, to declare his righteousness for the remission of sins that are past, through the forbearance of God." The other use is Hebrews 9.5, "And over it

---

[17] David Alan Black. "Who Wrote Hebrews? The Internal and External Evidence Reexamined." *Faith and Mission*, Vol. 18:2 (Spring 1999), pp. 32-51. Black notes many Pauline literary affinities in Hebrews. See also Daniel A. Penick. "Paul's Epistles Compared with One Another and with the Epistle to the Hebrews." *The American Journal of Philology*, Vol. 42, No. 1 (1921), pp. 58-72 (http://www.jstor.org/stable/pdf/289398.pdf).

the cherubim of glory shadowing the mercy seat (ἱλαστήριον); of which we cannot now speak particularly. Paul equated Christ's sacrifice with the mercy seat.

Hebrews also contains several rare words found in Paul's letters not found elsewhere in the New Testament or the Septuagint: αἰδώς (Hebrews 12.13; 1 Timothy 2.9), ἄναθεωρέω (Hebrews 13.7; Acts 17.23), ἀνυπότακτος (Hebrews 2.8; 1 Timothy. 1.9; Titus 1.6, 10), ἀπείθεια (Hebrews 4.6, 11; Romans 11.30, 32; Ephesians 2.2; Colossians 3.5), ἀπόλουσις (Hebrews 11.25; 1 Timothy 6.17), ἀφιλάργυρος (Hebrews 13.5; 1 Timothy 3.3), ἔνδικος (Hebrews 2.1; Romans 3.8), ἐνεργής (Hebrews 4.12; 1 Corinthians 16.9; Philemon 6), ἐφάπαξ (Hebrews 7.27; 10.10; Romans 9.10; 1 Corinthians 15.6), κοσμικός (Hebrews 9.11; Titus 2.12), μιμητής (Hebrews 6.12; 1 Corinthians 4.16, etc.), νεκρόω (Hebrews 11.12; Romans 4.19; Colossians 3.5), ὀρέγομαι (Hebrews 11.16; 1 Timothy 3.1; 6.10), παρακοή (Hebrews 2.2; Romans 5.10; 2 Corinthians 10.6), πληροφορία (Hebrews 6.11; 10.22; Colossians 2.2; 1 Thessalonians 1.5), φιλοξενία (Hebrews 13.2; Romans 12.13).[18]

The author's purpose in writing is revealed in Hebrews 13.22:

> Now I urge you brethren, endure the message of the exhortation, for I wrote to you with few words.

The word "exhortation" is παράκλησις. Only Luke and Paul used this word. Paul delivered such an exhortation (παράκλησις) to the Jews at Pisidia Antioch (Acts 13.15).

## Conclusion

Evidence for Pauline authorship of Hebrews is more than substantial: it is *overwhelming*. The weight of external and internal evidence easily overrides issues of style, particularly since Luke was Paul's constant companion and could have penned the letter. Objections against Pauline authorship are vapid. Alternate authors have all the weaknesses and none of the strengths of Paul.

---

[18] Schaff, Philip. *History of the Christian Church*. 3rd rev. Vol. 1, p. 824. Scribner, New York, 1889.

# Chapter 10
# Paul on Prayer

*Do not worry about anything. But in everything, by prayer and entreaty, with thanksgiving let your requests be made known to the God (Philippians 4.6).*

Prayer is talking with God. Prayer has always characterized godly men and women for it is through prayer that we communicate with our Creator and Savior. Through prayer, believers express their concerns, fears, joys, needs, thanks, and praise to the One who knows and loves us like no other.

## Jesus' Instruction on Prayer

During His earthly ministry the Lord instructed the Twelve how they should pray:

> [5] And when you may pray, you will not be as the hypocrites. For they love standing in the synagogues and on the corners of streets to pray so they might be seen by mankind. Truly I tell you, They have their reward. [6] But you, when you should pray, go to your room. And after you close your door, pray to your Father, the One in the secret. And your Father, the One who sees in the secret, will reward you openly. [7] Now do not use useless repetitions like the Gentiles when you pray. For they think that by their many words they will be heard. [8] Therefore, do not be like them. For your Father knows what things you need before you ask Him.
>
> [9] So therefore, pray this way: Our Father, the One in the heavens, Holy be your name. [10] Your kingdom come. Your will be done, as in heaven also on earth. [11] Give us our needed bread. [12] And forgive us our offences even as we forgive our offenders. [13] And do not bring us into *a* test, but deliver us from the evil one. For yours is the kingdom and the power and the glory forever. Amen. [14] For if should forgive mankind their trespasses, your heavenly Father will also forgive you. [15] But if you should not forgive mankind their trespasses, neither will your Father forgive your trespasses (Matthew 6.5-15).

While the content of this prayer was addressed to Jewish believers under the Law certain truths are applicable for the Church, the body of Christ. They include the following:

1. Do not pray to parade your godliness. Pray to God privately.
2. Do not use empty repetitions in prayer.
3. Recognize who God is your relationship to Him.

4. Pray to God recognizing where God is and His holiness.
5. Pray for daily provision.
6. Ask God not to bring us into trials but to deliver us.
7. Recognize God rules and all power and glory are His forever.

## Paul's Instruction on Prayer

Portions of the prayer Jesus taught His disciples *do not concern us* as members of the Church, the body of Christ. Indeed, parts of this prayer would be *wrong to pray* in light of Paul's instruction from the risen Lord. What are these?

God's prophetic program focused on Israel, particularly with regard to His earthly kingdom, Israel's great hope, manifested by hundreds of Old Testament passages. The Lord instructed His disciples to pray that His kingdom be established on earth (verse 10). We should desire this also but an earthly kingdom is not a promise God has given the Church. Heaven, not earth, is the destiny of members of the body of Christ.

The other matter altogether different is forgiveness. Jesus instructed the Twelve that to receive God's forgiveness required forgiving others (verses 12, 14, and 15). Under the gospel of the kingdom, one had to forgive another to be forgiven.

Paul taught the opposite. He wrote:

> In whom we have the redemption through His blood, the forgiveness [ἄφεσις] of the sins, according to the riches of His grace (Ephesians 1.7; cf. Colossians 1.14).
>
> And you, while you were dead in the trespasses and the uncircumcision of your flesh, He made you alive with Him, for He forgave [χαρίζομαι] all your trespasses (Colossians 2.13).

Under Paul's gospel of grace, believers *have been forgiven* by God. Forgiveness is an accomplished fact. For members of the body of Christ, forgiving others *results from* God's forgiveness rather than a *condition of* God's forgiveness. Thus, Paul wrote the Ephesians:

> But be kind, compassionate, to one another, forgiving [χαριζόμενοι] each other, as also the God by Christ also forgave [ἐχαρίσατο][1] you (Ephesians 4.32).

Jesus taught His disciples that God's forgiveness depended on forgiving others. Paul, from his instruction by the ascended Lord, taught that believers of his gospel have been forgiven and because of this should forgive. What a difference! This is yet another example of

---

[1] The verb χαριζόμενοι is a present middle participle and ἐχαρίσατο is an aorist middle indicative. Believers are to forgive one another because Christ forgave us.

the vast difference between God's program with Israel, evidenced in the Old Testament and Gospels, compared to His program with the Church, evidenced in Paul's letters.

## Paul's Prayers

Jesus in His earthly ministry gave a model prayer to His disciples and instructed them how to pray. With God's new program of the Church, the Lord needed to provide instruction for how *we* should pray. He did. The Lord in His heavenly ministry instructed Paul and Paul taught that members of the Church should copy or imitate him. Paul's prayers reveal how we should pray.

The first thing to note is that Paul taught that our praying should be *ceaseless*. In his first letter, he commanded the Thessalonians:

> Pray unceasingly (1 Thessalonians 5.17).

Paul practiced what he preached. Many verses—Romans 1.9; 1 Corinthians 1.4, 3.8; Ephesians 1.16, 5.20, 6.18; Colossians 1.3, 9; Philippians 1.4; Philemon 1.4; 1 Thessalonians 1.2, 2.13; 2 Thessalonians 1.3, 11—show Paul's unceasing prayers for believers. This should be our practice also. Let us examine some of Paul's prayers to learn how we, as members of the Church, the body of Christ, should pray.

## 1 Thessalonians 3.11-13

> 11 Now how we wish that our God and Father Himself and our Lord Jesus Christ, to direct our way to you. 12 And how we wish the Lord to increase and abound you in the love for one another and for everyone, even as we also for you, 13 so your hearts might be strengthened, blameless in holiness before our God and Father at the coming of our Lord Jesus Christ with all His saints.

Paul prayed that God would 1) direct (κατευθύνω)[2] his way in ministering to the Thessalonians, 2) for the Thessalonians to increase (πλεονάζω)[3] and abound or overflow (περισσεύω) in love towards one another and all people, even as Paul did towards them[4] and 3) this increase in love was to establish or firmly fix their hearts blameless, free from fault in holiness (dative of sphere), i.e., in the realm of holiness at the Lord's coming.

When the Lord returns for His Church, members of the body of Christ will receive resurrection bodies with no sin nature. Paul desired that believers experience holiness in anticipation of what they would become at Christ's return.

---

[2] The verb κατευθύνω means to guide or remove obstacles in one's path.
[3] Only used by Paul (7x) except in 2 Peter 1.8. It means to abound or increase.
[4] This is an example of Paul's command for believers to imitate or copy him.

## 1 Thessalonians 5.23-24

> [23] Now may the God of the peace Himself sanctify you completely. And may your whole spirit, and soul, and body be preserved blameless at the coming of our Lord Jesus Christ. [24] The One who calls you is faithful, who will also do *it*.

Paul prayed for 1) the Thessalonians' sanctification, 2) that their spirit (πνεῦμα), soul (ψυχή), and body (σῶμα) [5] be preserved blameless until Christ's coming, and 3) recognized God is faithful and will do this.

Paul wrote of the coming of the Lord, i.e., the Rapture, in each of these prayers. The Pre-Tribulational Rapture is the Church's "blessed hope" (Titus 2.13). Teaching this great doctrine cannot be overemphasized.

Believing the Pre-Tribulational Rapture is not essential for *salvation*. However, one cannot be a mature or *obedient* Christian apart from it since Paul *commanded* believers to encourage (present active imperative of παρακαλέω) one another with it (1 Thessalonians 4.18, 5.11). To not teach and encourage believers with the Pre-Tribulation Rapture is to disobey God.

## 2 Thessalonians 1.11-12

> [11] For which also we always pray for you, so our God might deem you worthy of the calling, and might complete every desire of goodness and work of faith with power, [12] so that the name of our Lord Jesus Christ might be glorified in you and you in Him, according to the grace of our God and *the* Lord Jesus Christ.

This prayer reveals Paul's praying without ceasing (1 Thessalonians 5.17) and Paul prayed that 1) God would consider the Thessalonians worthy of their calling, 2) complete (πληρόω) the desire of His goodness, 3) and the work of faith in power. The phrase, "faith with power" (πίστεως ἐν δυνάμει) reveals how a believer grows in Christ. Salvation begins by faith and continues that way. The believer matures and is made holy by a life of faith through the power of the indwelling Holy Spirit. Paul continued, praying that 4) the name of Christ might be glorified in them (through godliness and maturity), 5) that they might be glorified (ἐνδοξάζομαι) in Him (by faith and obedience) and that 6) this is to be accomplished according to the grace of our God and Christ.

Paul's statement, "The name of our Lord Jesus Christ may be glorified in you and you in him" refers especially to His return. The preceding verse reads:

---

[5] The believer is composed of body, soul, and spirit. We are tripartite beings.

> When He will come to be glorified [ἐνδοξάζομαι] by His saints and to be marveled at by all who believed, because our testimony to you was believed in that day.

Paul used the verb ἐνδοξάζομαι only twice, both times in these verses. Christ's glorification will be "by His saints." *We* are His inheritance.[6]

## Colossians 1.9-12

> [9] Because of this, we too, from the day we heard, do not stop
> praying for you and asking that you might be filled with the
> full knowledge of His will in all wisdom and spiritual
> understanding, [10] so you might walk worthily of the Lord for
> all pleasing, in every good work, by producing fruit and by
> growing in the full knowledge of the God, [11] since you are
> empowered with all power, in accord with His glorious
> might, for every endurance and patience with joy,
> [12] thanking the Father, the One who qualified us[7] for the
> share of the saints' inheritance in the light,

This is another prayer demonstrating Paul's unceasing occupation with prayer. He prayed the Colossians would be 1) filled up or complete (πληρόω) with the full knowledge of God's will in all wisdom and spiritual understanding. The text, "full knowledge of His will" reads τὴν ἐπίγνωσιν τοῦ θελήματος αὐτοῦ. The word "knowledge," ἐπίγνωσις, primarily used by Paul,[8] generally has a fuller, more *experiential* sense of understanding than γνῶσις. This is especially true of Paul's prison letters and afterwards. In this case, Paul prayed for the Colossians to have a full grasp of the truths he taught in all wisdom and spiritual understanding (σύνεσις).[9] The experiential thought is continued in the rest of the prayer, to 2) "walk worthy of the Lord for all pleasing, in every good work, by producing fruit and by growing in the full knowledge (ἐπίγνωσις) of the God."

Paul concluded the prayer 3) stating that believers are empowered (δυναμόω) with all power (δύναμις) "in accord with His glorious might" (κατὰ τὸ κράτος τῆς δόξης αὐτοῦ) 4) for every endurance and

---

[6] Paul wrote that believers are Christ's inheritance (Ephesian 1.18).

[7] Some manuscripts have "you," ὑμᾶς.

[8] See Romans 1.28, 3.20, 10.2; Ephesians 1.17, 4.13; Philippians 1.9; Colossians 1.9-10, 2.2, 3.10; 1 Timothy 2.4; 2 Timothy 2.25, 3.7; Titus 1.1; Philemon 1.6; Hebrews 10.26. Thus, 3x in Romans, 8x in the Prison Epistles, 4x in the Pastoral Epistles, and 1x in Hebrews. The key point is that Paul used ἐπίγνωσις in his later letters to signify a more complete knowledge in light of what he wrote the Corinthians in 1 Corinthians 13. This is discussed in the chapter, Paul and Sign Gifts. Peter used the word four times in his last letter (2 Peter 1.2, 3, 8, 2.20). The distinction between γνῶσις and ἐπίγνωσις, "knowledge," has received a fair amount of scholarly attention. See Robert E. Picirelli, "The Meaning of 'Epignosis'" *Evangelical Quarterly* 47.2 (April-June 1975): 85-93. See http://biblicalstudies.org.uk/pdf/eq/1975-2_085.pdf.

[9] The noun σύνεσις is a mental putting together—to comprehend, to grasp.

patience with joy and 5) thanking the Father who has qualified (ἱκανόω)[10] us to share in the inheritance of the saints in the light. What we will be, what we will have as heirs of God and joint-heirs of Christ (Romans 8.17) cannot be fully comprehended or imagined. But such an anticipated destiny should move us live godly lives, to endure, and give us joy as we contemplate our glorious future.

## Colossians 2.1-3

> [1] For I want you to know how great *a* struggle I am having for you and those in Laodicea, and as many as have not seen my face in the flesh, [2] so their hearts might be encouraged, since they have been united in love, and for all *the* riches of the full assurance of the understanding, for *the* full knowledge of the secret of the God, Christ, [3] in whom are hidden all the treasures of the wisdom and the knowledge.

Paul wished his readers to know how embattled he was for them—the Colossians, Laodiceans, and others who had not seen him. He prayed that their 1) hearts might be encouraged (παρακαλέω)[11] 2) for they had been united in love (ἀγάπη) and 3) for all riches of the full assurance of the understanding, for full knowledge (ἐπίγνωσις) of the secret of the God, of Christ (τοῦ μυστηρίου τοῦ θεοῦ Χριστοῦ). Paul concluded his prayer describing Christ: 4) in whom are hid all the treasures of the wisdom and the knowledge. These treasures are hidden in Christ.

## Ephesians 1.15-19

> [15] Because of this, I too, when I heard of your faith in the Lord Jesus and the love for all the saints, [16] do not cease giving thanks for you, by remembering you in my prayers, [17] so the God of our Lord Jesus Christ, the glorious Father, might give you *a* spirit of wisdom and revelation in *the* full knowledge of Him, [18] since the eyes of your understanding have been enlightened for you to know what is the hope of His calling and what *are* the riches of His glorious inheritance in the saints, [19] and what *is* the surpassing greatness of His power for us who believe, according to the working of the strength of His might,

As soon as Paul learned of the faith[12] of the Ephesians and their love for fellow believers, he prayed for them. Here is another example of unceasing prayer (1 Thessalonians 5.17). Paul said he 1) did not cease

---

[10] The verb ἱκανόω was used only by Paul, here and in 2 Corinthians 3.6, and means to render fit or adequate for a role. In the Corinthians passage, Paul spoke of being "a minister of the new covenant."

[11] The verb παρακαλέω here means to be encouraged or strengthened—comforted in the original Latin sense, "with strength," "fortified."

[12] What is in view is the gospel the Ephesians had believed, not their act of believing.

giving thanks for them and prayed that 2) God the Father, the glorious Father, would give them the spirit of wisdom and revelation in full knowledge (ἐπίγνωσις) of Him. He prayed that since the eyes of their understanding had been enlightened (πεφωτισμένους, perfect passive participle of φωτίζω), (by believing the gospel) for them to know[13] the hope of His calling and His inheritance in the saints.

Paul closed his prayer for believers to know 3) the surpassing (ὑπερβάλλω)[14] greatness of His power towards us who believe according to the working of the strength of His might. Paul prayed for believers to understand that God's power towards believers. Notice how much of Paul's prayers regard knowledge and understanding.

## Ephesians 3.13-21

> 13 Therefore, I implore, do not lose heart at my suffering for
> you, which is your glory. 14 For this reason, I bow my knees
> to the Father of our Lord Jesus Christ, 15 from whom every
> family in *the* heavens and on earth is named, 16 so He might
> give you, according to the riches of His glory, to be
> strengthened with power, through His Spirit, in the inner
> man, 17 so Christ might dwell through the faith in your
> hearts, since you have been rooted and established in love,
> 18 so you might have strength to comprehend with all the
> saints, what *is* the breadth, even length, and depth, and
> height, 19 so you might know the love of the Christ which
> surpasses the knowledge, so you might be filled up to all the
> fullness of the God. 20 Now to the One who can do all things
> exceedingly beyond what we ask or think, after the power
> working in us, 21 to Him *be* the glory in the Church in Christ
> Jesus, to all the generations forever and ever. Amen.

Paul loved believers. He was always concerned for their welfare and prayed that they not become discouraged over his trials. Indeed, he wrote that his tribulations were their glory. The Lord had told Ananias, "For I will show him how many things he must suffer for My name (Acts 9.16)." Paul's sufferings were part of his ministry and will be his glory (Colossians 1.24). Paul declared he bowed his knees to God from whom every family in the heavens and on earth is named. God is the Creator. He created everything. Paul prayed that 1) God would give the Ephesians, according to the riches of His glory, strength with

---

[13] Literally, the verse reads, "the eyes of your understanding having been enlightened for you to know the hope of His calling.... The word "know" is εἰδέναι, the perfect active infinitive of εἴδω, an obsolete form. Its present tense is supplied by ὁράω (to see). The tenses from εἰδῶ retained by usage form two families, one which signifies to see, the other to know. The verb comports with Paul's metaphor ὀφθαλμοὺς τῆς διανοίας, "eyes of understanding."

[14] Present active participle of ὑπερβάλλω from which we get "hyperbole."

power through His Spirit in the inner man,[15] 2) so that Christ might dwell in their hearts through the faith (διὰ τῆς πίστεως), Paul's doctrines, 3) for they had been rooted and grounded in love (God's love for us establishing us in Him), 4) that they might comprehend (καταλαμβάνω—to take hold of) with all the saints, the breadth, length, depth, and height (all that God possesses), and 5) know the love of Christ which surpasses knowledge—God's love is greater than anything (Romans 8.35-39) 6) that you may be filled with all the fullness of God. Believers are predestinated to be conformed to the image of Christ (Romans 8.29). This is the believer's *destiny*.

Paul concluded his prayer with a glorious doxology. He prayed 7) "now to the One who can do all things exceedingly beyond what we ask or think, according to the power working in us." God is beyond what we can ask or think. Jesus declared "for nothing will be impossible with God" (Luke 1.37). Believers are indwelled by the Holy Spirit, who is transforming us into the image of Christ. God's power works in us and 8) to Him be the glory in the Church in Christ Jesus, for all the generations forever and ever. Amen. God will receive eternal glory from all creation and the Church has its own special and unique glory and praise for God.

## Philippians 1.9-11

> [9] And this I pray, that your love may abound still more and more in full knowledge and every discernment, [10] for you to test the things that are different, so you may be pure and blameless for *the* day of Christ, [11] having been filled with *the* fruit of righteousness that *is* through Jesus Christ, for *the* glory and praise of God.

Paul prayed that 1) the Philippian's love might abound (περισσεύω)[16] more and more in full knowledge (ἐπίγνωσις) and every discernment (αἴσθησις),[17] 2) this increase in knowledge and judgment was "to test the things that differ" (δοκιμάζειν τά διαφέροντα). Other translations render the phrase something like "approve things that are excellent" but it is better understood as "testing or discerning what things differ." Elsewhere Paul used διαφέρω to distinguish between differing things (cf. Romans 2.18; 1 Corinthians 15.41; Galatians 2.6, 4.1). He had special reference to the difference between his doctrines and the teaching of others. Paul desired the Philippians to be 3) pure and without offense until the day of Christ (Rapture). Lastly, Paul prayed

---

[15] See the discussion on The Nature of Man.
[16] See the prayer in 1 Thessalonians 3.12.
[17] The word αἴσθησις is unique to Paul and means wisdom and discernment in moral and spiritual matters.

that believers 4) be filled with the fruit[18] of righteousness that is through Jesus Christ, to the glory and praise of God and most likely meant the "fruit of the Spirit" (Galatians 5.22-23; Ephesians 5.9-10).

## Philippians 4.4-7

> [4] Rejoice in *the* Lord always. Again, I will say, rejoice! [5] Let your gentleness be known to all men. The Lord *is* near. [6] Do not worry about anything. But in everything, by prayer and entreaty, with thanksgiving, let your requests be made known to the God. [7] And the peace of God, which surpasses all understanding, will guard your hearts and your minds in Christ Jesus.

Paul's prayers are characterized by *joy* and *thanksgiving*. Everything in a believer's life is not happiness (Paul was incarcerated when he wrote Philippians) but believers can experience joy in the midst of trials.[19] Happiness depends upon circumstances. Joy is a deeper reality, based on conviction of who God is, one's relationship to Him, and the hope of resurrection and future reward. Paul prayed that 1) the Philippians "gentleness" (ἐπιεικῆς) be known to all. This should characterize our attitude. Paul thought the Lord was "near," ἐγγύς."[20]

He continued his instruction, writing the Philippians 2) not to worry about anything. The μεριμνάω means "full of care," being troubled or anxious. The verb is a present active imperative, a command. It is natural and human to worry but believers rest of the truth that God is in control. He sees and knows all and He is good. Thus, we are not to worry. Instead, 3) in everything, by prayer (προσευχή) and entreaty (δέησις) with thanksgiving we are to make our requests (αἴτημα) known to God.[21] Instead of worrying, pray. Such prayers are to be made with "thanksgiving," thanking God for His goodness and trusting Him to deal with the matter. The result of such prayer is 4) the peace of God, which passes all understanding, will guard (φρουρέω) the believer's heart and mind through Christ Jesus.

---

[18] The KJV (Majority Text) reads καρπῶν "fruits" and the Critical Text (CT) reads καρπὸν "fruit." This is an auditory copy error—a long or a short "o," ω or ο. Paul usually wrote "fruit" so the CT is the more likely reading.

[19] In Philippi, Paul and Silas, after having been beaten and imprisoned, sang praises to God (Acts 16.20-25). That is the peace that passes understanding.

[20] The Twelve and Paul thought the Lord would return in their lifetimes (Mathew 3.2, 4.17; Acts 2.17; Romans 13.11-12, 16.20; 1 Corinthians 7.29; Philippians 4.5; 1 Thessalonians 4.15, 17; Hebrews 10.25, 37; James 5.7-9; 1 Peter 4.7; 1 John 2.18, 28; Revelation 1.1, 3, 22.20). Paul thought the Lord would return for His Church (Rapture) and wrote the Philippians that he hoped for the ἐξανάστασιν τὴν ἐκ νεκρῶν "out resurrection from the dead" (Philippians 3.11). He coined the word ἐξανάστασις as a synonym of ἁρπάζω, the Rapture, to express his personal hope. Every passing day the Lord is "nearer."

[21] A δέησις is an entreaty, a request, and αἴτημα is a petition—synonyms.

This is easy to write but difficult to practice. All of us are prone to worry—we live in an evil, dangerous world. But this is an exercise of faith, a discipline. God often is silent or answers prayers not as we expect. Many times, we do not understand what God is doing or why. But faith apprehends God's love and trusts He does what is best for us. Because of this, we can thank Him. Thanksgiving is the path to joy.

## Colossians 4.1-4

> [1] Masters! Give what *is* right and equal to the servants, since you know that you too have *a* Master in heaven. [2] Persist in the prayer by being attentive in it with thanksgiving, [3] praying at the same time also for us, that the God might open *a* door to us for the word, to speak the secret of the Christ, for which I have also been bound, so I might make it clear as I must speak.

## Ephesians 6.18-20

> [18] Through every prayer and request, pray at all times in *the* Spirit, even for this very thing, watching with all perseverance and request for all the saints, [19] and for me, so I might be given *a* message with boldness in opening my mouth, to make known the secret of the gospel, [20] for which I am *an* ambassador in *a* chain, so by it I might be bold to speak as I must.

The preaching of the cross was everything for Paul. He wrote the Corinthians, "For Christ did not send me to baptize but to proclaim the gospel—not by wisdom of speech so that the cross of the Christ might not be nullified" (1 Corinthians 1.17) and "For if I should proclaim the gospel, no boasting is for me. For necessity is laid on me. Woe is me if I should not proclaim the gospel" (1 Corinthians 9.16)!

In both prayers, Paul continued his instruction to 1) pray without ceasing and for God to 2) open doors for him to proclaim Christ. In the Colossians passage, he wrote of the "secret of the Christ." What was this? Likely, he meant the body of truth, his revelations, his secrets, he received from the ascended Lord. In the Ephesians passage, he wrote of the "secret of the gospel." This clearly was not the gospel of the kingdom proclaimed by John the Baptist, Jesus in His earthly ministry, or the gospel proclaimed by the Twelve for that gospel was not secret. What was secret was the gospel Paul proclaimed, that Christ died for our sins and rose from the dead and that by believing this one has forgiveness of sins and eternal life. This was the gospel Paul wrote about in Galatians 1.11-12. Lastly, Paul prayed that 3) he might speak boldly as he ought to speak. As imitators of Paul, these should be our prayers also: that God will open doors of opportunity to use to proclaim the wonderful good news of God's love, grace, and salvation, and that we might proclaim this message boldly and clearly. All Christian teachers and believers need to be sustained by such prayers.

## Conclusion

The above prayers are how members of the Church, the body of Christ, are to pray. They are our models. Praying such prayers is part of the growth and maturity process by which God conforms us into the image of His Son. Paul wrote these encouraging words to the Ephesians:

> Until we all should attain to the unity of the faith and the full knowledge of the Son of the God, to *a* completed man, for *the* measure of *the* stature of the completeness of the Christ (Ephesians 4.13).

# Chapter 11

# Paul and the Nature of Man

*Now may the God of the peace Himself sanctify you completely. And may your whole spirit, and soul, and body be preserved blameless at the coming of our Lord Jesus Christ (1 Thessalonians 5.23).*

## Man: A Tripartite Being

God created mankind with body, soul, and spirit. Paul wrote the Thessalonians for God to sanctify them completely: body, soul, and spirit (1 Thessalonians 5.23). Soul and spirit are invisible entities but the Word of God can to distinguish and divide between them:

> For the word of the God is alive and productive and sharper than any double-edged sword, piercing even to division of soul and spirit, of joints and marrows, and *a* discerner of thoughts and intentions of *the* heart (Hebrews 4.12).

| Creation of Mankind | |
|---|---|
| Constitution | Capabilities |
| Body | Sight, Smell, Touch, Hearing, Taste |
| Soul | Mind, Will, Emotion |
| Spirit | Communicator with God |

The body houses soul and spirit. Through the senses of sight, smell, touch, hearing, and taste we perceive the external world. The mind analyzes and associates information through the senses and emotion enjoys or dislikes that information. The spirit perceives and discerns spiritual realities and communicates with God.

Israel's Tabernacle was a representation of God's heavenly court and throne complex. It also pictured mankind's tripartite nature and Paul called our body a "tabernacle" (σκῆνος) in 2 Corinthians 5.1, 4).[1] The Tabernacle had three main parts: an outer court and an inner court composed of the holy place and holy of holies. The outer court represented man's body, the holy place the soul and spirit, and the holy of holies, man's spirit. In the holy place was the lampstand, showbread, and altar of incense, which pictured sight, taste, and smell of the soul. A veil divided the holy place from the holy of holies. It showed the immaterial closeness between soul and spirit. In the holy of holies was the ark of the covenant which represented God's throne

---

[1] The word σκῆνος was the word used in the LXX for "tabernacle."

and presence. It was the part of the tabernacle was where man's spirit communes with God.

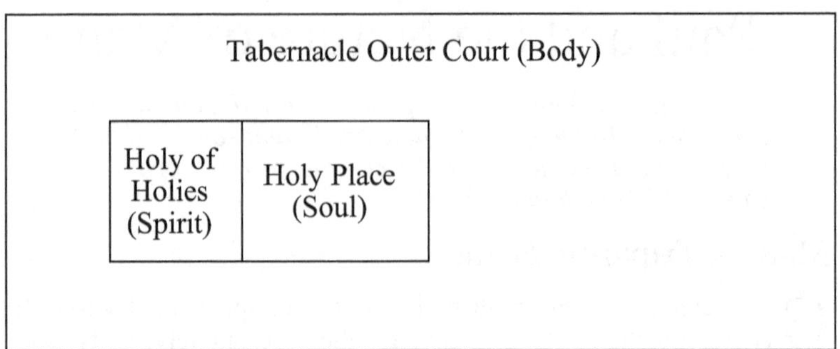


## The First Couple

God created Adam perfect. He gave the man and woman bodies capable of living forever, souls to enjoy the paradise He had provided, and spirits to delight in His fellowship and presence.

When Adam and the woman ate from the fruit of the Tree of the Knowledge of Good and Evil their constitution changed. God had warned Adam they could eat from every tree in the garden except one. Eating its fruit would result in death (Genesis 2.16-17).[2] When Adam ate from the forbidden fruit, he plunged the human race into a state of sin and death.[3]

| Fall of Mankind | |
|---|---|
| Constitution | Result of Disobedience |
| Body | Began to die |
| Soul | Damaged: became a nature in rebellion to God |
| Spirit | Died immediately |

## The Nature of Mankind

Moses revealed mankind was created in God's image (Genesis 1.26-27)[4] and wrote about mankind's Fall, the beginning of sin and death.

---

[2] Genesis 2.17 reads, מוֹת תָּמוּת, "dying you will die," a Qal infinitive absolute and Qal imperfect. The moment Adam ate the forbidden fruit, his spirit died, his soul acquired a sin nature in rebellion to God, and the process of physical death began. Adam lived to be 930 years old (Genesis 5.5) and died. Human death is scientific proof the Bible is true.

[3] Theologians call this disobedience the Fall.

[4] Both the man and woman were Adam (Genesis 1.27, 5.1-2).

His account provided a basic understanding of man's problem but Paul provided much more revelation about our condition.

> Wherefore, as by one man sin entered into the world, and death by sin; and so death passed upon all men, for that all have sinned (Romans 5.12).

Paul revealed Adam sinned willfully, unlike Eve, who was deceived (1 Timothy 2.14). He wrote that mankind has inherited a nature in rebellion to God (Romans 1.18-32, 7.14-24) which turned us into God's enemy (Romans 5.10; Colossians 1.21). He also revealed the principle:

WE ARE NOT SINNERS BECAUSE WE SIN;
WE SIN BECAUSE WE ARE SINNERS

Sin is mankind's *natural* state. As a result of Adam, we are bent to it. We sin by nature, doing "what comes naturally."

## Paul's Vocabulary For Mankind's Fallen State

Man's soul was ruined and became a sin nature from Adam's disobedience (Romans 7.18, 21). In addition, man's spirit died. All of us inherit Adam's sin nature, and Paul used several terms to describe it, shown in the following chart with representative verses:

| Term | Scripture |
|---|---|
| Natural Man ψυχικὸς ἄνθρωπος | Now the **natural man** does not receive the things of the Spirit of the God for they are foolishness to him. And he cannot understand for they are spiritually discerned. (1 Corinthians 2.14). |
| The Old Man ὁ παλαιὸς ἄνθρωπος | For we know this: our **old man** was crucified with *Him* so that the body of the sin may be rendered inactive, so that we are no longer enslaved by the sin. (Romans 6.6; cf. Ephesians 4.22; Colossians 3.9). |
| Flesh σάρξ | (I speak in human terms because of the weakness of your **flesh**). For just as you presented your members *as* servants to the uncleanness and to the lawlessness, so now present your members *as* servants to the righteousness for sanctification. (Romans 6.19; cf. 7.5, 18, 7.25, 8.1, 3, 4, 5, 8, 9, 12, 13, 13.14; 2 Corinthians 7.1, 10.3; Galatians 3.3, 4.29, 5.13, 16 Galatians 5.17, 19, 24, 6.8; Ephesians 2.3, 11; Philippians 1.22, 3.3; Colossians 2.13). |
| Fleshly σαρκικός | For we know that *the* Law is spiritual. But I am **fleshly**, since I have been sold as a slave under the sin (Romans 7.14; cf. 8.7). |
| The Body of the Sin | For we know this: our old man was crucified with *Him* so that **the body of the sin** may be rendered |

| | |
|---|---|
| ὁ σῶμα τῆς ἁμαρτίας | inactive, so that we are no longer enslaved by the sin (Romans 6.6). |
| The Sin ἁμαρτία | So you too. Reckon yourselves to be dead to **the sin** but alive to the God in Jesus Christ our Lord (Romans 6.11-14, 16-18, 20, 22-23, 7.5, 8, 11, 14, 17, 20, 23). |

Each of us is born as "natural man" (ψυχικὸς ἄνθρωπος). The "natural man" cannot receive the things of the Spirit of God. Why? Paul declared the things of the Spirit of God are "spiritually discerned." God can transmit but we cannot receive. Without a functioning human spirit, man cannot receive spiritual information.

The above terms are synonyms and each refers to our fallen state as children of Adam. Romans 6.6 provides two of the terms, "old man" and "body of sin." Paul wrote "the old man" was crucified with Christ to destroy "the body of the sin." God sees a believer's fallen nature as having died with Christ and his new nature as having risen with Christ (Romans 6.4-5). Paul wrote concerning Christ:

> Because the Law was powerless, in that it was continually weak through the flesh, the God sent His own Son in *the* likeness of sinful flesh, and concerning sin—condemned the sin in the flesh (Romans 8.3).

Christ came in the "likeness of sinful flesh" (ἐν ὁμοιώματι σαρκὸς ἁμαρτίας). He looked like us but He had no sin nature since He was virgin-born.[5] His human nature was like Adam's before he disobeyed.

A word should be said about Paul's phrase, "body of sin" as rendered by the KJV and most translations. The text reads, ὁ σῶμα τῆς ἁμαρτίας, "the body of the sin," not "body of sin." Paul's nomenclature, "the sin" referred to one particular sin—eating the forbidden fruit, Adam's disobedience We inherit this sin's consequences with a fallen nature, a dead human spirit, and bodies which will die. Paul described this unhappy condition:

> [12] Because of this, just as through one man the sin entered into the world, and through the sin the death, so also, the death passed through to all men, for all sinned: . . . [18] So, then, as through one offence condemnation *came* to all men, so also through one righteous act *came* to all men for justification of life [19] For just as through the disobedience of the one man, the many were rendered sinners, so also through the obedience of the One, the many will be rendered righteous (Romans 5.12, 18-19).

[5] The virgin birth was essential for Jesus to be a sinless human. Without the virgin birth, Christ would have had a sin nature and been no different from us.

Death proves the Bible is true. Every time a person dies, the Bible is proven true. Human death is the scientific, replicable experiment. But Paul declared that because of Christ's work, the free gift of salvation has come on all mankind. Christ has made eternal life available to anyone who will accept it (Romans 3.22).

Paul also described our fallen condition as affecting the body's "members" (τὰ μέλη ὑμῶν) (Romans 6.13, 19, 7.5, 23). We are born into slavery, servants of sin, our "old nature" being the slave master (Romans 6.6, 17, 19-20, 7.14; Galatians 5.1). Paul described our fallen nature as reigning as a king (βασιλεύω) (Romans 6.12) and having dominion (κυριεύω) (Romans 6.14). The old nature cannot obey or please God (Romans 8.7-8). When it comes in contact with the moral law, it rebels, and the law actually excites sin (Romans 7.7-10).

## What Changed Upon Believing the Gospel

### Regeneration of the Human Spirit

When one believes Paul's gospel (1 Corinthians 15.1-4), one becomes a different person. While this change may or may not be evident immediately, over time it becomes manifest.[6] The moment one believes, one's spirit is regenerated and one is indwelt with the Holy Spirit. Romans 8.16 describes the relationship between the believer's human spirit and the indwelling Holy Spirit:

> The Spirit Himself testifies to our spirit: we are God's children (Romans 8.16).

God created Adam with a human spirit designed to communicate with God. But when Adam sinned, his human spirit died immediately. Communication with God was broken. When the couple heard God walking in the garden they hid (Genesis 3.8). The cool of the day was a designated time when they communed with God. With a dead human spirit, this intimacy ended. They now feared God.

The indwelling Holy Spirit communicates with the regenerated human spirit of the believer. Paul wrote:

> For you did not receive *a* spirit of bondage again for fear. Rather, you received *the* Spirit of adoption by whom we cry, Abba—Father (Romans 8.15)!

> Now because you are sons, the God sent the Spirit of His Son into your hearts, who shouts, Abba, Father (Galatians 4.6)!

---

[6] God changes us *individually*. We become better than we were, not better than someone else.

The believer's human spirit recognizes God as his Father, and calls out, "Abba,[7] Father." This vocative occurs three times in the Scriptures—the two cases above and when Jesus prayed to His Father the night before His crucifixion and asked if it was possible to remove the cup He was about to drink (Mark 14.36). Such language reveals the intimate and personal communication between the human spirit and God.

Further attestation of this truth may be seen by Paul's words to the Romans and the Corinthians:

> For the God is my witness, whom I serve in my spirit in the gospel of His Son, that I mention you continually (Romans 1.9).
>
> But now, we were released from the Law, because we died to what we used to be bound, so we might serve in newness of *the* Spirit and not in oldness of *the* letter (Romans 7.6).
>
> 14 For if I pray in *an unknown* language, my spirit prays but my mind is unfruitful. 15 What should I do? I will pray with the spirit, but I will also pray with the mind. I will sing praise with the spirit, but I will also sing praise with the mind. 16 Otherwise, if you should bless with *the* spirit, how will the one who is in the place of the unlearned say the Amen at your thanksgiving, since he does not know what you say (1 Corinthians 14.14-16)?

## The Indwelling Holy Spirit

Another thing which occurs the moment one believes Paul's gospel is God the Holy Spirit comes to indwell the believer. God's Spirit is His down payment of our salvation. Paul wrote:

> 13 In whom you too, when you heard the word of the truth, the gospel of your salvation, in whom, when you too believed, you were sealed with the promised Holy Spirit, 14 who is *the* down payment of our inheritance, for *the* redemption of the possession, to *the* praise of His glory (Ephesians 1.13-14).

God seals the believer with the Holy Spirit. The verb σφραγίζω, "seal," denotes authentication, identification, and possession. The Holy Spirit is "down payment," ἀρραβών, of our inheritance in anticipation of the "redemption of the purchased possession,"[8] Christ's blood being the purchase price of redemption (Ephesians 1.7, 2.13; Colossians 1.14, 20). The redemption of which Paul speaks here is the redemption of

---

[7] The vocative Ἀββᾶ is an Aramaism of אַב, "father."

[8] Paul also wrote of the down payment of the Spirit in 2 Corinthians 1.22, 5.5.

our bodies, which occurs at the Rapture. Paul wrote of the indwelling Holy Spirit in the following verses:

> Now if the Spirit of the One who raised Jesus from *the* dead lives in you, the One who raised the Christ from the dead will also make your mortal bodies alive through His Spirit who lives in you (Romans 8.11).
>
> Do you not know that you are *the* temple of God and the Spirit of the God lives in you (1 Corinthians 3.16)?
>
> Consequently, the one who rejects *this* does not reject man, but the God, the One who also gives us His Holy Spirit (1 Thessalonians 4.8).
>
> Protect the good thing entrusted *to you* through the Holy Spirit, the One who lives in us (2 Timothy 1.14).

The Holy Spirit is also the One who baptizes us into the Church, the body of Christ:

> For by one Spirit we were all baptized[9] into one body, whether Jews or Greeks, whether servants or freemen, and all were made to drink one Spirit (1 Corinthians 12.13).

## The New Nature

In addition to making the believer's human spirit alive and indwelling the believer with the Holy Spirit, God creates a new nature in the believer. This new nature works in concert with the regenerated human spirit and indwelling Holy Spirit. Paul wrote:

> [22] to put off your former behavior, the old man, (τὸν παλαιὸν ἄνθρωπον) who is being corrupted according to the desires of the deceit, [23] and to be renewed in the spirit of your mind, [24] and put on the new man, (τὸν καινὸν ἄνθρωπον) the one made according to God, in righteousness and holiness of the truth (Ephesians 4.22-24).
>
> [9] Do not lie to one another, since you put off the old man (τὸν παλαιὸν ἄνθρωπον) with his practices, [10] and since you put on the new, (τὸν νέον) the one who is being renewed in full knowledge, (ἐπίγνωσις) after *the* image of the One who created him (Colossians 3.9-10).

Paul called this new nature, "the new man"[10] and "the inner man" (τὸν ἔσω ἄνθρωπον). In one of his prayers for the Ephesians, he wrote:

---

[9] This work identifies the believer as a member of Christ's body, the Church. See also Romans 6.3-4; Galatians 3.27; Ephesians 4.5; Colossians 2.12.

[10] Νέος is generally "new" in respect to time and καινός in respect to quality.

> So He might give you, according to the riches of His glory, to be strengthened with power, through His Spirit, in the inner man (τὸν ἔσω ἄνθρωπον) (Ephesians 3.16).

The Holy Spirit works with the "inner man" in concert with the human spirit.

| The Condition of the Believer | |
|---|---|
| Constitution | The Result of Believing the Gospel |
| Body | Will be raised to new life |
| Soul | Acquires a new nature (τὸν καινὸν ἄνθρωπον) |
| Spirit | Made alive |

## Warfare Between Old and New Natures

The above verses contrast the old man, our inherited Adamic nature, with the new man (τὸν καινὸν ἄνθρωπον), the new nature, which God creates when a person believes the gospel. Paul had much to say about these two natures and their conflict and reveled how the Law affects the old nature:

> [7] Therefore, what will we say? *Is* the Law sin? Never! But I did not understand the sin except through *the* Law. For I did not understand lust except the Law kept saying: You will not lust. [8] But the sin, since it took advantage through the commandment, produced in me every kind of lust. For apart from *the* Law sin *is* dead. [9] Now I was once alive apart from Law. But when the commandment came, the sin revived. Then I died. [10] And the commandment that *was* for life, I found *to be* death! [11] For the sin, which took advantage through the commandment, deceived me, and through it, killed *me*. [12] So, *the* Law *is* holy, and the commandment *is* holy, and righteous, and good (Romans 7.7-12).

The Mosaic Law was "holy, righteous, and good." But its effect upon the Adamic nature was to agitate and exacerbate sin. Paul continued:

> [13] Therefore, did the good become death to me? Never! But the sin, so that it might be shown to be sin through the good, produced death to me, so the sin might become extremely sinful through the commandment. [14] For we know that *the* Law is spiritual. But I am fleshly, since I have been sold as a slave under the sin (Romans 7.13-14).

What Paul meant by "the sin" was the "sin nature," the source of sinfulness. The Law exposes not only particular sins but the source of sin, the sin nature—"so the sin might become extremely sinful through the commandment."

<table>
<tr><th colspan="3">Warfare Within the Believer</th></tr>
<tr><td>Constitution</td><td colspan="2">The Result of Believing the Gospel</td></tr>
<tr><td>Body</td><td colspan="2">Will be raised to new life</td></tr>
<tr><td>Soul</td><td>New nature<br>(τὸν καινὸν ἄνθρωπον)</td><td>Old nature<br>(τὸν παλαιὸν ἄνθρωπον)</td></tr>
<tr><td>Spirit</td><td colspan="2">Made alive</td></tr>
</table>

Paul continued to describe this conflict:

> 15 For what I do, I do not understand. For what I do not want, this I do. But what I hate, this I do. 16 Now if what I do not want, this I do, I agree with the Law, that *it is* good. 17 But now, I no longer do it, but the sin which resides in me. 18 For I know that nothing good resides in me, that is, in my flesh. For to will is present with me, but I do not accomplish the good. 19 For I do not do *the* good that I wish, but *the* evil that I do not wish, this I practice! 20 Now if I do what I do not wish, I am no longer the one who accomplishes it, but the sin residing in me. 21 So, I find the law: when I want to do the good, that the evil is present in me. 22 For I delight in God's Law according to the inner man. 23 But I see another law in my members which wages war against the law of my mind and takes me captive to the law of the sin that is in my members. 24 I am *a* wretched man! Who will deliver me from this body of death? 25 Now I thank the God through Jesus Christ our Lord! So then, I myself serve God's Law in the mind, but in the flesh, sin's law (Romans 7.15-25).

Paul recognized that part of him, "the inner man," (verse 22) wished to obey God but that "the sin," the "sin nature" (verses 17, 20), opposed this desire. As a result, Paul did what he hated (verse 20). Our "sin nature" affects our entire body, i.e., "in my members" (verse 23). Paul languished under this reality, writing, "who will deliver me from this body of death!" This conflict is present in every believer. We are in a moment-by-moment fight—the old nature versus the new nature.

Paul wrote similarly to the Galatians:

> 16 Now I say, Walk by the Spirit so you might not fulfill *the* desire of *the* flesh. 17 For the flesh desires against the Spirit, and the Spirit against the flesh. For these oppose one another, so you may not do the things you may wish. 18 But if you are led by *the* Spirit, you are not under *the* Law (Galatians 5.16-18).

Mankind's greatest problem is our old nature. It affects us in every possible way: "so you may not do the things you may wish" (verse 17). Paul wrote:

> [7] Because the fleshly mind *is* hostile towards God for it is not subject to God's Law, nor can it *be*. [8] Now those who are in *the* flesh cannot please God (Romans 8.7-8).

The chapter, "Paul and the Law" discusses victory over sin in the Christian life.

<table>
<tr><th colspan="3">Victory in Christian Living</th></tr>
<tr><th>Constitution</th><th colspan="2">The Result of Believing the Gospel</th></tr>
<tr><td>Body</td><td colspan="2">Will be raised to new life</td></tr>
<tr><td rowspan="2">Soul</td><td>New nature<br>(τὸν καινὸν ἄνθρωπον)</td><td>Old nature<br>(τὸν παλαιὸν ἄνθρωπον)</td></tr>
<tr><td>Live by faith under the control of the indwelling Holy Spirit</td><td>Reckon the old nature as dead, crucified with Christ</td></tr>
<tr><td>Spirit</td><td colspan="2">Made alive</td></tr>
</table>

# Chapter 12
# Paul and Sign Gifts

> 22 Now Jews ask for signs and Greeks seek wisdom, 23 but we preach Christ who has been crucified—to Jews, an offense, and to Gentiles, foolishness. 24 But to those called, both Jews and Greeks, Christ is the power of God and the wisdom of God (1 Corinthians 1.22-24).

## Introduction

Some denominations and churches place great emphasis on the sign gifts of healing, prophecy, knowledge, and speaking in tongues. They maintain these gifts confirm the presence of the Holy Spirit and that believers should be exercising them as evidence of godly living. What is the history of miracles and signs and are they valid today?

## The Beginning of Signs and Miracles

Signs and miracles began with God's dealings with Abraham. In about 2,000 B.C., God called Abraham from Ur of the Chaldees and promised to make him a great nation (Genesis 12.1-3). For many years Abraham and his wife, Sarah, could not have a child. Frustrated, they took matters into their own hands and Hagar, a servant of Sarah, bore Abraham a son, Ishmael. When Abraham was a hundred years old and Sarah ninety, God performed a miracle and they had a son, Isaac. He became the child of promise and the child of the covenant line (Genesis 17.15-22).

After Jacob went to Egypt and the Jews became enslaved, God responded to their sufferings and performed miraculous signs to Pharaoh and the Egyptians through Moses. By these signs the God of the Jews revealed He was superior to the gods of Egypt. God told Moses:

> 19 And I am sure that the king of Egypt will not let you go, no, not by a mighty hand. 20 And I will stretch out my hand, and smite Egypt with all my wonders which I will do in the midst thereof: and after that he will let you go (Exodus 3.19-20).

Exodus records the miracles and signs God performed to bring Israel out of Egyptian bondage. These events took place about 1500 B.C.

| God's Miracles to Israel in the Book of Exodus |
|---|
| Aaron's rod changed into a serpent (Exodus 7.10-12). |
| The ten plagues of Egypt: 1) Waters turned to blood, 2) Frogs, 3) Lice, 4) Flies, 5) Murrain, 6) Boils, 7) Thunder and hail, 8) Locusts, 9) Darkness, 10) Death of the first-born (Exodus 7.20-12:30). |
| Red Sea divided: Israel passed through it while the Egyptian army was drowned (Exodus 14.21-31). |
| Waters of Marah sweetened (Exodus 15.23-25). |
| Daily manna, except on Sabbath (Exodus 16.14-35). |
| Water from the rock at Rephidim (Massah) (Exodus 17.5-7) and at Kadesh (Meribah) (Numbers 20.1-13). |

Throughout Israel's history, God performed miracles. Some periods had more signs and miracles than others but signs and miracles occurred throughout Jewish history.

When John the Baptist came on the scene, over 400 years had passed since a prophet had risen in Israel. During that period, God performed no miracles. This was a long time and may explain why the Sadducees did not believe in the miraculous and supernatural. But with the birth of John, God restarted signs and miracles. John's birth was like that of Isaac for Abraham and Sarah, for Zechariah and Elizabeth, John's parents, were past the time of child-bearing (Luke 1.5-25, 39-45 cf. Genesis 18.9-15). Six months after John, Mary gave birth to Jesus. His birth was both miraculous, Mary was a virgin (Luke 1.26-38) and unique, Jesus was wholly God and wholly man. Angels announced both miraculous births.

John the Baptist proclaimed the gospel of the kingdom and that the kingdom of God was near (Matthew 3.1-3). But after he was imprisoned by Herod, he began to wonder if Jesus truly was the promised Messiah. He could not reconcile his imprisonment with the kingdom of God being near. Matthew wrote:

> [2] Now when John heard in the prison about the works of the Christ, he sent two of his disciples. [3] They said to Him, Are you the Coming One? Or do we look for another? [4] So when Jesus answered, He said to them, After you leave, report to John what you hear and see: [5] Blind receive sight and lame walk. Lepers are cleansed and deaf hear. Dead are raised and the poor have good news proclaimed. [6] So blessed is he who is not offended by Me (Matthew 11.2-6).

Jesus' response to John was that He was the Promised One for He performed the signs of the Messiah according to the Scriptures (Isaiah 35.5; 61.1). These signs authenticated His identity and message. During His three-year ministry, Jesus performed thousands of miracles of which the gospels record but a sampling. John wrote:

> 30 Therefore, Jesus did many other signs also in the presence
> of His disciples that are not written in this book. 31 But these
> have been written so you may believe that Jesus is the
> Christ, the Son of the God, and that believing, you may have
> life in His name (John 20.30-31).

and

> 24 This is the disciple, the one who testifies about these
> things and the one who wrote these things. And we know
> that his testimony is true. 25 Now there are also many other
> things that Jesus did, which, if every one should be written,
> I do not think even the world itself could hold the books
> written. Amen (John 21.24-25).

The point of this brief overview is to recognize that God began His relationship with His covenant people with signs and miracles and continued them through Jewish history. It should also be noted that they were performed either by God or by Jews and their purpose was to prove that the God of Israel was the one true God.

## Signs in Acts

Jesus told His disciples that miraculous signs would continue among those who had believed in Him. Mark wrote:

> 17 Now signs will accompany the ones who believed these
> things: they will expel demons in My name, they will speak
> with new languages, 18 and they will pick up snakes, and if
> they should drink anything deadly, it will not hurt them, and
> they will lay hands on the sick and they will become well.
> 19 Therefore, after the Lord Jesus spoke to them, He was
> taken up into the heaven and sat at the right hand of the God.
> 20 Now they, after they left, preached everywhere, while the
> Lord worked with them by confirming the message through
> the accompanying signs (Mark 16.17-20).

The book of Acts confirms the truth of Jesus' statement.

| Miracles Associated With Peter |
|---|
| Peter and John healed a lame man at the Temple (Acts 3.1-11). |
| The Twelve performed many signs (σημεῖον) and wonders (τέρας) to the Jews in Jerusalem (Acts 5.12-16). |
| Peter healed Aeneas of paralysis at Lydda (Acts 9.32-35). |
| Peter raised Tabitha, or Dorcas, to life from the dead at Joppa (Acts 9.36-42). |
| An angel delivered Peter from prison in Jerusalem (Acts 12.7-17). |

| Miracles Associated With Paul |
|---|
| Paul caused Elymas, the sorcerer, to be blinded for a season at Paphos (Acts 13.6-11). |
| Paul healed a cripple Lystra (Acts 14.8-10). |
| Paul cast out a spirit of divination at Philippi (Acts 16.16-18). |
| God caused an earthquake to open Paul and Silas's prison doors (and all the other prisoners) at Philippi (Acts 16.25-26). |
| Paul healed and cast out demons at Corinth (Acts 19.11-12). |
| Paul raised Eutychus to life from death at Troas (Acts 20.9-12). |
| Paul unaffected by the venom of a viper on Malta (Acts 28.3-6). |
| Paul healed the father of Publius and others on Malta (Acts 28.7-9). |

## The Gift of Healing

The last account of healing in the Bible is Paul's healing of Publius' father and others on Malta (Acts 28.8-9). This occurred about 60 A.D. After he reached Rome, he could no longer heal (cf. Philippians 2.27; 1 Timothy 5.23; 2 Timothy 4.20).

The gift of healing disappeared much earlier among those who proclaimed and believed the gospel of the kingdom. James wrote Jewish believers (James 1.1) in the mid or late 40s:

> [14] Is anyone sick among you? Let him call the elders of the congregation and let them pray for him, after they anoint him with oil in the name of the Lord. [15] And the prayer of the faith will heal the one who is sick. And the Lord will raise him up. And if he should have committed sins, it will be forgiven him.[16] Therefore, confess your sins to one another and pray for one another, so you might be healed. Much prayer of a righteous man is strong and effective (James 5.14-16).

Instead of exercising the gift of healing, the elders were to anoint the ill with oil and pray for healing.

## The Gift of Tongues (Languages)

Two Greek words are used for languages: γλῶσσα and διάλεκτος.1 The word γλῶσσα may be used for the physical organ of speech, the tongue, or for a language. The word διάλεκτος is used only for a language. All languages have a discernable vocabulary and syntactical

---

[1] Γλῶσσα, see Acts 2.3, 4, 11, 10.46, 19.6; 1 Corinthians 12.10, 28, 30, 13.1, 8, 14.2, 4, 5, 6, 9, 13, 14, 18, 19, 21, 22, 23, 26, 27, 39. Διάλεκτος, see Acts 1.19, 2.6, 8, 21.40, 22.2, 26.14.

structure. The sounds spoken in the present "tongues movement" lack these characteristics. They are gibberish.

Paul knew all about tongues, i.e., languages (1 Corinthians 14.18). He loved the Corinthians but recognized they were immature. In addition of other problems, they had become enamored with the gift of tongues. To correct their excesses, he laid out specific instructions:

1. The value of tongues was in being understood (1 Corinthians 14.6-20).
2. Tongues were a sign for unbelievers, not believers (1 Corinthians 14.21-22).
3. Uncontrolled speaking in tongues would lead an unbeliever to conclude a church was composed of madmen (1 Corinthians 14.23).
4. No more than two or three were to speak in tongues (1 Corinthians 14.27).
5. No one should speak in tongues unless someone was present to interpret what was said (1 Corinthians 14.28).
6. Women were forbidden to speak in tongues (1 Corinthians 14.34).

No tongue-speaking church follows Paul's rules. This in itself shows it is outside God's will today. When Paul wrote Corinthians, tongues was a legitimate, God-given gift. But he also wrote them this gift and the other sign gifts, would soon cease.

## Paul and Sign Gifts

Paul wrote about spiritual gifts in 1 Corinthians 12-14. His great doctrinal discourse about the presence and future of sign gifts was 1 Corinthians 13, popularly known as the "love chapter." Paul declared sign gifts were presently useful, but temporary. He wrote:

> [8] The love never fails. Now if there are prophecies, they will be set aside, if languages, they will cease; if knowledge, it will be set aside. [9] For we know in part and we prophesy in part. [10] But when the complete (τὸ τέλειον) should come, the partial will be set aside. [11] When I was a child, I used to speak like a child, I used to think like a child, I used to reason like a child. When I become a man, I set aside the things of the child. [12] Now, we see through a mirror unclearly, but then, face to face. At present, I know in part. But then, I will know fully, as I am fully known. [13] But now these three remain: faith, hope, love. have been fully known (1 Corinthians 13.8-13).

Paul wrote that while gifts of prophecy, tongues, and knowledge would cease, faith, hope, and love would continue. The sign gifts he mentioned were likely a metonymy for all the gifts he mentioned in 1 Corinthians 14.8-11. Paul likened sign gifts to things a child puts aside at adulthood and that they were "partial"—useful at the present time but would cease when "the complete" (τὸ τέλειον) came.

## What Did Paul Mean by τὸ τέλειον?

Much discussion has taken place over the meaning of "the complete," "the perfect," in some translations. Understanding what Paul meant by this expression requires examining how he used the word elsewhere.

| Paul's Use of τέλειος | Verse |
|---|---|
| So do not become conformed to this age but become transformed by the renewing of the mind so you might prove what is the good, and pleasing, and complete [τέλειον] will of the God. | Romans 12.2 |
| Now we speak wisdom among the mature, [τελείοις] but not the wisdom of this age, nor of the rulers of this age, who are being set aside. | 1 Corinthians 2.6 |
| But when the complete [τὸ τέλειον] should come, the partial will be set aside. | 1 Corinthians 13.10 |
| Brethren, do not be children in your thinking. But be children in the evil. Be grownups [τέλειοι] in your thinking. | 1 Corinthians 14.20 |
| Until we all should attain to the unity of the faith and the full knowledge of the Son of the God, to a completed [τέλειον] man, for the measure of the stature of the completeness of the Christ. | Ephesians 4.13 |
| Therefore, all who are mature [τέλειοι] should think this. And if you think anything differently, the God will also reveal this to you. | Philippians 3.15 |
| whom we proclaim, warning every man, and teaching every man, in all wisdom, so we might present every man complete [τέλειον] in Christ Jesus. | Colossians 1.28 |
| Epaphras, servant of Christ Jesus, who is from you, greets you who always struggles for you in his prayers, so that you might stand complete [τέλειοι] and fully accomplished in every will of the God. | Colossians 4.12 |
| But the solid food is for the mature, [τελείων] of those who have trained the faculties through use for discernment of both of good and of evil. | Hebrews 5.14 |
| But when Christ came, as high priest of the good things to come, through the greater and more complete [τελειοτέρας] tabernacle not made by hands, that is, not of this creation | Hebrews 9.11 |

These passages reveal Paul used τέλειος for that which had reached its end, maturation, completion, or intended goal. The presence of sign gifts when Paul wrote 1 Corinthians indicated maturity or completion had not yet been realized. What did he mean?

Paul revealed that sign gifts would cease when τὸ τέλειον came. It is noteworthy that only in this verse did Paul include the definite article with τέλειος, τὸ τέλειον, "the complete," indicating something specific. Greek can create nouns from adjectives by adding an article in the neuter case, putting the adjective into that case. Thus, the adjective, τέλειος, becomes an abstract noun or concept with the addition of the article, τὸ τέλειον and can be translated "the perfect" or "the complete." The article τό, nominative (or accusative) neuter singular of ὁ, indicated "the mature" or "the complete" was a thing that would come. When this thing occurred, sign gifts would disappear.

What was τὸ τέλειον? Paul received revelations from the Lord throughout his ministry. At the time he wrote the Corinthians, he had not received all that the Lord was going to show him. During his imprisonment in Rome, however, he received the full scope of God's revelation (Ephesians 1.8-10, 3.8-11). Once this occurred, sign gifts and miracles ceased. Thus, Paul wrote:

> Now, we see through a mirror unclearly, but then, face to face. At present, I know (γινώσκω) in part. But then, I will know fully (ἐπιγινώσκω), as I am fully known (ἐπιγινώσκω) (1 Corinthians 13.12).

Paul distinguished γινώσκω (know) from ἐπιγινώσκω (know) and wrote a more complete knowledge would come with τὸ τέλειον. Paul's use of ἐπίγνωσις, the noun associated with the verb ἐπιγινώσκω,2 is the key to understanding the cessation of the gifts of tongues, knowledge, prophecy, word of wisdom, discerning spirits, working miracles, and healing, as well as the practice of water baptism found in Acts and Paul's earlier letters. Paul wrote the Colossians and Philippians:

> [9] Because of this, we too, from the day we heard, do not stop praying for you and asking that you might be filled with the full knowledge (ἐπίγνωσις) of His will in all wisdom and spiritual understanding, [10] so you might walk worthily of the Lord for all pleasing, in every good work, by producing fruit and by growing in the full knowledge (ἐπίγνωσις) of the God (Colossians 1.9-10; cf. Ephesians 1.9-10, 16-17).

> So their hearts might be encouraged, since they have been united in love, and for all the riches of the full assurance of

---

[2] Paul letters after Acts show that he focused far greater attention upon ἐπίγνωσις, completed knowledge than before. He used ἐπίγνωσις three times in Romans. In the Prison Epistles he used it eight times and in the Pastorals four times (Ephesians 1.17, 4.13; Philippians 1.9; Colossians 1.9-10, 2.2, 3.10; 1 Timothy 2.4; 2 Timothy 2.25, 3.7; Titus 1.1; Philemon 1.6).

> the understanding, for the full knowledge (ἐπίγνωσις) of the secret of the God, Christ (Colossians 2.2).
>
> And this I pray, that your love may abound still more and more in full knowledge (ἐπίγνωσις) and every discernment (Philippians 1.9).

## Tongues: A Sign of Judgment

In his instructions on the use of tongues (languages), Paul wrote they were a sign of judgment to Israel:

> 21 In the Law it has been written: With other languages and with other lips I will speak to this people. And not even then will they hear Me, says the Lord. 22 So, the languages are for a sign, not for believers, but for unbelievers. But the prophecy is not for unbelievers but for believers (1 Corinthians 14.21-22).

Paul quoted Isaiah 28.11-12 and declared the speaking in other languages by Gentiles was a sign of God's judgment on Israel, a fulfillment of prophecy. Thus, he wrote, "tongues are for a sign, not to them that believe, but to them that believe not," i.e., Israel.

Luke recorded Paul's last meeting with and communication to the Jews while imprisoned in Rome:

> 25 And when there was discord with one another, they began leaving after Paul spoke one word: The Holy Spirit correctly spoke through Isaiah the prophet to our fathers, 26 saying, Go to this people and say, Hearing you will hear so you might never understand. And seeing you will see so you might never perceive. 27 For the heart of this people is thick and they barely hear with their ears, and they closed their eyes, lest they should see with their eyes and hear with their ears, and perceive with their heart, and turn so I will heal them. 28 Therefore, know this: This salvation of the God is sent to the Gentiles. And they will listen! 29 And after he said these things, the Jews went away and had a great argument among themselves (Acts 28.25-29).

Paul's statement pronounced judgment on national Israel. He recognized the nation would not repent or listen. Jesus had performed thousands of signs and miracles, the Twelve had performed signs and miracles, Paul had performed signs and miracles, and Gentile believers had spoken in tongues as a sign of judgment. Paul's words, "Now Jews ask for signs" (1 Corinthians 1.22) was fulfilled. Paul recognized his ministry to Israel had ended. After this, he would minister only to Gentiles. Thus, he wrote the Ephesians that he was the prisoner of Jesus Christ for Gentiles (Ephesians 3.1).

## First and Last Letters

Paul wrote seven letters during the Acts period: 1 and 2 Thessalonians, Hebrews, Galatians, 1 and 2 Corinthians, and Romans. During this period, miracles and sign gifts were present, e.g., Acts 19.6, 11-12, 21.10-14, 28.8-9; 1 Thessalonians 5.20; Galatians 3.5; 1 Corinthians 12, 13, 14; Romans 12.6.

After Acts, during Paul's imprisonment in Rome, he wrote four letters: Ephesians, Colossians, Philemon, and Philippians. After he was released, he wrote three more letters: Titus, 1 and 2 Timothy. Paul's last seven letters contain no miracles or sign gifts.[3] Thus, the first seven letters include miracles and sign gifts; the last seven letters do not. This is a strong indicator signs and miracles ceased by the time of Paul's Roman imprisonment.

Paul gave Timothy and Titus selection criteria for elders and deacons (Titus 1.6-9; 1 Timothy 3.1-10). Strikingly absent is any mention of miracles or sign gifts. If the gifts of tongues, wisdom, prophecy, knowledge, healing, and other miracles were still operating one would expect Paul to have noted them for those in leadership and service positions. This is another strong indicator they had ceased.

## Conclusion

The Bible is a progressive revelation. Paul's ministry was no different. God did not reveal everything to him at once. There was a process.

After Paul concluded his ministry recorded in Acts, in which he was still engaging in Jewish evangelism, he received the full revelation of God. Paul's speech to the Jews in Jerusalem was his final declaration of judgment to the nation. God had given the Jews signs for over sixty years beginning with the birth of John the Baptist and Jesus' birth. Signs continued throughout Christ's earthly ministry, the ministry of the Twelve, and Paul's ministry in Acts. After Acts, signs and miracles ceased. Paul wrote that what happened to Israel was for our instruction (Romans 15.4; 1 Corinthians 10.11). As such, Israel's entering the promised land provides an instruction on sign gifts.

The generation of Jews who came out of Egypt with Moses wandered forty years in the desert and died. They could not enter the promised land because of unbelief (Hebrews 3.7-19). Throughout this time, however, God graciously, and miraculously, fed them with manna. Manna, while life-sustaining, was not what God wished for them. He wanted them to enjoy the milk and honey of the promised land.

God dried the Jordan River and the new generation crossed it on dry ground under Joshua (Joshua 1.1-3, 3.14-17, 4.23-24) even as their

---

[3] Paul mentions prophecy in 1 Timothy 1.18, 4.14 but the prophecies about Timothy had been made years before.

fathers crossed the dry Red Sea under Moses. God then commanded the people to be circumcised for they had neglected the sign of the Abrahamic Covenant for forty years (Joshua 5.2-10). After this circumcision, God told Joshua, "This day have I rolled away the reproach of Egypt from off you" (Joshua 5.9). The nation also celebrated the Passover (Joshua 5.10). Then we read:

> [11] And they did eat of the old corn of the land on the morrow after the passover, unleavened cakes, and parched corn in the selfsame day. [12] And the manna ceased on the morrow after they had eaten of the old corn of the land; neither had the children of Israel manna any more; but they did eat of the fruit of the land of Canaan that year (Joshua 5.11-12).

The "manna ceased." Manna was like the sign gifts: transitory. It provided temporary sustenance until the people were prepared to go into the promised land and enjoy the fruit of the land. So it is with us. We have God's full revelation—the milk and honey of Paul's secrets and the completion of the Word of God.

God continues to heal today but the *gift* of healing has ceased. Instead of seeking "healers," believers are to pray to God for healing. God sometimes will heal immediately, sometimes it will be gradual, and sometimes He will not heal because He has a greater purpose in mind. No "healers" exist in the Church. Apparent gifts of prophecy, tongues, knowledge, etc. are counterfeits: products of fakery, psychological manipulation, emotionalism, or the powers of darkness. No believer should be involved in such deceit.

The baptism of the Holy Spirit was "the complete" and replaced "the partial" of water baptism. Paul baptized in his early ministry but after he received Christ's full revelation, he wrote that *one* baptism exists in the Church: the baptism of the Holy Spirit (Ephesians 4.5). Water baptism was required for salvation under the gospel of the kingdom (Mark 1.4, 16.16; Acts 2.38, 22.16) but for us, the baptism of the Holy Spirit is the divine part of our salvation. In addition, the Word, not water, cleanses believers. Paul wrote the Ephesians that Christ loved and gave Himself so He might sanctify the Church: "He cleansed her by the washing of the water by the word" (Ephesians 5.26).

We have the full revelation of Paul's secrets. We have the completed Word of God (Colossians 1.25). We can enjoy the "full assurance of understanding" (Colossians 2.2) and the "unity of the faith" (Ephesians 4.13). Paul is our apostle and all Church doctrine comes from him. We live the Christian life by following Paul's doctrines, by faith, through the power of the Holy Spirit. This is our pathway, not experiences, not the gifts of tongues, knowledge, prophecy, not water baptism, not the gift of healing. God set these aside with τὸ τέλειον, the full assurance of the understanding (Colossians 2.2). We no longer are children (1 Corinthians 13.11) for we see "face to face" (1 Corinthians 13.12).

What remains is far greater: the faith, the hope, and the love,[4] God's full revelation to His Church.

A final, but important concluding remark is needed about sign gifts in Paul's ministry. Acts records Paul exercise of sign gifts, during which time he wrote six letters to the Church, Romans, Galatians, 1-2 Corinthians, 1-2 Thessalonians and one letter to the Jews, Hebrews. Throughout the Acts period when Paul wrote the above letters, sign gifts were operational and water baptism occurred. But his last seven letters, Ephesians, Philippians, Colossians, 1-2 Timothy, Titus, and Philemon, contain no mention of sign gifts regarding himself, believers in general, or among those in church leadership, i.e., pastors, teachers, deacons, elders, etc. He also declared there was now "one baptism," the baptism of the Holy Spirit, ending water baptism.

Paul's ministry thus falls in two parts. Throughout Acts, he went to Jews first, then turned to Gentiles when the Jews rejected his message. This is noted three times in Acts 13, 19, and 28. After this, Paul ceased going to Jews first but concentrated his ministry on Gentiles. He wrote the Ephesians he was a prisoner of Christ Jesus for Gentiles (Ephesians 3.1). Thus, a correspondence exists between Paul's earlier ministry and operation of sign gifts and practice of water baptism and his latter ministry with no sign gifts and no water baptism.

How are we to understand this? According to the Lord's words in Acts 9.15, Paul's commission included ministry to both Jews and Gentiles but his primary mission was to Gentiles (Romans 11.13). Paul initially went to Jews for he loved them and thought that if he, Jesus' chief opponent, could be saved, his nation could also. But as Acts 28 reveals, it was not to be. Paul finally realized this and ceased going to the Jews.

How does this fit with sign gifts and water baptism? Paul wrote the Corinthians, "Now Jews ask for sign and Greeks seek wisdom" (1 Corinthians 1.22). God allowed Paul to exercise sign gifts to prove to the Jews, and the Twelve, that he was a genuine apostle. He continued to practice water baptism, though he declared this practice was quite limited (1 Corinthians 1.14-17) for Christ did not send him to baptize but to proclaim the gospel (1 Corinthians 1.17). Had Paul not been able in his early ministry to exercise the sign gifts of prophecy, languages, knowledge, healing and practice water baptism, he would not have been accepted by the Jews as a genuine apostle to minister to Jews.

Once it became clear the Jews would not accept Paul's testimony that Jesus was the promised Messiah, the sign gifts ceased. Water baptism ceased also for it was the key work in the gospel of the kingdom for repentance and belief that Jesus was the Messiah, the Son of God. In this sense, "the complete," τὸ τέλειον, was the end of Paul's ministry to Jews in particular.

---

[4] All the nouns are articular, denoting their source is God.

Those who maintain the sign gifts of prophecy, knowledge, languages, healings are operational today fail to understand this division in Paul's ministry and fail to understand Paul was God's unique apostle, not an appendage to the Twelve. Furthermore, those who teach the Church, the body of Christ, began in Acts 2 face an insurmountable theological barrier in arguing sign gifts have ceased since speaking in languages was the preeminent divine sign at Pentecost of the coming of the Holy Spirit. Pentecostals are right in maintaining that if the Church began at Pentecost, the power of speaking in languages should be present today among believers as evidence of the Holy Spirit. And if this is true, then the other sign gifts should also be operational among believers.

However, if the Church did not begin in Acts 2, everything changes. If the Church did not begin in Acts 2, the sign gifts and water baptism that Paul practiced in his early ministry were not defining components of the Church but gifts and practices God gave him to exercise (for Jews ask for signs) to authenticate his ministry to Jews during the Acts period. These things continued so long as Paul ministered to Jews. It must also be remembered that Luke's primary purpose in writing Acts was to explain to Jews why Christ did not return and why the kingdom of God did not come (cf. Acts 3.19-21; Matthew 23.37-39). If this is the case (and it is) a sound theological basis exists to refute the claims of Pentecostals that sign gifts are operational today. But, on the contrary, if one maintains the Church began in Acts 2, solid ground turns to sand.

# Chapter 13

# Paul: Adversaries and Suffering

> [15] *But the Lord said to him, Go. For this man is a chosen vessel to Me, to carry My name before the Gentiles, and kings, and the sons of Israel.* [16] *For I will show him how many things he must suffer for My name (Acts 9.15-16).*

## Introduction

Shortly after Paul met the risen Lord on the road to Damascus, God told the fearful Ananias that Paul was a "chosen vessel" to reveal God to the Gentiles, kings, and the children of Israel and that he would suffer greatly for Him (Acts 9.15-16). Truer words were never spoken.

Few have suffered for Christ as Paul. For thirty years he endured enormous physical, mental, and emotional pressures. Yet throughout his suffering, he remained joyful and the Lord was with him.

Paul wrote he was "*a* pattern for those about to believe on Him for eternal life" (1 Timothy 1.16). As that pattern, members of the Church, the body of Christ, are to imitate him (1 Corinthians 4.16). How Paul met suffering and adversity is an inspiring example of faithfulness for all who desire to live godly lives in Christ. His endurance should cheer and encourage each of us to be faithful to the One who loved us and gave Himself for us.

## False Teachers

Paul faced detractors and false teachers throughout his ministry. Immediately following his conversion, he taught what he formerly fought—that Jesus of Nazareth was the Son of God (Acts 9.20). This led to fierce disputes with the Jews who resolved to kill him (Acts 9.23, 26). Acts records their conflicts with Paul and plots to murder him.

Throughout the centuries, the Church has been afflicted by numerous heresies. Paul's letters reveal the earliest heresies were 1) attempts to bring believers under the administration of the Mosaic Law and 2) the denial of the Pre-Tribulational Rapture.

### Bringing Believers Under the Mosaic Law

Paul wrote the Galatians:

> [4] because of the false brethren who infiltrated us, who came in secretly to spy on our liberty that we have in Christ Jesus, so they could enslave us, [5] to whom we did not give way in subjection, not even for *an* hour, so the truth of the gospel might continue with you (Galatians 2.4-5).

The Galatian problem concerned whether the Christian life should be lived under the administration of the Mosaic Law or under the administration of grace through the Holy Spirit. The "party of the circumcision," also known as the Judaizers (Galatians 2.12), wished to control believers through circumcision and the Mosaic Law. Paul also wrote of these false teachers:

> 10 I am confident for you in *the* Lord that you will not think otherwise. But the one who troubles you will bear the judgment, whoever he might be. 11 Now I brethren, if I still proclaim circumcision, why am I still persecuted? In that case, the offense of the cross has been abolished. 12 I wish those who trouble you will castrate themselves (Galatians 5.10-12)!

Paul did not mince language against these circumcision advocates. He wrote that he wished those who were troubling the Galatians to go all the way and castrate themselves in their zeal for circumcision.[1] He also wrote of them:

> 12 Those who want to impress in *the* flesh force you to be circumcised only so they may not be persecuted for the cross of the Christ. 13 For not even those who are circumcised keep *the* Law themselves, but they wish you to be circumcised, so they may boast in your flesh. 14 But for me, may I never boast except in the cross of our Lord Jesus Christ, through which *the* world has been crucified to me and I to *the* world. 15 For in Christ Jesus neither circumcision nor uncircumcision avails anything: Instead, *a* new creation (Galatians 6.12-15).

## Denial of the Rapture

Paul's letters to the Thessalonians were his first letters and the first doctrine he taught them after they believed the gospel was the Pre-Tribulation Rapture, the principal subject of 1 and 2 Thessalonians. In the second letter, he defended it and addressed the false teaching that the Day of the Lord, the Tribulation, had come. Paul wrote:

> 1 Now we ask you, brethren, concerning the coming of our Lord Jesus Christ and of our gathering to Him, 2 that you might not be easily shaken in your mind or be troubled, by neither spirit, or by word, or by *a* letter as if through us, that the day of the Lord has arrived [ἐνίστημι][2] (2 Thessalonians 2.1-2).

---

[1] The verb ἀποκόπτω (cut off, amputate) is a future middle indicative. The middle voice indicates the subject is both the cause and receiver of the action.

[2] Paul alone used the verb ἐνίστημι (Romans 8.38; 1 Corinthians 3,22, 7.26; Galatians 1.4; 2 Thessalonians 2.2; 2 Timothy 3.1; Hebrews 9.9). He always used the word for that which was present.

The Thessalonians had received a forged letter, purportedly from Paul, which said the suffering they were experiencing was the Tribulation. This was highly upsetting because it meant 1) the Thessalonians had missed the Rapture, i.e., they were not true believers, or 2) there was no Pre-Tribulation Rapture. Such a claim contradicted Paul's teaching that Christ would return and rescue them from the Tribulation (1 Thessalonians 1.10, 5.9). As a result, Paul encouraged them:

> Do not let anyone deceive you in any way. For the departure must come first and then the man of the sin should be revealed, the son of the destruction (2 Thessalonians 2.3).

Before the Tribulation can come, the Rapture (the departure) must come. After that, the "man of the sin," the Beast, is revealed. Paul's last letter corrected another false teaching regarding the Rapture:

> [16] But avoid worldly, pointless babbling, for they will lead to more impiety [17] and their talk will spread as gangrene, of whom are Hymenaeus and Philetus, [18] who went astray from the truth, by asserting the resurrection has already occurred. So they are undermining the faith of some (2 Timothy 2.16-18).

Hymenaeus and Philetus taught "the resurrection," the Rapture, had occurred. These false teachers wished to frighten Paul's converts and bring them under their control. The attack on the Pre-Tribulational Rapture has a long history that continues today. Its denial is an easy and clear mark of a false teacher.

## Counterfeit Christians

Many in Christendom appear to be Christians but are pretenders. They profess Christ but do not possess Christ. They belong to churches, teach in seminaries, use Christian vocabulary, have Christian titles, and may wear robes of authority. Paul warned about such deceivers:

> [12] Now what I do, I will do, so I might cut off the chance of those who want *a* chance so they might be found *to be* as we by what they boast. [13] For such *are* false apostles, deceitful workers, masquerading as apostles of Christ.[14] And no wonder—for Satan himself masquerades as *an* angel of light. [15] Therefore, it is not surprising if his servants also masquerade as servants of righteousness—whose end will be according to their works (2 Corinthians 11.12-15).

Paul also warned Timothy of such false teachers:

> [19] By holding faith and *a* good conscience, which some, who have rejected the faith, became shipwrecked, [20] among whom are Hymenaeus and Alexander, whom I delivered to Satan, so they might be taught not to blaspheme (1 Timothy 1.19-20).

> [14] Alexander the coppersmith showed me much harm. The Lord will repay to him according to his works. [15] You too watch out for him. For he greatly opposed our words (2 Timothy 4.14-15).

Paul instructed the Church how to deal with such individuals. Believers are to pray to God that they be "delivered to Satan" and "rewarded according to their works." To follow false doctrine is bad. To teach it is worse. To tolerate it is faithlessness.

## Abandonment of Paul's Doctrines

One of the saddest passages in all Scripture is the following which Paul wrote Timothy, shortly before he was executed:

> [13] Hold to the pattern of sound words which you heard from me by faith and love which *are* in Christ Jesus. [14] Protect the good thing entrusted *to you* through the Holy Spirit, the One who lives in us. [15] You know this: everyone in Asia deserted me—among whom are Phygellus and Hermogenes (2 Timothy 1.13-15).

All Asia abandoned Paul's teachings. The places he had worked so hard and established churches—Ephesus, Colossae, Galatia, Iconium, Derbe, Lystra, Antioch Pisidia, and Laodicea—all these congregations abandoned his teachings. Only a few years before, the Ephesian elders had wept and kissed him when he told them he would likely never see them again (Acts 20.36-38). How fragile is the faith of some and how fickle human nature! How easily some are swayed by false teachers! Today is no different. The failure to understand Paul's unique apostleship and secrets, that he founded the Church, the body of Christ, and that all Church doctrine is from Paul, began with this desertion.

Perhaps the most heart-breaking truth is that many who do not recognize the unique nature of Paul's apostleship think they are teaching the truth. In reality, they have abandoned the Scriptures for tradition, what has been handed down for centuries.

Some even teach that Paul was a false apostle, that he perverted the teachings of Christ and the Twelve. They do not realize that without Paul there is no Church, no Church doctrine, no message of salvation. Peter, James, John, Luke, and Mark all recognized Paul was God's "chosen vessel," "the apostle of the Gentiles." One who rejects Paul must reject them also. Who remains? The only writers with no known contact with Paul are Matthew and Jude. Rejecting Paul means one's New Testament has two books: Matthew's Gospel and Jude's letter.

## Murder Plots

Paul had to contend with attempts on his life throughout his ministry. These plots begin shortly after his salvation, in Damascus. Luke wrote:

> [23] Now when many days had passed, the Jews plotted to kill him. [24] But their plot became known to Saul. Now they kept watching the gates both day and night, so they might kill him. [25] But his disciples took *him* at night and let him down through the wall by lowering *him* in *a* basket. [29] He also kept speaking and debating with the Hellenists.[3] But they kept trying to kill him (Acts 9.23-25, 29).

Having narrowly escaped being torn to pieces by the mob incited by Demetrius the silversmith in Ephesus (Acts 19.22-41), Paul traveled to Greece where he stayed for three months. During this time, the Jews "made *a* plot against him" (Acts 20.3).

Going to Miletus, in southwestern Turkey, Paul addressed the Ephesian elders and told them of his determination to go to Jerusalem for Pentecost (Acts 20-17-24). When he arrived in Jerusalem, Paul agreed to James' counsel to take a vow. It did no good.

> [27] Now when the seven days were about to be completed, after the Jews from Asia saw him in the Temple, they began stirring up the whole crowd and grabbed him with their hands, [28] shouting, Men, Israelites, help! This is the man, the one who teaches everyone, everywhere against the people, and the Law, and this place. And besides this, he led Greeks into the Temple and has defiled this holy place. [29] (For they had previously seen Trophimus the Ephesian in the city with him and assumed that Paul brought him into the Temple). [30] So the whole city became agitated and the people rushed together. And after they grabbed Paul, they began dragging him outside the Temple. And immediately the doors were locked. [31] So while they were trying to kill him, news went up to the commander of the cohort that all Jerusalem was in an uproar (Acts 21.27-31).

When the Roman battalion commander received news of the riot, he arrested Paul. Paul convinced him he was not the Egyptian who had caused an earlier insurrection and to allow him to address the Jews. Paul's speech went fine until he said one word: Gentiles. Luke wrote:

> [21] Then He said to me, Go! For I will send you far away to *the* Gentiles. [22] Now they kept listening to him until this word. Then they raised their voice, saying, Away from the earth with such! He is not fit to live! [23] And when they shouted, and threw off their cloaks, and tossed dust into the air (Acts 22.21-23).

The commander was going to whip Paul but stopped when he learned he was a Roman citizen (Acts 22.25-29). As a result, he freed him and placed him before the Jewish rulers. When Paul perceived it was not

---

[3] Hellenists were Jews who spoke Greek and had adopted Greek culture.

possible to get a fair hearing, he changed the dynamics of the meeting. He declared he was on trial for the resurrection. This initiated a fight between the Pharisees and Sadducees and the commander had to move Paul to safety in the fortress (Acts 23.6-10). The Jews, however, would not be deterred and organized a group of assassins:

> [12] Now when it was day, some of the Jews made *a* plot and
> put themselves under *a* curse, swearing not to eat or drink
> until they should kill Paul. [13] Now more than forty made this
> plot, [14] who, after they came to the chief priests and the
> elders, said, We placed ourselves under *a* curse not to eat or
> drink anything until we should kill Paul. [15] Now therefore,
> you with the Sanhedrin, request that the commander should
> bring him down to you tomorrow as if you want to examine
> the issues surrounding him more carefully. Then, before he
> comes near, we are ready to kill him (Acts 23.12-15).

Paul's nephew learned of the plot, told Paul, and Paul notified the Roman commander. To ensure Paul's safety as a Roman citizen, the commander, Claudius Lysias, ordered 200 infantry, 60 cavalry, and 200 spearmen to escort Paul from Jerusalem to Caesarea. Such a heavy military force revealed the scope of the threat Paul. Arriving in Caesarea, Paul was imprisoned two years. At the end of this time, he had to appeal his case to Caesar because Festus would have returned him to Jerusalem to be tried by the Jews (Acts 25.6-12). Paul knew they would kill him. His appeal led to a long, perilous sea voyage to Rome.

In addition to these plots, Paul had to contend with mobs who wished to kill him (Acts 17.1-10, 19.23-41, 21.27-31, 22.21-25). It should be mentioned that the Jews *succeeded* in killing or nearly killing him. Luke wrote:

> [19] Then Jews from Antioch and Iconium came. And after
> they persuaded the crowds and stoned Paul, they dragged
> him out of the city, because they thought he had died. [20] But
> when the disciples surrounded him, he got up, entered the
> city, and the next day went with Barnabas to Derbe (Acts
> 14.19-20).

Whether Paul actually died and God resuscitated him is unclear. What is clear, is that God supernaturally healed him. One does not survive stoning and be able to travel the next day without divine intervention.

## Sufferings

Paul wrote the Corinthians of his sufferings in about 57 A.D. His list was representative, not comprehensive for he would continue to suffer until his execution. Paul recounted:

> [22] Are they Hebrews? I too! Are they Israelites? I too! Are
> they descendants Abraham? I too! [23] Are they ministers of

> Christ? (I speak as unhinged), I more. Exceeding in labors,
> exceeding in imprisonments, in stripes beyond measure, in
> deaths many times. [24] Five times I received from *the* Jews
> forty lashes minus one. [25] Three times I was beaten with
> rods, once was I stoned, three times I was I shipwrecked. I
> spent *a* night and *a* day in the deep. [26] In many journeys, in
> dangers of rivers, in dangers of robbers, in dangers from *my*
> people, in dangers from Gentiles, in dangers in *the* city, in
> dangers in *the* wilderness, in dangers on *the* sea, in dangers
> among false brethren, [27] in labor and toil, in many sleepless
> nights, in hunger and thirst, many times without food, in
> cold and without clothing. [28] Besides these external things *is*
> the daily stress on me, the concern for all the churches.
> [29] Who is weak, and I am not weak? Who is offended, and I
> do not burn? [30] If I must boast, I will boast in the things of
> my weakness. [31] The God and Father of our Lord Jesus
> Christ knows, the One who is blessed forever, I do not lie!
> [32] In Damascus, the governor under Aretas the king kept
> guarding the city of the Damascenes to capture me [33] but I
> was lowered through *a* window in *a* basket through the wall
> and escaped his hands (2 Corinthians 11.22-33).

Paul's questions, "Are they Hebrews? Are they Israelites? Are they descendants of Abraham? Are they ministers of Christ?" reveal the attacks of his opponents. They claimed he had abandoned Judaism and was not a true minister. Paul wrote, "I lie not" because his enemies declared he was a liar. Despite this abuse, Paul knew the risen Christ and knew he was obedient to Him. Paul's attitude should be that of all godly believers who are persecuted for the faith.

## Defend Apostleship

Paul's opponents and critics were relentless in slandering and discrediting him. As a result, he had to defend his apostleship constantly. He wrote the Corinthians:

> [1] I must boast. Though it is not appropriate I will go on to
> visions and revelations from *the* Lord. [2] I know *a* man in
> Christ, who fourteen years ago, whether in *the* body I do not
> know, whether out of the body I do not know—the God
> knows—such *a* man was caught up to *the* third heaven. [3] and
> I know such *a* man, whether in the body or out of the body,
> I do not know—the God knows—[4] that he was caught up
> into the Paradise and he heard unspeakable words, which it
> is not permitted for man to speak. [5] I will boast about this
> man, but about myself I will not boast, except in my
> weaknesses. [6] For if I should wish to boast, I will not be *a*
> fool, for I will speak *the* truth. But I refrain, lest anyone
> should think more than what he sees in me or hears from me.
> [7] And so I might not become arrogant because of the
> superiority of the revelations, *a* thorn in my flesh, *an* angel

> of Satan, was given to me so he might torment me, so I might not become arrogant. [8] Three times I pleaded with the Lord about this, that it might leave me. [9] But He said to me, My grace is sufficient for you. For My power is completed by weakness. Therefore, I will most gladly rather boast in my weaknesses, so the power of the Christ might reside on me. [10] So, I take pleasure in weaknesses, in insults, in hardships, in persecutions, in stresses for Christ. For when I may be weak, then I am powerful (2 Corinthians 12.1-10).

God took Paul to the third heaven[4] and he heard things which he could not disclose. These revelations were so profound that God gave him a "thorn in the flesh," allowing Satan to "torment" him. Paul declared God allowed this to prevent him from becoming arrogant in the face of all the abuse he received from those who attacked Paul's gospel and doctrines of grace. This suffering was so trying that Paul begged the Lord three times to remove it. He would not. From this, Paul learned, as should we, that when we are weak, then we are powerful. When we rely wholly on the Lord, then we have power.

## Provided For Own Needs

Paul was acutely sensitive to avoid any appearance of financial impropriety. For this reason, he labored as much as possible to provide for his own needs. Nothing is more damaging to a believer's testimony than to have one's reputation undermined by avarice. Paul's words instruct us in this matter.

> [33] I coveted no one's silver, or gold, or clothing. [34] You yourselves know that these hands ministered to my needs and to those who were with me. [35] I showed you by everything, that by hard work, we must help those who are weak and remember the words of the Lord Jesus, that He Himself said, It is more blessed to give than to receive [5] (Acts 20.33-35).

The reason Paul wrote he "coveted no man's silver," etc. was because his critics accused him of being in the ministry for the money. Just how ridiculous this charge was is apparent from the following:

> [10] We *are* fools for Christ but you *are* wise in Christ. We *are* weak but you *are* strong. You *are* honored, we *are* dishonored. [11] To the present hour we are hungry, and thirsty, and poorly clothed, and beaten, and homeless. [12] And we toil, by working with own hands. When we are reviled,

---

[4] The first heaven is the sky, the second is space, and the third is the abode of God and the angelic host. Subtracting 14 years from when Paul wrote 2 Corinthians, about 57 A.D., means Paul went to the third heaven in about 43 A.D., before his first missionary journey, probably while in Antioch, Syria.

[5] This statement is not in the Gospels.

> we bless; when we are persecuted, we endure; [13] when we are slandered, we entreat. We became as *the* filth of the earth, *the* offscouring of all, until now. [14] I do not write these things to shame you, but as my beloved children, to counsel you. [15] For though you may have ten thousand guardians in Christ, yet not many fathers. For I fathered you in Christ Jesus through the gospel. [16] Therefore, I urge you, become imitators of me (1 Corinthians 4.10-16).

Paul wrote the Thessalonians:

> For you remember brethren, our labor and toil: by working night and day so we might not burden any of you, we declared the gospel of the God to you (1 Thessalonians 2.9).

> [7] For you yourselves know how you must imitate us for we did not act disorderly among you [8] or eat bread from anyone without payment, but by labor and toil, we worked night and day not to burden any of you (2 Thessalonians 3.7-8).

As a Pharisaic Jew, Paul was respected, wealthy, on the fast track of success. He gave it all up for Christ.

The next two passages drip with sarcasm but Paul knew the Corinthians could handle it. The Macedonians, the poor Greek hillbillies, were helping support Paul while the wealthy, sophisticated Corinthians were lagging behind. Paul's well-placed barbs were aimed to awaken the Corinthians to their financial responsibilities.

> [4] For if the one who comes proclaims another Jesus whom we did not proclaim, or you receive *a* different spirit which you did not receive, or *a* different gospel which you did not accept— you put up with it fine. [5] For I reckon to have been inferior in nothing to "the super apostles." [6] Now even if *I am* unpolished in speech, yet not in knowledge. But in everything we were manifested to you in all things. [7] Or did I commit *a* sin by humbling myself so you might be exalted, because I proclaimed the gospel of the God free of charge? [8] I robbed other churches when I received support for ministry to you! [9] And when I was present with you and was in need, I burdened no one. For my need was completely supplied when the brethren came from Macedonia. (2 Corinthians 11.4-9).

> [13] For how is it that you were inferior to the rest *of the* churches except that I myself did not burden you? Forgive me this injustice! [14] Behold, this *is the* third time I am ready to come to you, and I will not be *a* burden to you. For I do not seek what is yours, but you. For the children ought not to save up for the parents, but the parents for the children. [15] Now I will most gladly expend and be spent for your souls. If I love you even more, am I loved less? [16] So be it. Yet I

> did not burden you. But, being crafty, I caught you with
> trickery. 17 Did anyone whom I have sent to you—did I
> exploit you by him (2 Corinthians 12.13-17)?

Christian leaders must sometimes goad their congregations to recognize their responsibilities, even as Paul did.

## Church Problems

In addition to assassination plots, imprisonments, beatings, and false teachers, Paul had to contend with internal church problems. Many of these are revealed in his letters to the Corinthians. They included factions, immorality, lawsuits, questions about marriage, questions regarding eating foods sacrificed to idols, women praying unveiled, abuses of the Lord's supper, proper exercise of spiritual gifts, and questions regarding the resurrection.

## False Accusers

Every time Paul was arrested and came to trial was a result of injustice: the suborning of false witnesses and mob rule. Those whom Satan has blinded (2 Corinthians 4.4) use such devices to hinder truth. Nothing is a greater target for Satan's attacks than Paul's gospel and doctrines for they are the power of God to all who believe (Romans 1.16 cf. 1 Corinthian 1.18). Luke wrote the following regarding false witnesses:

> 12 Now when Gallio was proconsul of Achaia, the Jews
> united against Paul and brought him to the judgment seat,
> 13 saying, This man incites men to worship the God against
> the Law. 14 Now as Paul was about to open his mouth, Gallio
> said to the Jews, Now Jews, if this was some unrighteous or
> evil crime, I would accept your case. 15 But if it is *a* question
> about *a* word and names, and of your Law, you will see to it
> yourselves. I do not intend to be *a* judge of these things. 16 So
> he dismissed them from the judgment seat (Acts 18.12-16).

> 1 Now after five days, Ananias, the high priest, came down
> with some of the elders and *a* certain orator, Tertullus, and
> brought the case against Paul to the governor. 2 Now when
> he was called, Tertullus began to accuse *him*, saying, We are
> enjoying great peace because of you and worthy
> achievements are being done to this nation because of your
> foresight. 3 Most noble Felix, we recognize this in every way
> and everywhere with all gratitude. 4 Now, so that I may not
> delay you any longer, I beg you to hear us briefly with your
> customary indulgence. 5 For because we found this man *a*
> pest who stirs up dissent among all the Jews in the world, *a*
> ringleader of the sect of the Nazarenes, 6 who even attempted
> to desecrate the Temple, whom we also seized and wanted
> to try according to our Law, 7 but Lysias the commander
> arrived with great violence and took him from our hands
> 8 and ordered his accusers to come to you. After you

> examine him yourself, you will be able to understand from him about all these things of which we accuse him. [9] Then the Jews also joined in by asserting these things to be so (Acts 24.1-9).

> [6] Now after he stayed with them more than ten days, he went down to Caesarea. On the next day, after he sat on the judgment seat, he commanded Paul to be brought. [7] Now after he came, the Jews who had come down from Jerusalem stood around him and brought many serious charges against Paul, which they kept not being able to prove (Acts 25.6-7).

## Failure of Believers

One of the most painful (and saddest) incidents in Paul's life was his confrontation with Peter in Antioch. Paul wrote:

> [11] Now when Peter came to Antioch, I stood up against him to his face, because he was wrong. [12] For before some came from James, he used to eat with the Gentiles. But when they came, he began to withdraw and kept separating himself, because he was afraid of those of the circumcision. [13] And the rest of the Jews joined in this hypocrisy with him also, so that even Barnabas was carried away by their hypocrisy. [14] But when I saw they were not behaving properly, after the truth of the gospel, I said to Peter before everyone, If you are *a* Jew and live like *a* Gentile and not like *a* Jew, why do you make the Gentiles live like Jews (Galatians 2.11-14)?

Peter visited Antioch after the Council of Jerusalem. At the Council, he had supported Paul and declared Paul's Gentile believers did not have to be circumcised and keep the Law to be saved. Even more, he stated that Jews from that day forward must be saved like Paul's Gentiles (Acts 15.11). This declaration overturned 2,000 years of Jewish theology and ended the gospel of the kingdom. From then until when God completes the Church, only Paul's gospel was a valid message of salvation.

While the matter of the gospel and salvation was settled at the Council, how to live the Christian life was not. When Peter came to Antioch, he ate and fellowshipped with Gentile believers. But representatives of James, those of the "party of the circumcision," came to Antioch and confronted him about his behavior. As a result, Peter withdrew from eating with Gentile believers and told them they had to keep the Mosaic Law, contrary to what Paul had taught. Paul had no choice but to rebuke Peter. Paul declared:

> [14] But when I saw they were not behaving properly, after the truth of the gospel, I said to Peter before everyone, If you are *a* Jew and live like *a* Gentile and not like *a* Jew, why do you make the Gentiles live like Jews? [15] We are Jews by nature and not sinners from *the* Gentiles, [16] but we know that

> *a* man is not declared righteous except through *the* faithfulness of Jesus Christ, not from works of *the* Law. And we believed in Christ Jesus so we might be declared righteous from *the* faithfulness of Christ and not by works from *the* Law. For no flesh will be declared righteous from *the* works of *the* Law (Galatians 2.14-16).

The actions of these Judaizers and the cancer of legalism poisoned even Barnabas (Galatians 2.13). This reveals how vulnerable truth is and why we must be constantly reminded of Paul's doctrines of grace. Paul wrote the Galatians: "a little leaven leavens the whole lump" (Galatians 5.9). Even strong believers such as Barnabas, who had ministered with Paul, and Peter became intimidated by the party of the circumcision from James. The Christian life is never Law *and* Grace. It is Law *or* Grace. They cannot coexist. No hint of legalism must invade the Christian life. Choosing Law means one is a debtor to keep the whole Law (Galatians 5.3). To live a godly, Christian life, we must heed and obey Paul's admonition:

> Stand fast, therefore, in the freedom in which Christ set us free. And do not become entangled again with *a* yoke of bondage (Galatians 5.1).

> For sin will not rule over you. For you are not under Law, but under grace (Romans 6.14).

This truth is difficult for many and much of the weight of Christendom is against it. Paul knew it well. Consider his last words:

> [10] For Demas deserted me because he loved the present age and went to Thessalonica, Crescens to Galatia, Titus to Dalmatia. [11] Luke alone is with me. When you pick up Mark, bring *him* with you for he is useful to me for ministry. [12] Now Tychicus I sent to Ephesus. [13] Bring the cloak which I left in Troas with Carpus when you come, and the books, especially the parchments. [14] Alexander the coppersmith showed me much harm. The Lord will repay to him according to his works. [15] You too watch out for him. For he greatly opposed our words. [16] In my first defense no one stood with me. Instead, everyone deserted me. May it not be reckoned against them. [17] But the Lord stood with me and strengthened me so the preaching might be fully accomplished through me so all the Gentiles might hear. So, I was delivered from *the* mouth of *the* lion. [18] The Lord will rescue me from every evil work and will save *me* into His heavenly kingdom. To whom *be* the glory forever and ever! Amen (2 Timothy 4.10-18).

Following Paul will be costly. Most of Christendom adheres to tradition, knows nothing of Paul's secrets, and has little desire to learn about them and enjoy the "full assurance of understanding" (Colossians 2.2) and the "unity of the faith" (Ephesians 4.13). The vast majority are content to accept what their church or denomination teaches and live by tradition rather than the Scriptures. But Christ will judge us according to faithfulness to His word, not tradition. Such knowledge should galvanize us to obeying what God has revealed to the Church through Paul. When Paul wrote 2 Timothy, Luke alone was with him. He wrote that at his first defense trial *all* forsook him. Courage is required to hold to and live by Pauline truths against the majority. But Paul is our example and wrote, "the Lord stood with me and strengthened me." God is always with us and gives strength to those who stand with Him in the truth. God remembers faithfulness and will reward it.

## Suffering and God's Justice

Paul wrote the Thessalonians:

> 4 So that we ourselves boast[6] about you in the churches of the God about your endurance and faith in all your persecutions and in the afflictions that you are enduring.
> 5 *This is* evidence of the righteous judgment of the God so you might be deemed worthy of the kingdom of the God for which you suffer. 6 For *it is* right for God to repay those who afflict you with tribulation, 7 and to you who are being afflicted, *to give* rest with us in the revelation of the Lord Jesus from heaven, with His powerful angels, 8 by inflicting vengeance with flaming fire on those who do not know God and on those who do not obey the gospel of our Lord Jesus Christ, 9 who will pay the penalty of eternal destruction away from the face of the Lord and from the glory of His strength,
> 10 when He should come to be glorified by His saints and to be marveled at by all who believed, because our testimony to you was believed in that day (2 Thessalonians 1.4-10).

Paul boasted about the Thessalonians' endurance and faith due to suffering persecution and declared it was evidence of God's righteous judgment so they might be deemed worthy of God's kingdom. Such suffering also demonstrates that God is just in punishing persecutors. God is now dealing in grace but His case against unbelieving humanity continues to build. He will not allow injustice to go on forever. A point comes in which He will punish unbelievers—the Tribulation, the Day of the Lord. Penal justice is also in view in this passage. God will judge every person individually. Unlike Christ, Paul rarely spoke of hell, but here, he declared that those who reject Christ will be punished with "eternal destruction away from the face of the Lord and from the glory

---

[6] Paul wrote the Romans he gloried in tribulations for they resulted in patience (Romans 5.3). The noun καυχάομαι means to glory or boast.

of His strength" (ὄλεθρον αἰώνιον ἀπὸ προσώπου τοῦ κυρίου καὶ ἀπὸ τῆς δόξης τῆς ἰσχύος αὐτοῦ).[7]

Paul wrote similarly to the Philippians:

> 27 Only live worthily of the gospel of the Christ, so whether I come and see you, or whether I am absent, I may hear these things about you: that you stand fast in one spirit, with one soul, striving together in the faith of the gospel. 28 So do not be frightened by anything from those who oppose—which is *a* proof of destruction to them, but to you, of salvation—and this *is* from God. 29 For it was granted to you on Christ's behalf, not only to believe in Him, but also to suffer for Him, 30 since you have the same conflict, that you saw in me and now hear by me (Philippians 1.27-30).

Paul continued with this word to the Thessalonians:

> 11 For which also we always pray for you, so our God might deem you worthy of the calling, and might complete every desire of goodness and work of faith with power, 12 so that the name of our Lord Jesus Christ might be glorified in you and you in Him, according to the grace of our God and *the* Lord Jesus Christ (2 Thessalonians 1.11-12).

Suffering and persecution by believers is to be expected in a world aligned against God and His Christ (Psalm 2.1-3). When believers suffer for Christ, they are deemed "worthy" of Christ's calling for suffering and persecution identify true believers. In spiritual matters, the majority is always wrong.

---

[7] The word translated "destruction," ὄλεθρος, does not mean annihilation but ruin. The word translated "everlasting" is αἰώνιος, the same word the Scriptures use for "eternal life." See John 3.16 (ζωὴν αἰώνιον), 5.24 (ζωὴν αἰώνιον), 6.47 (ζωὴν αἰώνιον), etc. The Bible consistently teaches believers have eternal life and unbelievers suffer eternal punishment.

# Chapter 14
# Paul: Extent of the Atonement and Predestination

## Introduction

Over the centuries great theological arguments have waged over the extent of the atonement and predestination. Regarding the atonement, the issue is whether Christ died for everyone or only believers. These two views are known as 1) unlimited atonement and 2) limited or definite atonement. Intertwined with this subject is predestination. Some maintain God has predestinated some to eternal bliss and some to eternal condemnation.

How one defines God's sovereignty and man's will determines one's views on these subjects. Historically, these views have known as Calvinism verses Arminianism, named for their theological founders, John Calvin and Jacob Arminius. Arguments about these subjects have been based largely on "either-or" presuppositions but the Bible reveals them as "both-and." The Bible reveals God *always* takes the initiative in salvation. Mankind can only respond to or reject God.

These subjects are not exclusive to Paul but they will be examined with a focus on Paul's writings. Paul provides the solution to the problem—to the degree it can be solved.

To begin, one must recognize two fatal weaknesses attend limited or definite atonement. The first is Scriptural and the second, logical.

## Limited Atonement: The Scriptural Problem

### The Old Testament View of the Messiah's Death

How did the Old Testament present the Messiah's redemptive work? Most of the Old Testament concerns 1) God's kingdom on earth in which the Messiah will reign and 2) God's judgment of the earth. Little was revealed concerning the "suffering Messiah" and what was revealed was veiled in secrecy. Indeed, only *one passage*, Isaiah 53, dealt with the Messiah's death with regard to sin. And *no one* understood it.[1] The passage reads:

---

[1] Phillip's encounter with the Ethiopian eunuch, a godly Jew in charge of the finances of Candice, queen of Ethiopia, reveals this clearly. He had travelled to Jerusalem to worship and while returning read Isaiah 53. The Lord sent Philip to explain the passage concerned Jesus of Nazareth (Acts 8.26-40).

> [1] Who has believed our report? and to whom is the arm of the LORD revealed? [2] For he will grow up before him as a tender plant, and as a root out of a dry ground: he has no form or comeliness; and when we will see him, there is no beauty that we should desire him. [3] He is despised and rejected of men; a man of sorrows, and acquainted with grief: and we hid as it were our faces from him; he was despised, and we esteemed him not. [4] Surely he has borne our griefs, and carried our sorrows: yet we did esteem him stricken, smitten of God, and afflicted. [5] But he was wounded for our transgressions, he was bruised for our iniquities: the chastisement of our peace was on him; and with his stripes we are healed. [6] All we like sheep have gone astray; we have turned every one to his own way; and the LORD has laid on him the iniquity of us all (Isaiah 53.1-6).

Isaiah wrote to Jews. The personal pronouns in the above passage referred to *Jews*: verse 2, "**we** will see him," "**we** should desire him," verse 3, "**we** hid as it were our faces," "**we** esteemed him not," verse 4, "he has borne **our** griefs, and carried **our** sorrows," "yet **we** did esteem him stricken," verse 5, "wounded for **our** transgressions," "bruised for **our** iniquities," "chastisement of **our** peace," "with his stripes **we** are healed," verse 6, "all **we**," "**we** have turned," "the iniquity of **us** all." Gentiles were *not in view* in this passage. However the passage was understood, it concerned *only Jews* and *all Jews*.

## The Levitical Sacrifices

The Old Testament provided pictures or types of the reality that would be fulfilled by Christ.[2] God commanded the Levitical sacrifices as the means of propitiation, כָּפַר, with regard to sin. Through these sacrifices Jews were reminded constantly that sin's penalty was death (Genesis 2.17; Ezekiel 18.4; Romans 6.23) and required the shedding of blood. As soon as Adam and Eve sinned, God had revealed the necessity of a blood sacrifice and had covered them with the hides of animals He had killed (Genesis 3.21 cf. Isaiah 61.10). Moses wrote:

> For the life of the flesh is in the blood: and I have given it to you upon the altar to make an atonement for your souls: for it is the blood that makes an atonement for the soul (Leviticus 17.11 cf. Hebrews 9.22).

The text states, "So the priest will make atonement, or more accurately, a propitiation, כָּפַר, on his behalf for his sin which he has committed, and it will be forgiven him" (cf. Leviticus 4.20, 26, 31, 35, 5.6, 10, 13, 16, 18, 6.7, etc.). In addition to individual animal sacrifices, God instituted a Day of Atonement, יוֹם הַכִּפֻּרִים, *for all the people* (Leviticus

---

[2] Paul revealed this great truth in his letter to the Hebrews.

16.17, 22). The Day of Atonement (Leviticus 16) had a sin offering and a burnt offering for both priests and the people. In addition, two goats were chosen for the people, one as a sin offering and the other for a scapegoat released into the wilderness. The sin offering signified propitiation of sins and the scapegoat expiation of sins for *all Jews*.[3]

The Day of Atonement was a picture, a type, of Christ's atoning work for all Jews.[4] The Jews had no understanding their sacrifices were types. For them, the sacrifices were the realities. God kept hidden how He was going to deal ultimately with sin. Were the sacrifices effective? From the divine perspective they were for they were what God commanded. From the human perspective they were effective *if* a Jew offered the sacrifice in faith—if he believed God was propitiating his sin by means of the sacrifice. If no faith accompanied the sacrifice, it was not effective. Paul wrote the Jews:

> 2 For we also had good news proclaimed, even as they, but the word which they heard did not benefit their hearing, because it was not joined with the faith by those who heard.
> 3 For the ones who believed enter into the rest. Even as He has said, As I swore in My wrath, They will not enter into My rest. And yet the works were done from *the* foundation of *the* world (Hebrews 4.2-3).

Again, he wrote,

> Now without faith *it is* impossible to please *Him*, for the one who comes near to the God must believe He exists and is *a* rewarder to those who seek Him (Hebrews 11.6).

God has *always* required faith for salvation to be effective.

The Isaiah 53 passage had in view 1) only Jews and 2) all Jews. The Levitical sacrifices revealed three things regarding salvation:[5] They were for 1) only Jews, 2) all Jews, and 3) required obedience/faith.[6]

## The Death of Christ in the Gospels

What did the Gospels reveal concerning salvation? The angel of the Lord told Joseph that Jesus would "save His people from their sins" (Matthew 1.21). This statement agreed with Isaiah's words that the extent of the atonement included *only* Jews and *all* Jews.

---

[3] The LXX used ἀποπομπή, "send away" or "get rid of" for the goat.

[4] The Old Testament only reveals how God dealt with the sins of Jews.

[5] I have found no one who has considered the question of the extent of the atonement as presented in the Old Testament and in the Gospels.

[6] Undoubtedly proselytes followed the Mosaic Law and offered sacrifices. What is in view here is Jewish theology—what the Scriptures revealed about the extent of the atonement in the Old Testament.

"His people" were Jews. Jesus was of the tribe of Judah, of the royal line of the house of David. The wise men inquired, "Where is the One born King of the Jews" (Matthew 2.2)?

Zechariah, the father of John the Baptist, responded to the miraculous happenings surrounding the birth of his own son and Jesus' birth by recounting God's promises of salvation. Luke wrote:

> 67 Then Zachariah, his father, was filled with *the* Holy Spirit
> and prophesied, saying, 68 Blessed *be* the Lord God of Israel,
> because He helped and redeemed His people 69 and raised *a*
> horn of salvation for us in *the* house of David, His servant.
> 70 As He spoke through the mouth of His holy prophets from
> long ago: 71 Salvation from our enemies and from *the* hand
> of all who hate us. 72 To perform mercy with our fathers and
> remember His holy covenant, 73 *the* oath which He swore to
> Abraham our father: 74 To let us, after we have been rescued
> from the hand of our enemies, serve Him without fear, 75 in
> holiness and righteousness before Him, all the days of our
> life. 76 And now you, child, will be called Prophet of *the*
> Highest. For you will go before the Lord to prepare His
> ways, 77 to give knowledge of salvation to His people by *the*
> forgiveness of their sins, 78 through the compassionate
> mercies of our God, in which the Sunrise from on high will
> visit us, 79 to illumine those who sit in darkness and *the*
> shadow of death; to guide our feet into *the* way of peace
> (Luke 1.67-79).

Notice Zechariah's words focused on *Israel*, not the world. In verses 69-76, he spoke of Israel's salvation from its *enemies*, a prophecy of Moses written in Deuteronomy 28.1, 7, 13. Verses 77-78 prophesied John would give the knowledge of salvation to Jews by God's forgiving their sins. Jews *alone* were the subject here. Israel and the Messiah were prophesied to be the agents to give light to the Gentiles (Isaiah 42.6, 49.6, 60.3). Verse 79 has this in view as God would "guide our (Jews) feet into the way of peace."

Angels announced the Messiah's birth to Jewish shepherds:

> 8 And shepherds were in the same region camping in the
> fields and keeping night watches over their flock. 9 And
> behold, *an* angel of *the* Lord stood by them and *the* glory of
> *the* Lord shined around them. And they were greatly afraid.
> 10 And the angel said to them, Do not be afraid. Behold, I tell
> you good news of great joy that will be to all the people.
> 11 For *a* Savior was born to you today in David's city who is
> Christ *the* Lord (Luke 2.8-11).

Good news was announced to *all*, but to Jews, was born a Savior.

When Joseph and Mary took the baby Jesus to the Temple where Simeon gave a prophecy. Luke wrote:

> 25 And behold, *a* man was in Jerusalem whose name *was*
> Simeon. And this man *was* righteous and devout, waiting for
> the consolation of Israel. And the Holy Spirit was on him.
> 26 And it had been revealed to him by the Holy Spirit that he
> would not die before he should see the Christ of *the* Lord.
> 27 And he came in the Spirit into the Temple when the
> parents brought the child Jesus, doing what was customary
> by the Law for Him. 28 And he took Him into his arms and
> blessed the God, and said, 29 Now release your servant in
> peace, Lord, according to your word. 30 For my eyes have
> seen your salvation, 31 which you prepared in the presence
> of all the peoples: 32 Light, for revelation of the Gentiles, and
> glory of your people, Israel. 33 And His father and mother
> were amazed at the things spoken about Him (Luke 2.25-
> 33).

As in the Zechariah passage, Simeon extended salvation beyond Israel with his statement, "For my eyes have seen your salvation, which you prepared in the presence of all the peoples: Light, for revelation of the Gentiles, and glory of your people, Israel" (verses 30-32). Salvation of Gentiles would come *through Israel* (Genesis 12.3; Isaiah 42.1-6, 60.1-3; Micah 4.2; Zechariah 8.20-23). The nature of this salvation, for Jews or Gentiles, was veiled with regard to the matter of sin.

Before God gave Israel the Law, He spoke to Moses and the people:

> 4 You have seen what I did to the Egyptians, and how I bore
> you on eagles' wings, and brought you to myself. 5 Now
> therefore, if you will obey my voice indeed, and keep my
> covenant, then you will be a peculiar treasure to me above
> all people: for all the earth is mine: 6 And you will be to me
> a kingdom of priests, and a holy nation. These are the words
> which you will speak to the children of Israel (Exodus 19.4-
> 6).

God's plan for Israel was for every Jew to be a priest in a holy nation. The primary role of a priest is a go-between, a representative. Israel, in its covenant relationship to God, would represent God to Gentiles in accord with the Abrahamic Covenant.

Jesus spoke of Himself as the Good Shepherd and taught the Good Shepherd lays down His life for His sheep. Who were the sheep? They were Jews. John wrote:

> 11 I am the good shepherd. The good shepherd lays down His
> life for the sheep. 12 And the hired servant, since he is not *the*
> shepherd, who does not own the sheep, sees the wolf coming
> and leaves the sheep and flees. And the wolf snatches them
> and scatters the sheep. 13 But the hired servant flees because
> he is *a* hired servant and does not care about the sheep. 14 I
> am the good shepherd. So I know My own and am known
> by My own. 15 As the Father knows Me, I also know the

> Father, and I lay down My life for the sheep. [16] And I have other sheep that are not of this fold. I must bring those also. And they will hear My voice and there will become one flock *with* one shepherd (John 10.11-16).[7]

Jesus' words agreed with other Gospel accounts of salvation to Jews. Gentiles were not in direct view of salvation.

John revealed a fascinating conversation among the Jewish leadership in their discussions about the "Jesus" problem. He wrote:

> [49] But one of them, Caiaphas, who was high priest that year, said to them, You know nothing. [50] Do you not recognize that it is advantageous to us that one man should die for the people so the whole nation should not perish? [51] (Now he said this, not from himself, but since he was high priest that year, he prophesied that Jesus was about to die for the nation—[52] and not for the nation alone, but that He might also gather into one the children of the God, the ones who had been scattered abroad) (John 11.49-52).

Caiaphas plotted Jesus' death as an expedient political act. But God used him to accomplish His will.[8] Note the text limited Jesus's death "for the people," i.e., Jews—within the nation and abroad—"the children of God who are scattered abroad"—Jews of the Diaspora (Acts 2.5; 1 Peter 1.1-2; James 1.1).

We would be remiss if we failed to address a passage that seems not to fit the above analysis, John 1.29:

> On the next day, John saw Jesus coming to him and said, Look! The Lamb of the God, who takes away the sin of the world!

What are we to make of John the Baptist's statement about Jesus taking away the sins of the world? The only reasonable explanation is that John understood his proclamation according to what had been revealed in the Old Testament and prophets in the same sense as Zechariah and Simeon, who stated Jesus was "a light to lighten the Gentiles." John had no understanding about how Jesus would solve the problem of sin and death through His death and resurrection (cf. Luke 18.31-34).

We must also recognize that the Old Testament prophets (which is what John was) often said or wrote things they did not understand. Daniel did not understand what the pre-incarnate Christ revealed to him in Daniel 12.9-13. The Twelve did not understand Jesus would die

---

[7] The "other sheep" are not Gentiles or the Church but a future generation of Jews (the Tribulation generation) who will "hear My voice" and become "one fold" with the rest of believing Israel (Matthew 23.37-39; Ezekiel 37.19-22).

[8] Joseph spoke similar words concerning the actions of his brothers (Genesis 50.20).

and be resurrected (Luke 18.31-34; John 20.8-9). It is impossible that John understood what the Twelve did not. John prophesied a truth that would only be understood later.

John 3.16 is probably the most well-known verse in the Bible. What about it? It reads:

> For the God so loved the world, that He gave His Only Begotten Son, so that everyone who believes in Him should not perish, but may have eternal life.

Jesus spoke these words to Nicodemus. Notice what the verse says and what it does not say. It says God so loved the world that He gave His Only Begotten Son so that everyone who believes in Him should not perish but may have eternal life. It does *not* say God so loved the world that He gave His only begotten Son *to die* for us or *to rise from the dead*. The context of the passage is that Jesus came as Israel's Messiah. To be saved, one had to believe He was the Messiah, the Son of God. The significance of Jesus' death and resurrection with regard to solving the problem of sin and death was not yet been revealed.

In the previous two verses, Jesus told Nicodemus:

> [14] And as Moses lifted up the serpent in the wilderness, so must the Son of the Man be lifted up [15] so that everyone who believes in Him should not perish, but should have eternal life.

Jesus knew this meant He would go to the cross and die but Nicodemus did not. What he knew was that when Moses lifted up the brass serpent, whoever looked at it was healed. Nicodemus understood Jesus' statement to mean that anyone who saw and believed Jesus was the Christ, the Son of God, would have eternal life.

## Paul Confirmed Jesus Died for the Jews in Hebrews

Paul wrote:

> [16] For assuredly, He is not helping angels but He helps *the* seed of Abraham. [17] For this reason, He had to be made like His brethren in all things, so He might become *a* merciful and faithful high priest *in* the things related to the God, to propitiate (ἱλάσκομαι) the sins of the people (Hebrews 2.16-17).

To whom did Paul refer with "made like His brethren?" Again, the answer is the Jewish people. He "propitiated the sins of the people."[9] The phrase "the people" in Scripture referred to the Jewish people.

Paul confirmed this addressing the Galatians:

---

[9] The word ἱλάσκομαι means propitiation and was used in the LXX for animal sacrifices. Jesus was the effective Lamb of God, the antitype of the types.

> [4] But when the fullness of the time came, the God sent His Son, born of *a* woman, born under the Law, [5] so He might redeem those under *the* Law, so we might receive the adoption as sons (Galatians 4.4-5).

Jesus ministered under the Law of Moses to those "under the Law"—*Jews*—not Gentiles. Notice the next part of the verse: "so we might receive the adoption as sons." Who is "we?" The "we" are Gentiles. Paul was a Jew but spoke representing his office as "the apostle to the Gentiles" (Romans 11.13). Thus, Christ redeemed Jews so Gentiles could be adopted as sons. This was how God would bless Gentiles in accord with the Abrahamic Covenant (Genesis 12.1-3).

## Conclusion: Death of Christ in the Old Testament and Gospels

The above examination of the Old Testament and the Gospels reveals God promised a Savior and salvation to Jews and that Gentiles would be saved through them (Isaiah 42.1-9, 49.5-7; 60.1-3; Zechariah 8.20-23). The Old Testament and Gospels taught both a limited atonement—salvation of Jews—and an unlimited atonement—all Jews were included. But neither the Old Testament nor the Gospels revealed *how* Gentiles, or for that matter, how Jews, would be saved with regard to sin. All that God revealed was that salvation would somehow come through Israel and the Messiah.

## The Death of Christ in Pauline Texts

God saved Saul of Tarsus and commissioned him as the apostle of the Gentiles (Romans 11.13). The risen Lord revealed to Paul what His death and resurrection meant concerning sin—it solved the problem of sin and death for all—Jew and Gentile—and salvation was by faith alone.

Because Paul wrote to believers, statements made that Christ died for them are not conclusive to make a case for unlimited atonement. However, if a passage declares Christ died *for more than believers*, the limited atonement position is doomed.

Paul's *primary* purpose in writing about Christ's death was to teach its significance to believers, not to unbelievers. Thus, we have passages such as the following:

> [6] For when we were yet weak, at the right time, Christ died for *the* ungodly. [7] (For rarely indeed will anyone die for *a* righteous man, though for the good *man*, perhaps someone would even dare to die). [8] But the God shows His love to us: that while we were yet sinners, Christ died for us. [9] Much more, therefore, since we were now declared righteous by His blood, we will be saved from the wrath through Him. [10] For if, when we were enemies, we were reconciled to the God through the death of His Son, much more, because we were reconciled, will we be saved by His life. [11] Now not

> only *this*, but we are also boasting in the God through our Lord Jesus Christ, through whom now we received the reconciliation (Romans 5.6-11).

A case *can* be made from Paul's statements, "Christ died for the ungodly," "while we were yet sinners," and "when we were enemies" to include everyone. But those who teach limited atonement maintain these phrases mean Christ died for the elect while in unbelief. Other texts are less easily dismissed.

## Problem Texts in Paul for Limited Atonement

The above passage continues and reads:

> 12 Because of this, just as through one man the sin[10] entered into the world, and through the sin the death, so also, the death passed through to all [πᾶς] men, for all [πᾶς] sinned. .
> . . 18 So, then, as through one offence condemnation *came* to all [πᾶς] men, so also through one righteous act *came* to all [πᾶς] men for justification of life. 19 For just as through the disobedience of the one man, the many [πολύς] were rendered sinners, so also through the obedience of the One, the many [πολύς] will be rendered righteous (Romans 5.12, 18-19).

Those who argue for limited atonement maintain that expressions of "all" do not mean "*every person*" but "*all kinds of persons*," a sense required sense for their argument. If true, Romans 5.12 cannot mean Adam's sin affected "every person" but only "all kinds of persons." This means Adam's sin did not cause the death of all mankind but only some and Adam was *not* the federal head of the human race—some after Adam were born without sin. The same may be seen in Romans 5.18-19. These verses show the Jewish proclivity towards parallelism found in the prophets and psalms.[11] Paul wrote in verse 18 that by the offense of one, "all" were condemned and by the righteousness of one, justification came upon "all." If the latter "all" does not mean "every person" the former "all" does not mean "every person." But Paul wrote in Romans 5.14, "death ruled from Adam to Moses." The case for "all" being "all kinds" collapses. Verse 18 interprets verse 19 according to Hebrew parallelism. The "many," (πολύς) are "all."

Consider the following passage:

> 3 For this *is* right and acceptable before the God, our Savior,
> 4 who wants all [πᾶς] men to be saved and come to *the* full knowledge of *the* truth. 5 For *there is* one God and One agent between God and men, *the* man Christ Jesus, 6 the One who

---

[10] Throughout Paul's writings, the articular construct "the sin," ἡ ἁμαρτία, denotes Adam's sin.
[11] Cf. 2 Kings 19.31; Isaiah 2.3, 62.1.

> gave Himself *a* ransom for all, [πᾶς] the witness in their proper times, [7] for which I was appointed preacher and apostle. I speak truth. I do not lie: teacher of Gentiles by faith and by truth (1 Timothy 2.3-7).

Paul wrote that God is the Savior of believers, "our Savior" (verse 3). In the next verse he declared God desires *all* to be saved. What sense does it make for God to wish "all" to be saved if "all" means "all kinds of men," i.e., the elect? Such a rendering is nonsense, particularly in light of verse 5, in which Paul declared one mediator exists between God and mankind: Christ Jesus. If one argues Paul was speaking of believers in verse 4, one must argue Christ is the mediator of believers only (verse 5). This argument means one of two things: unbelievers have 1) another mediator or 2) no mediator. But Paul wrote "one mediator" exists between God and men. Paul did not write, "believers" or "some men." He wrote, "men." A normal reading of the passage is Paul meant all men, i.e., mankind (ἄνθρωπος).[12] Another passage from the same letter provides additional clarity to Paul's meaning:

> For this we toil and strive, for we have hope upon *the* living God, who is Savior of all [πᾶς] men, especially of believers (1 Timothy 4.10).

Paul stated that God is the Savior of all men, *especially* believers. The normal reading of the verse is that God is the Savior of all, "every person." The word "especially" is μάλιστα, the neuter plural superlative of the adverb μάλα which means "chiefly," "especially," or "particularly" (Galatians 6.10; Philippians 4.22; 1 Timothy 4.10, 5.8, 17; 2 Timothy 4.13; Titus 1.10; Philemon 1.16). For "all" (πᾶς) to mean "all kinds" the passage must read: "We trust in the living God, who is the Savior of all kinds of men, especially of believers." Such a reading is nonsense. The only *reasonable* reading is that Christ died for every person but that believers benefit from Christ's work *because they have believed.*

One benefits from Christ's work by faith. One believes the gospel, that Christ died our sins and rose from the dead. Christ's work is *sufficient* for *all* but *efficient* or *effective* for those who *believe.*

Lastly, we will examine one of Paul's greatest texts, the Church's "great commission."[13] It reads:

> [18] Now all the things *are* from God, the One who reconciled us to Himself through Jesus Christ and gave us the ministry of the reconciliation [19] how God was in Christ reconciling

[12] The word ἄνθρωπος means human beings, i.e., mankind.

[13] The "great commission" Jesus gave in Matthew 28.16-20 was to the Eleven, who were apostles of Israel (Matthew 19.28) under the Mosaic Law. They were *not* apostles of the Church, the body of Christ, for the Church did not yet exist, and which is under grace, not Law (Romans 6.14).

> *the* world to Himself, not reckoning to them their trespasses and who put in us the word of the reconciliation (2 Corinthians 5.18-19).

In verse 18, Paul stated God reconciled "us," i.e., believers, the elect. He then defined the "ministry of reconciliation" given to believers: "God was in Christ reconciling the world to Himself." The "world" is not "believers," "the elect," or "all kinds of men." The "world" is the human race. If "world" does *not* mean the entire human race, who are "them" and "their" in verse 19? This is yet another passage, where Paul clearly distinguished between *us* and *them*, believers and unbelievers.

If language means *anything*, God has reconciled the entire human race to Himself and given the Church, the body of Christ, this glorious message of reconciliation. Those who refuse to proclaim Christ died for every person are *unfaithful stewards* of God's grace and proclaim *another gospel*. They are cursed (Galatians 1.6-9).

## Problem Texts in Hebrews for Limited Atonement

Paul wrote the Jews:

> 9 But, we see Jesus, who has been made lower than angels for a little while, because of the suffering of the death, who has been crowned with glory and honor, so that by *the* grace of God He might taste death for everyone [ὑπὲρ παντὸς].
> 10 For it was fitting to Him, for whom *are* all the things and through whom *are* all the things, who brought many sons to glory, to make the author of their salvation complete through sufferings (Hebrews 2.9-10).

In verse 9, Paul explicitly stated Jesus died for every person. The phrase construction is ὑπὲρ παντὸς. The preposition ὑπέρ is a substitutionary word, "for," "on behalf of" and is coupled with παντὸς, the genitive singular of πᾶς, "all" or "everyone." Verses 9 and 10 show the same distinction between believers and unbelievers as other passages: Christ died for every person (verse 9) but only *some*, "many sons to glory" benefit from His death and resurrection (verse 10).

## More Problem Texts for Limited Atonement

Paul's writings have been the focus of examining the extent of the atonement, but Peter and John agreed with Paul. Peter wrote:

> 18 For Christ also suffered once for sins, righteous for unrighteous, so He might lead us to the God, for He was put to death in *the* flesh but has been made alive in *the* spirit (1 Peter 3.18).

Notice again the distinction between unbelievers and believers: "Christ suffered once for sins, righteous for unrighteous" versus "so He might bring us to God." Who was "righteous?" Christ. Who was "unrighteous?" Everyone. Who is "led to God?" Those who believe.

> [1] Now false prophets also came among the people, even as false teachers will be among you, who will subtly introduce destructive heresies, and deny the Master who bought them, bringing swift destruction to themselves (2 Peter 2.1).

Peter declared Christ "bought," i.e., redeemed (ἀγοράζω) false teachers. Would those who teach limited atonement have us believe false teachers who deny Christ are the elect?

John's testimony also agrees with Paul and Peter:

> [1] My little children, I write these things to you so you might not sin. And if anyone should sin, we have *an* Advocate with the Father, righteous Jesus Christ. [2] And He is *the* propitiation for our sins. But not for ours only, but also for the whole world (1 John 2.1-2).

The Greek text of 1 John 2.2 reads:

| καὶ αὐτὸς ἱλασμός ἐστιν περὶ τῶν ἁμαρτιῶν ἡμῶν οὐ περὶ τῶν ἡμετέρων δὲ μόνον ἀλλὰ καὶ περὶ ὅλου τοῦ κόσμου. |
|---|
| And He is propitiation for our sins and not for our sins alone but even for the whole world. |

The connective καί is translated in its ascensive sense, "even" or "also." Christ is the propitiation for "our," i.e., believer's sins, and even or also of "the whole world." In 1 John 4.14, John wrote He was "Savior of the world," σωτῆρα τοῦ κόσμου. Can language be clearer? Christ died for everyone's sins and rose from death for every person.

## The Logical Problem of Limited Atonement

The Scriptural case has been made for unlimited atonement. What about the logical case? Logically, the case for limited atonement is a *far* more difficult case to make than the case for unlimited atonement. If Christ died for ALL, He died for SOME since SOME is a subset of ALL. If Christ died for some, He did not die for all. ALL is not a subset of SOME. Those who hold to limited atonement must demonstrate that *every verse* that states Christ died for "all" *always* means "some." If this cannot be done, the limited atonement argument collapses.

The *only* way limited atonement can be proven is to find a Scripture that *explicitly* states Christ died for believers *and no one else*. Nothing less will succeed. Such a verse does not exist. The limited atonement argument has *no* Scriptural support. It is false teaching.

### The Logical Fallacy of Limited Atonement

Definite or limited atonement is a false gospel. It is based on *false logic.* It has no Scriptural support. What do those who hold to limited atonement think Christ accomplished by His death and resurrection? Those who argue for limited atonement offer the following syllogism to support their position:

| Major premise | If Christ died for all then all are saved. |
|---|---|
| Minor premise | All are not saved. |
| Conclusion | Therefore, Christ did not die for all. |

This syllogism is unsound. Consider the following syllogism:

| Major premise | If all have medicine all will be healed. |
|---|---|
| Minor premise | All are not healed. |
| Conclusion | Therefore, all do not have medicine. |

The argument is unsound because medicine may be available for all but this does not mean all will be healed. Unless medicine is *taken*, it does no good.

Those who hold to definite atonement also argue if Christ died for all and all are not saved, then Christ's death was ineffective. But the Scriptures teach Christ did die for all and His work *was* effective. From *God's* perspective, Christ's death was effective because it satisfied His justice. Jesus paid the penalty of sin for all. He reconciled the world to Himself. From *an individual's* perspective, Christ's work is effective if a person accepts His work by faith and is consistent with the record and pattern throughout the Scriptures.

## The Fallacy of the Limited Atonement Argument

The reason those who maintain limited or definite atonement and arrive at the syllogism above is that they have a flawed, unscriptural understanding of God's sovereignty, His love, and man's will.

God is sovereign. God is love. His sovereignty and love must accommodate human will. God's genius allows Him to accommodate all possible human choices, real or potential—a near infinite number of permutations and have His plan work out as He intended. Man's role in resolving the angelic conflict requires him to be able to freely respond to God. God's love requires that man be able to choose God freely since love is *impossible* apart from free will. One cannot force another to love. Without free will, man is an automaton, a robot.

Consider this example:

> John tells George, "I have a check of $1,000 for you at the bank." George does not believe John and does not go to the bank. John's check was at the bank but it did George no good because he did not believe John.

A gift provides no benefit unless accepted. What does the Bible teach about how one receives God's blessing? God's blessing is received by obedience, by faith. Paul wrote the Romans of the "obedience of faith" (Romans 1.5, 16.26), a genitive of apposition and means "obedience which is faith." Faith is believing or doing what God has said, i.e., obedience. The benefit of Christ's death and resurrection remains an unclaimed gift if one refuses to accept it, to believe it. For such a person, Christ's work is *ineffective* for he refuses it. Does a person who refuses Christ's work affect God's justice or Christ's victory over sin and death for him? No. It *only affects his relationship with God.*

Did Christ die for Saul of Tarsus? We know He did. Was Saul saved while he was seeking to destroy those who were believing in Jesus? We know he wasn't. When was Paul saved? He was saved on the road to Damascus when he believed Jesus of Nazareth was the Messiah. People are lost *not* because Christ did not die for them. People are lost because *they refuse to believe God.*

## The Mechanics of Belief

The specific mechanics of salvation are unknown. The Scriptures do not provide enough information for us to understand how the divine will interacts and cooperates with the human will. All we can know is that when God reveals Himself in some way, an individual has a choice. In the case of the gospel, one will or will not believe it. Faith is a decision. Divine and human wills are involved in salvation but God is *always* the initiator. A person can respond or reject God's revelation and prompting but the details of this cooperation are beyond our ken. The Word of God is a divine book. The Word of God is a human book. God the Son is wholly divine. God the Son is wholly human. Who understands this? Both are true. The following verses reveal both the divine will and the human will:

> [39] You search the Scriptures, for you think in them to have eternal life. And these are they that testify about Me. [40] And you do not want to come to Me so you may have life (John 5.39-40).
>
> No one can come to Me unless the Father who sent Me should draw him. And I will raise him up in the last day (John 6.44).
>
> Then He began saying, Because of this, I have told you, No one can come to Me unless it may have been given to him from My Father (John 6.65).
>
> And *a* certain woman named Lydia, *a* seller of purple cloth, of *the* city of Thyatira, who worshipped the God, was listening, whose heart the Lord opened to heed the things spoken by Paul (Acts 16.14).
>
> Then he believed in the LORD; and He reckoned it to him as righteousness (Genesis 15.6).
>
> Now those along the road are those who heard. Then the Devil comes and removes the word from their heart, so they might not believe and be saved (Luke 8.12).
>
> But, as many as received Him, He gave to them authority to become children of God—to those who believe in His name (John 1.12).

> For the God so loved the world, that He gave His Only Begotten Son, so that everyone who believes in Him should not perish, but may have eternal life (John 3.16).
>
> She said to him, Yes, Lord. I believe that you are the Christ, the Son of the God, the One who comes into the world (John 11.27).
>
> Then they said, Believe on the Lord Jesus Christ and you will be saved—you and your household (Acts 16.31).
>
> But to the one who does not work, but believes on the One declaring righteous the ungodly, his faith is reckoned for righteousness (Romans 4.5).
>
> [37] Jerusalem, Jerusalem, the one who kills the prophets and stones the ones who have been sent to her! How often I wished to gather your children, as *a* hen gathers her chicks under her wings, and you would not! [38] Behold, your house is left to you desolate! [39] For I tell you, you should never see Me from now until you should say, Blessed *is* the One who comes in *the* name of *the* Lord (Matthew 23.37-39)!
>
> [14] And as Moses lifted up the serpent in the wilderness, so must the Son of the Man be lifted up [15] so that everyone who believes in Him should not perish, but should have eternal life (John 3.14-15).

The Scriptures teach God wishes all be saved. What does this mean if He did not provide for all?

Paul wrote that what happened to Israel was for our instruction (Romans 15.4; 1 Corinthians 10.11). The Levitical sacrifices taught about Christ's work: they were for all Jews. The Passover taught the Jews that a lamb's blood had to be applied to the doorposts and lintel to be saved from the destroying angel (Exodus 12.7, 12-13). The brazen serpent had the power to heal for those who would look at it (John 3.14-16 cf. Numbers 21.8). Each of these taught that God had made provision but that His provision required faith, a free will response to be effective. Each was a type of Christ and His salvation. Christ died and rose again for all and men and women are saved by believing Paul's gospel (1 Corinthians 15.1-4). If one believes one is saved. If one will not, one is lost. It is a choice. It is that simple.

## Predestination

### Introduction

The subject of "predestination" troubles many. The primary reason for distress is because some have been told that God has chosen some for heaven and some for hell and that one's destiny is fixed. The Bible does not teach this. Furthermore, this is not what the Bible means by predestination.

A study of predestination requires examination of God's sovereignty, foreknowledge, election, and how divine and human wills interact. A *full* understanding of these subjects is impossible. But we can have a *sufficient* understanding.

## Biblical Terms Concerning Predestination

1. Προγινώσκω (v.) means to know beforehand.[14]
2. Ἐκλέγομαι (v.) means to elect or choose.[15]
3. Ἐκλεκτός (n.) means that which is chosen.[16]
4. Καλέω (v.) means to call or be named.[17]
5. Κλητός (n.) means one called.[18]
6. Προορίζω (v.) means to predestine or predetermine.[19]

Paul used the terms "elect" (ἐκλέγομαι, ἐκλεκτός), "call" (καλέω, κλητός), and "predestine" (προορίζω) *only* of believers with respect to salvation. *Only believers* are chosen and predestined. Furthermore, one is not predestined, elected, or called to heaven or hell but to a *position* and *relationship* with God. God has predestined believers to be "conformed to the image of His Son" (Romans 8.29), to "adoption as sons" (Ephesians 1.5), and to "an inheritance" (Ephesians 1.11). Believers have been elected to be "holy and without blame" (Ephesians 1.4), called "into the fellowship of His Son" (1 Corinthians 1.9), "to liberty" (Galatians 5.13), "in one body" (Colossians 3.15), "into His own kingdom and glory" (1 Thessalonians 2.12), "in holiness" (1 Thessalonians 4.7), and to "eternal life" (1 Timothy 6.12).

## All Enlightened

While God predestines, elects, and calls *only* believers, the Bible declares God has revealed Himself to *every* human being. Each of us is born with an innate knowledge of God and God holds us responsible to respond or to reject Him. Consider the following:

> The true Light, who enlightens everyone who comes in the world (John 1.9).
>
> 19 Because the knowledge of the God is evident among them—for the God revealed *it* to them. 20 For His invisible attributes from *the* creation of *the* world are clearly seen because they are understood by the things made, both His

---

[14] Romans 8.29.
[15] Ephesians 1.4.
[16] Romans 8.33, 16.13; Colossians 3.12; 2 Timothy 2.10; Titus 1.1.
[17] Romans 8.30, 9.11, 25; 1 Corinthians 1.9, 7.17, 22, 15.9; Galatians 1.6, 15, 5.8, 13; Ephesians 4.1, 4; 1 Thessalonians 2.12, 4.7, 5.24; 2 Thessalonians 2.14; 1 Timothy 6.12; 2 Timothy 1.9; Hebrews 9.15, 11.8.
[18] 1 Corinthians 1.26. Ephesians 1.18, 4.4. Philippians 3.14. 2 Thessalonians 1.11. 2 Timothy 1.9
[19] Romans 8.29-30; Ephesians 1.5, 11.

> eternal power and divinity. So, they are without excuse (Romans 1.19-20).
>
> For the saving grace of the God was revealed to all men (Titus 2.11).

Since God has given the knowledge of Himself to every person, those who become atheists or reject God suppress their innate knowledge of God. They *choose* to reject God.

God is not limited by geography or circumstances. Every person who has ever lived has an equal opportunity to know God. A person can live in a Christian community and be lost and a person can live 1,000 miles from any Christian witness and be saved. Everyone has an equal chance. If a person wants to know God, God will supply the needed information. The Ethiopian eunuch desired to understand Isaiah 53 and God sent Philip to explain it (Acts 8.26-39). We may not be able to understand this fully, but God knows all hearts and is not limited by time or space. Jesus declared *nothing* is impossible with God.

## Predestination and the Angelic Conflict

Discussion of predestination is incomplete without recognizing that one of God's chief purposes in creating mankind was to resolve the angelic conflict and the problem of evil. The book of Job reveals this purpose. Job is the story of a righteous man whom God used as a type to show how man's choice vindicates God justice.

Satan's case against God was that Job feared God because of what He had given him, rather than for who God is. Job persevered and trusted God despite slander and sufferings (Job 13.15). God vindicated Job before Satan, his wife, his friends (Job 42.7-9), and rewarded him for faithfulness (Job 42.10-17).

Mankind's role in resolving the angelic conflict choosing God for Himself, even against seemingly illogical and unfair circumstances, testifies against Satan and demonstrates to the angelic host that God is righteous and good. Man's choice for God reveals God will be fair in sending Satan and the rebellious angels to the Lake of Fire.

## How Predestination and Election Work

Two key verses solve the issue of the divine will and man's will and the nature of predestination and election. One is from Paul and the other from Peter. This is appropriate. Paul represented Gentiles, as the apostle of the Gentiles, and Peter represented Jews, as an apostle of Israel. Paul wrote the believers in Rome:

> [28] Now we know that for those who love the God, all things work together for good, for those who are called [κλητός] after *His* purpose. [29] Because whom He foreknew, [προγινώσκω] He also predestined [προορίζω] *to be* conformed [σύμμορφος] to the image of His Son, so He

> might be Firstborn among many brethren. 30 Now whom He predestined, [προορίζω] these also He called [καλέω]. And whom He called, [καλέω] these He also declared righteous [δικαιόω]. And whom He declared righteous, [δικαιόω] these He also glorified[δοξάζω] (Romans 8.28-30).

Peter wrote Jewish believers scattered abroad in Asia:

> 1 Peter, apostle of Jesus Christ, to the chosen [ἐκλεκτός] resident foreigners of *the* Dispersion of Pontus, Galatia, Cappadocia, Asia, and Bithynia, 2 according to *the* foreknowledge [πρόγνωσις] of God *the* Father, by sanctification of *the* Spirit for obedience and sprinkling of *the* blood of Jesus Christ: May grace and peace be multiplied to you (1 Peter 1.1-2)!

The first thing of note in these verses is that predestination, calling, justification, and glorification apply *only* to *believers*. The second thing of note is that God's *foreknowledge* governs all the other actions: predestination, election, justification, glorification. The chart below outlines this great truth revealed in Romans 8.28-30:

<table>
<tr><th colspan="5">How Predestination and Election Work</th></tr>
<tr><td rowspan="2">Whom He Foreknew (v. 29) →</td><td>Predestined (v. 29) →</td><td colspan="3">Conformed to the image of His Son (v. 29)</td></tr>
<tr><td>Predestined (v. 30) →</td><td>Called (v. 30) →</td><td>Justified (v. 30) →</td><td>Glorified (v. 30)</td></tr>
</table>

God inhabits eternity. Eternity is *not* a long time. Eternity is non-time, i.e., timelessness. No one really understands time but scientists tell us it is a physical property of space-matter, a fourth dimension related to length, height, and width. For man, the present is *now*. For God, past, present, and future are *now*. In eternity, outside time, God experiences all events as *now*. God sees all human decisions and events as *now*. From God's perspective, He has all eternity to contemplate each moment we experience in time.

The following chart illustrates God's relationship to time.

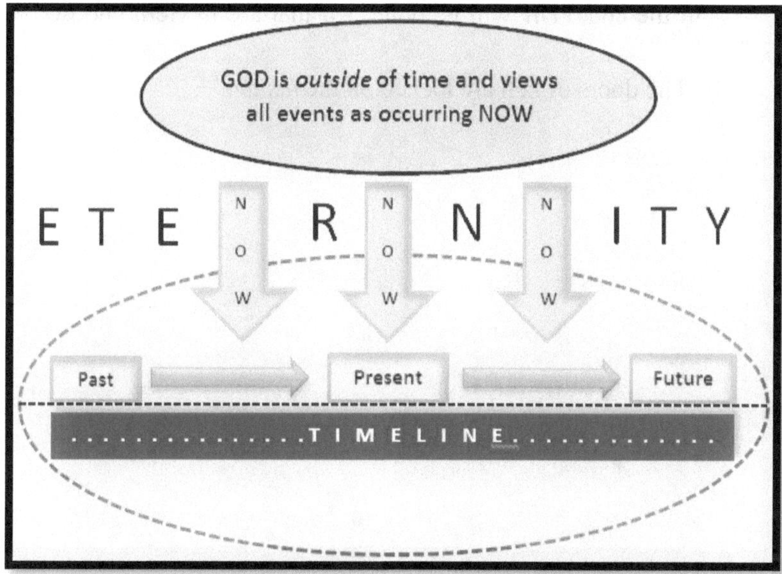


*God inhabits eternity. Past, present, and future are NOW for Him.*

God's foreknowledge sees and knows all choices we will make. His foreknowledge contemplates all possible decisions and actions, real and potential. God predestines, conforms, calls, justifies, and glorifies on the basis of man's choices, which He foresees. The Scriptures speak of these actions only with reference to *believers*, not unbelievers.

## Conclusion

While God knows what choice unbelievers will make, they are outside His predestination. The Bible does not teach that God predestines unbelievers. The theories of limited atonement and predestination of unbelievers are without Scriptural support.

God gives every person a knowledge of Himself. One can respond or reject Him. God foresees each person's response through His foreknowledge. If a person responds to the light he has, God will provide more light. Scriptural examples of this are Naaman (2 Kings 5.1-19), Lydia (Acts 16.14), and the Ethiopian eunuch (Acts 8.26-39). Over and over, we find such examples of salvation. You are one of them. God desires all to be saved but forces Himself on no one. Salvation is a free-will choice.

Since God has given mankind free will, God's will is not uncontested. Every person chooses or rejects salvation. C. S. Lewis summed the matter succinctly:

> "There are only two kinds of people in the end: those who say to God, 'Thy will be done' and those to whom God says,

in the end, '*Thy* will be done. All that are in Hell, choose it."[20]

"The doors of hell are locked on the *inside*."[21]

---

[20] C. S. Lewis. *The Great Divorce*. New York. Macmillan. 1946. p. 69.
[21] C. S. Lewis. *The Problem of Pain*. New York. Macmillan. 1973. p. 115.

# Appendix 1: Chronology of Paul

When one examines the various chronologies of Paul one fact becomes evident: no one agrees. David Brown wrote:

> Certainty in these dates is not to be had, the notes of time in the Acts being few and vague. It is only by connecting those events of secular history which it records, and the dates of which are otherwise tolerably known to us—such as the famine under Claudius Cæsar (Acts 11.28), the expulsion of the Jews from Rome by the same emperor (Acts 18.2), and the entrance of Porcius Festus upon his procuratorship (Acts 24.27), with the intervals specified between some occurrences in the apostle's life and others (such as Acts 20.31; 24.27; 28.30; and Galatians 1.1-2.21)—that we can thread our way through the difficulties that surround the chronology of the apostle's life, and approximate to certainty. Immense research has been brought to bear upon the subject, but, as might be expected, the learned are greatly divided. Every year has been fixed upon as the probable date of the apostle's conversion from A.D. 31 [Bengel] to A.D. 42 [Eusebius]. But the weight of authority is in favor of dates ranging between 35 and 40, a difference of not more than five years; and the largest number of authorities is in favor of the year 37 or 38. Taking the former of these, to which opinion largely inclines, the following Table will be useful to the student of apostolic history:[1]

[1] Jamieson, Robert, A R. Fausset, and David Brown. *A Commentary, Critical, Experimental, and Practical, on the Old and New Testaments*. 1871. pp. 26-27.

| Pauline Chronology | | |
|---|---|---|
| A.D. | Events | Scripture |
| 37 | Paul's Conversion | Acts 9, 22, 26 |
| 40 | First Visit to Jerusalem | Acts 9.26; Galatians 1.18-19 |
| 41-44 | First Residence at Antioch | Acts 11.25-30 |
| 45-47 | First Missionary Journey | Acts 13.2, 14.26 |
| 47-51 | Second Residence at Antioch | Acts 14.28 |
| 51 | Second Visit to Jerusalem Council of Jerusalem | Acts 15.2-30; Galatians 2.1-10 |
| 51 | Second Missionary Journey | Acts 15.36, 18.22 |
| 54-58 | Third Missionary Journey | Acts 18.23, 21.15 |
| 58-60 | Third Visit to Jerusalem Imprisonment at Caesarea | Acts 21.15, 23.35 |
| 60-61 | Voyage and Arrival in Rome | Acts 27.1-2, 28.16 |
| 61-63 | Roman Imprisonment | Acts 28.30 |
| 63-67 | Post-imprisonment journeys: Corinth, Miletus, Troas, etc. | 1 Timothy, 2 Timothy, Titus |
| 67-68 | Martyrdom at Rome | |

| Dates of Paul's Fourteen Letters | | | |
|---|---|---|---|
| A.D. | Letters | A.D. | Letters |
| 52 | 1st Thessalonians | 62 | Ephesians |
| 52 | 2nd Thessalonians | 62 | Colossians |
| 53 | Hebrews | 62 | Philemon |
| 55 | Galatians | 63 | Philippians |
| 57 | 1 Corinthians | 65 | Titus |
| 57 | 2 Corinthians | 66 | 1 Timothy |
| 57 | Romans | 67 | 2 Timothy |

Paul expressed his desire to go to Spain (Romans 15.24, 28). Clement of Rome (c. 35-99 A.D.) wrote that Paul went to the "extreme limit of the west" *(1st Epistle of Clement to the Corinthians*, Chapter 5). This could have been Spain.

| Books Associated with God's Programs | | | |
|---|---|---|---|
| Mankind | Israel (Prophetic Program) | | Church (Secret Program) |
| Genesis 1-11 | Genesis 12-Malachi | Matthew<br>Mark<br>Luke<br>John<br>Acts<br>Hebrews<br>James<br>1 Peter<br>2 Peter<br>1 John<br>2 John<br>3 John<br>Jude<br>Revelation | Romans<br>1 Corinthians<br>2 Corinthians<br>Galatians<br>Ephesians<br>Philippians<br>Colossians<br>1 Thessalonians<br>2 Thessalonians<br>1 Timothy<br>2 Timothy<br>Titus<br>Philemon |

# Appendix 2:
# A Conversation With Paul

## Introduction

We sat down with Stachys to interview Paul about his life, ministry, teaching, and concerns for today's world.[1]

## Interview

Stachys: Paul, you had quite a life. Tell us a bit about your story.

Paul: Thank you. I grew up in Tarsus, in Cilicia, located in south-central Turkey. I was born a Jew of the tribe of Benjamin (Philippians 3.5) and named Saul, after Israel's first king, who was of my tribe. I also was born with Roman citizenship, a benefit which would save my life (Acts 22.25-30). I demonstrated academic promise and went to Jerusalem to study to be a Pharisee under the famous Rabbi Gamaliel, grandson of the great Hillel (Acts 22.3).

Stachys: How did that go? Were you a good student?

Paul: Yes. I excelled. I became a member of the Council as soon as it was possible and advanced in Judaism above my peers (Galatians 1.14). I was (*smiling*) a "rising star."

Stachys: You were present when Stephen came to trial before the Sanhedrin?

Paul: Yes. Quite a day. Stephen gave a brilliant summary of Israel's history. He knew his Tanakh and one could not but be impressed with him. We killed him. I stood by the robes of those who stoned him (Acts 7.58).

Stachys: How did you feel about that?

Paul: I applauded it (Acts 8.1). I was zealous to uphold the Law.

Stachys: Was this action legal?

Paul: No. But as Dr. Luke recounted, we were enraged. Blasphemy was punishable by death. The Council would have convicted Stephen and it was easy to rationalize our actions.

---

[1] This fictional interview serves as a vehicle to present Paul's life and doctrines. Luke's account in Acts is distinctly Jewish and differs in emphasis from Paul's letters. Luke wrote primarily to Jews to explain Israel's fall from God's favor and why the kingdom of God did not come. Paul's letters primarily addressed Gentiles. They contain all Church doctrine—doctrines the risen Lord revealed to Paul for the Church, the body of Christ.

Stachys: So, you were ok with this?

Paul: Definitely. I was committed to destroying those following Jesus of Nazareth, all of “the Way.” I broke into their houses, imprisoned, tortured, and killed them.

Stachys: Did you confine your actions to Jerusalem?

Paul: Initially, yes. But I had a burning zeal for our traditions. I went to the high priest and requested documents to authorize me to pursue followers of the Way beyond Israel’s borders. Once I obtained these papers I left for Damascus.

Stachys: How did that go?

Paul: Not as expected.

(*laughter*)

Paul: As I neared Damascus—it was about noon—an intense light shown around me—so bright it dimmed the sun. I fell to the ground and heard a voice speaking to me in Hebrew which said, “Saul, Saul, why are you persecuting me? It is hard for you to kick against the goads.” I replied, ‘Who are You, Lord?’ The voice replied, ‘I am Jesus whom you are persecuting. Get up and stand on your feet; for this purpose I have appeared to you, to appoint you a minister and a witness not only to the things which you have seen, but also to the things in which I will appear to you; rescuing you from the Jewish people and from the Gentiles, to whom I am sending you, to open their eyes so that they may turn from darkness to light and from the dominion of Satan to God, that they may receive forgiveness of sins and an inheritance among those who have been sanctified by faith in Me’” (Acts 9.3-9, 22.6-11, 26.13-18).

Stachys: Wow. What next?

Paul: I was in shock. And I was blind.

Stachys: What about those with you? How were they affected?

Paul: They saw the light but were not blinded. They heard the sound of a voice but did not understand it. Since I was blind, they led me to Damascus to a house on Straight Street owned by a man named Judas. I was without sight for three days and did not eat or drink. All I could do was pray. While praying, I had a vision: a man named Ananias came and laid his hand on me to give me my sight (Acts 9.11-12, 22.6-11).

Stachys: So, did this happen?

Paul: Yes. While recovering, the Lord also appeared to Ananias. He told him about me, where I was, and to come to me.

Stachys: Did he come?

Paul: Yes—but not without protest. He knew my reputation for ruthlessness. Ananias objected, saying, “Lord, I have heard from many about this man, how much harm he did to your saints at Jerusalem; and here he has authority from the chief priests to bind all who call on your name" (Acts 9.13-14). But the Lord calmed Ananias' fears and said, "Go, for he is a chosen instrument of Mine, to bear My name before the Gentiles and kings and the sons of Israel; for I will show him how much he must suffer for My name's sake" (Acts 9.15-16). Ananias obeyed and came to the house.

Stachys: Then what happened?

Paul: He placed his hands on me and said, "Brother Saul, the Lord Jesus, who appeared to you on the road by which you were coming, has sent me so that you may regain your sight and be filled with the Holy Spirit." 'Brother Saul, receive your sight!' When I looked at him he said, 'The God of our fathers has appointed you to know His will and to see the Righteous One and to hear an utterance from His mouth. For you will be a witness for Him to all men of what you have seen and heard. Now, why do you delay? Get up and be baptized, and wash away your sins, calling on His name'" (Acts 9.17-18, 22.13-16).

Stachys: Then what happened?

Paul: As soon as he spoke, I regained my sight. I was baptized. After this, I ate and began to regain my strength. While recovering, I visited with other believers and told them what had happened. As soon as I was strong enough, I went to the synagogue and proclaimed Jesus was the Son of God (Acts 9.20).

Stachys: *That* must have been a shock!

Paul: Quite. Those who heard me could not believe they were hearing Saul of Tarsus. They said, "Is this not he who in Jerusalem destroyed those who called on this name, and who had come here for the purpose of bringing them bound before the chief priests?" The Jews confronted me. They were what I had been just a few days before. When I showed them from the Scriptures that Jesus was the Christ they were confounded (Acts 9.20-22).

Stachys: The Lord has quite a sense of irony. After this happened, did you go to Jerusalem and consult with the Twelve?

Paul: It is logical to think this would have been the first thing I did. But God had other plans. He sent me to Arabia—to the desert—to Sinai, where Moses received the Law (Galatians 1.16-17, 4.25). The risen Lord kept me isolated from the Twelve. He had a totally different purpose for me. He began to reveal what being "the apostle of the Gentiles" (Romans 11.13) meant. After I received His instruction, I left Arabia and returned to Damascus.

Stachys: What did you do there?

Paul: I continued to teach in the synagogues. The Jews could not refute my arguments so they plotted to kill me. I had become Stephen.

Fortunately, I learned of this plot and escaped at night with the help of the disciples. They lowered me down the city wall in a large basket.

Stachys: More excitement!

Paul: Well, more was to come.

Stachys: What next?

Paul: I went to Jerusalem. I wished to fellowship with the believers there but they were afraid of me and doubted I was a believer. Barnabas, however, believed me and took me to other believers and described how I had seen the Lord on the road, that He had spoken to me, and how I had proclaimed His name in Damascus (Acts 9.26-27).

Stachys: Did you meet with the Twelve?

Paul: Only Peter. I also met James—the Lord's half-brother, known as "James the Just." I stayed with Peter for fifteen days (Galatians 1.18).

Stachys: What did you do in Jerusalem?

Paul: I proclaimed Jesus as the Messiah. The Hellenistic Jews opposed me and tried to kill me (Acts 9.29). One day, while praying in the Temple, I fell into a trance and saw the Lord saying to me, 'Make haste and get out of Jerusalem quickly because they will not accept your testimony about Me.' I protested saying, 'Lord, they know that in one synagogue after another I used to imprison and beat those who believed in you. When the blood of your witness Stephen was being shed, I also was standing by approving, and watching out for the coats of those who were slaying him.' But the Lord said, 'Go! For I will send you far away to the Gentiles'" (Acts 22.17-21). It took me a long time to learn the truth of His words. I loved my people. I thought, if I, Saul of Tarsus, could be changed, they could. Surely, they will listen to *me*! It was not to be.

Stachys: So how long did it take to learn this truth?

Paul: It took a long time. I did not appreciate it fully until the Lord imprisoned me in Rome (Ephesians 3.1, 4.1). Luke recorded our missionary journeys in Acts and my priority of going to Jews first with the gospel. When they rejected it, I turned to the Gentiles (Acts 13.13-47, 18.5-6, 28.17-29). I resisted God's warnings about going to Jerusalem (Acts 20.22-23, 21.4, 7-14) and got into trouble, just as the Holy Spirit had warned. To save myself from being killed by the Jews, I had to use my Roman citizenship and appeal my case directly to Caesar (Acts 22.22-29, 25.11). The Roman commander moved me from Jerusalem to Caesarea to foil another Jewish plot to kill me. I was imprisoned there for two years and during that time I met Governors Felix, Festus, and King Agrippa and Bernice. Finally, they sent me to Rome for the Emperor to hear my appeal. During the voyage, a terrible storm arose. It wrecked our ship but the Lord was with us and lost no lives. When I arrived in Rome, I immediately met with the Jews—my final meeting with them. It became clear, as the Lord had said, that they would not listen (Acts 28.17-29). This was in about 62 A.D. For the next two years I was under house arrest (a rented house) as Rome's prisoner. During this time, I spoke with many of Caesar's guards and several came to know the Lord (Philippians 4.22). Sometimes they wondered who was the prisoner.

(*laughter*)

Stachys: Can we talk about your teachings?

Paul: By all means. The risen Lord revealed to me doctrines, which I called "secrets" (μυστήριον). I designated them so because that is what they were. The Lord had not given these revelations to Israel's prophets. He had also kept them hidden in His earthly ministry and to the Twelve. They were revelations He gave exclusively to me.

Stachys: What were these secrets?

Paul: One was the gospel of the grace of God—that Christ died for our sins and rose from the dead (Acts 20.24; Galatians 1.11-12). Another was salvation by faith alone—believing the good news that Christ died for our sins and rose from the dead for our justification (1 Corinthians 15.1-4).

Stachys: Peter and the Eleven did not know this gospel and salvation by faith alone?

Paul: Peter and the rest preached the gospel of the kingdom which began with John the Baptist. That gospel focused upon the *identity* of Christ—who He was—the Messiah, the Son of God. They looked for the establishment of the kingdom of God on earth with Christ ruling as King (Matthew 6.10). My gospel, the gospel I received directly from the risen Lord (Galatians 1.11-12) focused upon His *work*—He died for our sins and rose from the dead. The faith part of the gospel of the kingdom was to believe Jesus was the Messiah, the Son of God (Matthew 16.16; John 11.27; Acts 8.37). That gospel also required repentance, keeping the Law, and water baptism for salvation (Mark 1.4, 16.16; Luke 10.25-28; Acts 2.38; Acts 15.1, 5). My gospel (Romans 2.16, 16.25; Galatians 2.2, 7; 2 Corinthians 4.3; 2 Thessalonians 2.14; 2 Timothy 2.8) required only one thing: faith, trusting in the death and resurrection of Christ. When Peter preached the Lord's death at Pentecost, he did not proclaim it as good news but as a Jewish crime (Acts 2.22-24, 3.13-15). He demanded the nation repent (Acts 2.36-38). For Peter, the significance of the Lord's resurrection was He was alive and could return and establish His kingdom on earth—if the Jewish people would repent (Acts 3.19-20, 25-26). The gospel the Lord gave me proclaims His death and resurrection as *good news* (1 Corinthians 15.1-4). My gospel is a gospel of grace and faith alone (Romans 1.16-17, 3.22, 26, 28, 4.5; Ephesians 2.8-9; 1 Corinthians 15.1-4). The Twelve had no idea Christ's death and resurrection had paid for the sins of the world and that God had reconciled the world to Himself (2 Corinthians 5.14-21).

This truth remained hidden until the glorified Lord revealed it to me. The Twelve learned this truth from me (2 Peter 3.15-16).

Stachys: Wow. That's not what most people have been taught.

Paul: Well, that's not my fault (*smiling*). I wrote all these things in my letters and they are there for anyone to read. The Lord also revealed to me many other truths He had kept hidden.

Stachys: What were these?

Paul: Well, another was the Church, the body of Christ, in which those who believe my gospel become members of His body, in which no difference exists between Jew and Gentile (Galatians 3.27-28). This was unknown to the Twelve.

Stachys: Peter did not know about the Church? Some teach that the Church began with Peter.

Paul: Well, no one thought so in my day, especially Peter. Peter knew nothing of the Church. Peter and the Twelve never had a ministry to Gentiles. Peter, James, John, and Jude wrote to Jews. They never mention the Church, the body of Christ, in their letters. Remember, Peter left Jerusalem to visit Cornelius only through a direct order and prodding from the Lord. And after he returned, the believing Jews in Jerusalem upbraided him for going to a Gentile (Acts 10-11). The Lord designated the Twelve as apostles of Israel (Matthew 19.28; Galatians 2.7-9). But God designated me as the apostle of the Gentiles (Romans 11.13). The ascended Christ revealed to me, not Peter or the other apostles, the secret of the Church, the body of Christ (Ephesians 3.2-7; 1.22-23; Colossians 1.19; 1 Corinthians 12.12-27; Galatians 3.28).

Stachys: The Church did not begin at Pentecost?

Paul: Read Luke's account. What is the definition of the Church? It is that body in which Jew and Gentile are equal in Christ, indwelt by the Holy Spirit. Whom did Peter address at Pentecost? Jews or Gentiles? He addressed Jews. Pentecost, the Festival of Weeks, was a Jewish feast day, held fifty days after Passover. Peter called on the Jewish nation to repent from the murder of the Messiah (Acts 2.5, 14, 22, 36-39). If this was the birth of the Church, why did Peter not address Gentiles? The same is true for Peter's second sermon, in Acts 3. He only addressed Jews (Acts 3.12, 25). If the Church came into existence at Pentecost, why did no Gentile evangelism occur? Peter and the Twelve never had a ministry to Gentiles. I wrote Timothy that I was the first (πρῶτος), God's prototype or pattern (ὑποτύπωσις), of those who would follow in this new salvation by faith alone in the death and resurrection of Christ (1 Timothy 1.15-16). To the Corinthians, I wrote, "as a wise master-builder, I laid the foundation" (ὡς σοφὸς ἀρχιτέκτων θεμέλιον ἔθηκα, 1 Corinthians 3.10-11). I laid the foundation of the Church. God began it with me.

Stachys: Few seem to know this. What else?

Paul: The Lord revealed to me that when one believes my gospel he is identified in Christ's death and in His resurrection (Romans 6.3-5, 8). This identification is the basis of our hope of resurrection and the key to victory in the Christian life (Romans 6.6-7). Peter and the other apostles knew nothing of this identification truth—of believers being baptized and identified in Christ's death and resurrection.

Stachys: Other truths?

Paul: Several more. The Lord revealed that the one who believes my gospel is under new administration: Grace, not Law (Romans 6.14). God gave the Mosaic Law to Israel, not to Gentiles. The Law's primary purpose was to reveal sin and condemn. It had no power to make one better. Peter and the Eleven continued to practice Judaism under the Law of Moses. They knew nothing of a new administration of Grace which replaced the Mosaic Law. At the Council of Jerusalem, after much argument, the Lord moved Peter to remember how Cornelius had been saved and he sided with me (Acts 15.7-11). Peter's statement ended the gospel of the kingdom. From that point onward, only my gospel was valid (Galatians 1.6-9).

Stachys: What about the Law? The Law was bad?

Paul: Not at all. The Law is holy, righteous, and good (Romans 7.12). The problem is not with the Law but with *us*. This is another truth the Lord revealed to me alone. The nature we inherit from Adam cannot keep the Law. I learned this truth through hard experience and wrote about it in Romans 7. When the Law encounters our fallen, Adamic nature it excites sin. It does so because our fallen nature, which I called "the flesh," is in rebellion against God (Romans 7.8, 11, 21, 23, 25). To counter this and conform us into the image of Christ, God has regenerated our spirit (Romans 8.15-16; 1 Corinthians 6.20), given us a new nature (Romans 7.22; 2 Corinthians 5.17), and the indwelling Holy Spirit (1 Corinthians 3.16). He has placed us under the administration of grace (Romans 6.14). Under this arrangement, we live by faith under the control of the Holy Spirit. The love of Christ constrains us (2 Corinthians 5.14) and through the superintending work of the Holy Spirit, God sanctifies and transforms us to Himself (Romans 8.29) in a way the Law could not (Galatians 5.16-26). We are to "reckon" or "consider" (λογίζομαι) ourselves dead to sin but alive to God (Romans 6.11). This is an act of faith, the key to sanctification, and the key to victory in living the Christian life.

Stachys: What about national Israel? What is their future? Do they have a future?

Paul: Yes! God will fulfill His covenants promises to Israel. When God establishes a plan and makes a promise, He keeps it (Romans 11.29). At present, national Israel is blind. God revealed this secret to me and I wrote about it in Romans 9-11. When God called Abraham, He began a new program. He laid the foundation for the creation of the Jewish people. He revealed Himself to them and gave them covenant promises. God promised they would become a kingdom of priests and a holy nation (Exodus 19.6; Isaiah 61.4-6). He promised they would become the preeminent nation on earth and that He will reign as their King and rule the earth (Deuteronomy 28.1, 13; Zechariah 14.9). Because they refused to repent, God removed them from their place of blessing and placed Gentiles into the position of favor. But God will re-establish them (Romans 11.11-12, 25-27). At the end of the Tribulation, they will recognize Jesus of Nazareth as their Messiah and repent (Matthew 23.37-39; Zechariah 12.10-14, 13.6; Romans 11.26). God will fulfill all the prophecies and promises to Israel. This cannot occur until the Lord removes the Church, the body of Christ (Romans 11.25-26). It has been a long time but the future of Israel is bright!

Stachys: What do you mean, "removes the Church?"

Paul: We can close with this secret—the believer's great hope (Titus 2.13)—the Lord's return and the resurrection of our bodies. Many are confused about the subject of the Lord's return. The Lord revealed to me His return for His Church, the body of Christ. This return was another *secret*—an entirely new and different event from His return known as His second coming (1 Corinthians 15.51). That return was well-known. The prophets taught it and the Lord taught in His earthly ministry. It occurs at the end of the Tribulation when the Lord will deliver Israel and the nations. The return the Lord revealed to me occurs *before* the Tribulation. He will deliver the Church from His wrath (Romans 5.9; 1 Thessalonians 1.10, 5.9; 2 Thessalonians 2.3, 7-8). I described the Lord's return for His Church to the Thessalonians with the word ἁρπάζω. It means a snatching away and has come to be known as "the Rapture" (1 Thessalonians 4.13-18). The Lord will snatch members of the Church, the body of Christ, who have died from the grave and resurrect them. An instant later, He will transform living believers and give them resurrection bodies. Both meet the Lord in the air. In my second letter to the Thessalonians, I corrected the false teaching that the Thessalonians' suffering was the Tribulation, the Day of the Lord (2 Thessalonians 2.1-3). In that letter, I described the Rapture with the word ἀποστασία (departure).

Stachys: Can you say a bit more why you used these words? Snatch away and departure from what?

Paul: Jewish theology has two great themes: One is the kingdom of God on earth, in which Christ will rule and Israel will be supreme among the nations. The other is God's wrath, usually spoken of as the Day of the Lord. David was the first to write about it in Psalm 2—a summary of Jewish theology—no extra charge for that (*laughter*). But before God pours His wrath on the earth He will remove His body, the Church. No believer of my gospel will experience the judgments in those terrible years. I taught the Thessalonians this comforting truth (1 Thessalonians 1.10, 5.9) and used ἁρπάζω to describe how the Lord will "snatch away" believers to meet Him in the air before He begins His judgment of the earth. This amazing truth means one generation of believers will not experience physical death. I had hoped to experience this myself but had no idea the Lord would extend His program of the Church for so long. I used ἀποστασία to correct the false teaching the Thessalonians had received that they were experiencing the Tribulation. Believers will depart (ἀποστασία) *before* the Antichrist, the Beast is revealed (2 Thessalonians 2.1-3, 7-8). God's removal of the Church is a sign His judgment is near.

Stachys: Why do so few know these things? Why is there so much confusion?

Paul: Several reasons account for the confusion. The primary reason is Christendom's failure to differentiate my ministry from the ministry of Peter and the Eleven. Put another way, it is the failure to recognize the differences between God's program for Israel and the nations and His program for the Church. When one mixes the doctrines I received from the ascended Christ, the secrets of the Church, with God's covenant, prophetic program with Israel, confusion results. Israel and the Church are two distinct divine programs. Mix them and the result is theological disaster. At the Council of Jerusalem, my gospel became the only gospel. The gospel of the kingdom ended until God returns to His program with Israel. With regard to the believer's sanctification, I wrote the book of Galatians to combat the false teaching that believers of my gospel were under the administration of the Mosaic Law. The Judaizers taught that living the Christian life required one to live under the Mosaic Law rather by faith through the power of the Holy Spirit. I fought that battle but lost. I lost all Asia. All the time I had spent in Galatia, Ephesus, Colossae, Iconium, Derbe, Lystra, Antioch Pisidia—I lost them all.

Stachys: You lost them?

Paul: Yes. It was a bitter pill and heart-wrenching to see believers abandon their freedom in Christ and the truths of grace for the yoke of the Law. I wrote Timothy about this great tragedy (2 Timothy 1.15, 4.14-16). The syncretism in Christendom today—mixing of Law and Grace, conflating God's program for the Church and His program for Israel, failure to distinguish the Rapture and the Second Coming, not understanding salvation by faith alone from salvation by faith and works, thinking God has replaced Israel with the Church, believing Peter and I preached the same gospel, thinking that Peter and the Eleven ministered to Gentiles—I could go on—all these errors have their roots in the battle I fought in my lifetime. Confusion results from failure to understand the Scriptures—to understand my letters—to understand God saved and commissioned *me* as the apostle of the Gentiles and that with *me* God began an entirely new program, the Church, the body of Christ.

## Conclusion

Stachys: Thank you. This is sobering. It also is an encouragement to concentrate on your letters and study the truths the Lord revealed to you. Finally, what are your thoughts about today, what concerns you most?

Paul: As a Pharisee, I thought I was doing God's will but I had become a religious fanatic. But God in His grace chose and commissioned me to reveal His grace and demonstrate that no one is beyond His love. God saved me to become the prototype of a new program in which Jews and Gentiles are equal in Christ—the Church, the body of Christ. I became to the Church what Abraham, Moses, and the prophets were to Israel.

My greatest concern is for those without Christ, without hope, and without eternal life. God wishes all to be saved (1 Timothy 2.4). Christ has done all the work. One need only believe my gospel—trust in Christ's death and resurrection (1 Corinthians 15.1-4). My second concern is for believers to understand the secrets God revealed to me and be filled with the knowledge of his will in all wisdom and spiritual understanding. This is the key to living a victorious Christian life.

The Christian life is not easy—but it is a life of joy. We are to live by faith through the power of the indwelling Holy Spirit. The more we trust God the more He conforms us, transforms us, into the image of His Son. He is our blessed hope—and He is coming—soon!

## About the Author

Don Samdahl received his Th.M. degree from Dallas Theological Seminary, majoring in Semitics and Old Testament Studies.

He has written numerous articles on various Biblical subjects which can be found at Doctrine.org. The goal of those studies is to reveal the knowledge of Christ, the hope of His calling, and the riches of His glory.

Book proceeds and contributions support the ministry of Doctrine.org and help finance the website, articles, books, conference travel and other ministries which proclaim Paul's unique apostleship and the gospel of the grace of God.

## Author's Books

*God's Programs: An Introduction to Understanding the Bible*
*Paul: Apostle of Secrets*
*The New Testament Study Bible (BDV)*
*Understanding the Jewish Writings: An Examination of Hebrews, James, 1-2 Peter, 1-3 John, Jude, and Revelation*

## Good News

All have sinned and fall short of God's glory (Romans 3.23). Death is the result of sin but God gives eternal life in Christ Jesus (Romans 6.23). God loves you. He demonstrated His love when He sent His Son to die for your sins, to pay sin's penalty, death. Jesus Christ satisfied divine justice. He did all the work. Because of this, all one can do for salvation is accept God's work—believe Christ died for your sins and rose from the dead. This is the "good news." The clearest message of salvation is the following:

> [1] Now I declare to you, brethren, the gospel that I proclaimed to you, which you also received, by which also you stand,
> [2] through which also you are saved, if you possess that message I proclaimed to you, unless you believed in vain.
> [3] For I delivered to you first, what I also received: Christ died for our sins, according to the Scriptures, [4] and that He was buried, and that He has been raised on the third day, according to the Scriptures (1 Corinthians 15.1-4).

Do you wish to know God, have His forgiveness, eternal life, live with Him forever? If so, tell God you are trusting in Christ's death, burial, and resurrection for you. Trust Him. It is that simple

Made in United States
Troutdale, OR
10/19/2024